Albert Camus

The Artist in the Arena

Albert Camus

The Artist in the Arena

EMMETT PARKER

The University of Wisconsin Press
Madison • Milwaukee • London • 1966

Published by the University of Wisconsin Press
Madison, Milwaukee, and London

U.S.A.: Box 1379, Madison, Wisconsin 53701
U.K.: 26-28 Hallam Street, London, W. 1

Paperback Edition 1966

Printed in the United States of America
Library of Congress Catalog Card Number 65–13502

To Alice

Acknowledgments

I SHOULD LIKE to express my thanks to all those who helped in the preparation of this book; in particular, for their special advice and assistance: Mme. Albert Camus, who kindly granted me access to documents in her possession and who authorized the citation of passages from *Alger-Républicain, Soir-Républicain, Combat,* and *Rivages;* M. Henri Smadja, directeur of *Combat,* who authorized citation of passages from *Combat;* M. Jean Bloch-Michel, directeur of *Preuves;* M. Albert Ollivier, directeur des Programmes de Télévision, Radiodiffusion-Télévision Française; M. Roger Grenier of *France-Soir;* M. Marcel Gimont; Mme. Suzanne Agnely of Gallimard Editeurs; M. Jean Sénard of *Le Figaro;* Professor Germaine Brée of the Institute for Research in the Humanities, University of Wisconsin; Professor Alexander Y. Kroff, Department of French and Italian, University of Wisconsin; Professor Robert F. Roeming, Department of French and Italian, University of Wisconsin-Milwaukee; Miss Marguerite A. Christensen, assistant reference librarian, University of Wisconsin; M. T. Chouet of the Bibliothèque Publique et Universitaire, Geneva, Switzerland.

E. P.

Madison, Wisconsin
June 1, 1963

Contents

Introduction

HERE IS no doubt that Albert Camus has had a great influence on his own generation and on that which grew to maturity during the years of World War II and the beginning of the cold war. The body of critical literature written about him and his works is a clear indication of the degree to which he succeeded in capturing the interest and imagination of a worldwide audience. Critics have probably devoted more printed pages to discussing his personality and his writings than he himself published.

Camus first attracted international attention in 1945–46, when *L'Etranger* and *Le Mythe de Sisyphe* became known outside France; he was quickly hailed as one of the leading writers of the postwar period. Soon after World War II it became known that this new young author was not only a talented writer but a man passionately interested in the social and political problems of his century. Along with Jean-Paul Sartre, he became one of the leading figures among that group of French writers who, following the example of André Malraux, insisted upon the artist's responsibility as a spokesman in defense of human rights.

Such writers as Malraux, Sartre, and Camus accepted *engagement* (commitment) as a moral obligation for the artist; their respective concepts of commitment served as a kind of *ars poetica*. If it did not always prescribe the form of their creative works, it greatly influenced the content, especially in Camus's case. Camus believed that the artist is obliged by his very art to bear witness to man's basic right to freedom and justice in the face of the historical aberrations of his time. To reject this premise means a refusal to accept Camus as an artist on his own terms. If one accepts it, then the record of his testimony must be studied in its entirety. Some of Camus's testimony is embodied in his fiction and in his essays, but it is also expressed in his journalism, which is more extensive than is sometimes realized. Camus considered his work as a journalist important enough to merit four volumes of collected publication. Three appeared under the title *Actuelles;* he was working on a projected fourth volume at the time of his death.

Camus's first writing for newspapers dates from 1938–39 in Algeria, when he worked for the left-wing *Alger-Républicain,* then edited *Soir-Républicain.* After leaving Algeria in 1940 he became a rewrite man for *Paris-Soir.* His experience had thus prepared him to play an active role in editing and disseminating the clandestine newspaper *Combat* during the Nazi occupation of France and to become its editor in the final stages of the occupation. He was editor-in-chief of the postliberation daily *Combat* until 1947. From then on he devoted most of his time to his literary work; but he continued to write frequently for journals and newspapers and for a short period in 1955–56 contributed regularly to the left-wing weekly *L'Express.* A large number of his lectures and prefaces as well as the essay on twentieth-century revolution, *L'Homme révolté,* are by their political nature very closely related to his journalistic writings. Portions of *L'Homme révolté* were in fact first published as articles in journals: "Les Meurtriers délicats" in *La Table ronde* (1948), "Le Meurtre et l'absurde" in *Empédocle* (1949), and "Nietzsche et le nihilisme" in *Les Temps modernes* (1951); "Remarque sur la révolte," later revised as Chapter 1 of *L'Homme révolté,* was also published separately in *Existence,* a collection of essays edited by Jean Grenier and published in 1945.

Camus's articles and editorials, although less well known than his literary works, are of interest for several reasons. They form an important adjunct to the literary works, complementing and often adding a new dimension to them. Some of the same themes appear in the novels, plays, and essays, but stated more ambiguously and couched in more universal language than in the articles, where Camus expressed his ideas and opinions directly in relation to the day-to-day course of events. The articles often furnish new insights into his fictional world. In this study I have indicated from time to time what I think are some of the more important of these insights, although the book is devoted mainly to Camus's journalistic writings and their relation to his other political writings, especially *L'Homme révolté*. A detailed survey of these writings is essential before real progress can be made in the revaluation of Camus's work that his death in 1960 has made necessary.[1]

Camus's journalism and related political writings deal with some of the most important social and political problems that have confronted the world in recent times: the Spanish Civil War; World War II and its aftermath; the cold war and world peace; the Algerian conflict and the problem of decolonization; the Hungarian revolt; etc. As such these writings are of interest to anyone who shares a concern for the present state of world affairs. They are of very great interest to the student of French literature since they contain the record, over a twenty-two-year period, of Camus's commitment.

In spite of the popularity of his literary works, Camus has often been severely criticized by other left-wing intellectuals in France. The controversy that has surrounded him since 1952—and continues after his death—indicates that those intellectuals who attacked him and his ideas recognized, envied, and perhaps even feared his influence, especially on the younger generation. Their criticism was aimed primarily at his political thought and at his concept of commitment, but it frequently took the form of violent attacks against Camus personally and against his reputation as an artist. In retrospect the title of his first novel becomes ironically prophetic, for Camus was destined in many ways to become himself a "stranger" insofar as the Parisian literary-intellectual "Establishment" was concerned.

I do not mean to imply that Camus was at any time without sympathizers and defenders. While no coterie of disciples such as surrounds Sartre formed around him, he had a number of loyal friends; and his literary works were, on the whole, well received by the critics. However, that portion of the left-wing press which attacked him most sharply is also influential and widely read in intellectual circles in France and abroad: *Les Temps modernes, France-Observateur,* and *L'Express* among others.

Many of the misunderstandings surrounding Camus and his work resulted from and reflected early misinterpretations of his thought as expressed in such works as *L'Etranger, Le Mythe de Sisyphe, Caligula,* and others. The labels "pessimistic" and "nihilistic" were incorrectly applied to these writings and to their author when the works first appeared, and they have persisted in the criticism of nearly all of Camus's writing to the present day.

Thus, important as Camus's political thought is, not only in relation to the rest of his work but as a lucid and passionate commentary on the present state of the human condition, it has often been misconstrued. In America, where the reading public is far removed from the Haymarket atmosphere of Parisian intellectual and political debate, readers and critics have sometimes been unaware of the full issues involved in political disputes in which Camus took part, or they have received a distorted impression of them. This is also partially due to the fact that Camus's American audience has not always had access to newspapers and journals in which they could follow the day-to-day expression of ideas by the dissenting parties.

Even in France the articles from *Alger-Républicain* and *Soir-Républicain* are still little known. Many of the editorials Camus wrote for *Combat* were unsigned and remained unidentified until the present time.[2] The later articles and editorials, except for the limited number that Camus had reprinted in the three volumes of *Actuelles,* were often read and discussed at the time of their appearance only to be subsequently forgotten. In addition, most of the discussion of Camus's ideas in various periodicals took place in a heatedly partisan atmosphere. As a result the continuity and evolution of his thought, along with the fundamental beliefs that inspired it, were often missed. In this study I have attempted to trace that evolution in the hope that many misunderstandings concerning this facet of Camus's works will be clarified.

Even after clarification, there will be many who cannot agree with Camus in all his positions and pronouncements. This is inevitable. But the importance of his career of commitment resides less in what he said concerning specific political events as such than in the example he set for those who refuse to accept without question the dogmas derived from systematic ideologies and from ready-made political party platforms. In an age when concerted political action has become a necessary means to the achievement of further social progress, we should value all the more highly men like Camus who remind us constantly that the aim of social progress and of political action is the attainment of ever greater human freedom.

Albert
Camus

The Artist in the
Arena

. . . il y a toujours eu dans le cirque
de l'histoire le martyr et le lion. Le
premier se soutenait de consolations
éternelles, le second de nourriture his-
torique bien saignante. Mais l'artiste
jusqu'ici était sur les gradins. Il
chantait pour rien, pour lui-même, ou,
dans le meilleur des cas, pour encourager
le martyr et distraire un peu le lion de
son appétit. Maintenant, au contraire,
l'artiste se trouve dans le cirque. Sa
voix, forcément n'est plus la même; elle
est beaucoup moins assurée.

DISCOURS DE SUÈDE
© Editions Gallimard, 1958

1

Between Art and Commitment
A Balance Sought

CAMUS INITIATED his apprenticeship in journalism in the fall of 1938 as literary critic for the daily *Alger-Républicain,* which styled itself "The Popular Front newspaper, that is the newspaper of democracy." This sheet under the editorship of Pascal Pia began publication on 6 October 1938, and ran until 27 October of the next year; then it merged with its evening edition, *Soir-Républicain,* which had started publication on 15 September 1939. The evening paper was closed on 9 January 1940 as the result of a government ban imposed because of its violation of censorship regulations. *Alger-Républicain* was later revived as an extreme left-wing daily with strong Marxist leanings, but this was long after Camus and Pascal Pia had ceased to be associated with it.

Camus's first assignment at *Alger-Républicain* was writing book reviews. He progressed rapidly, and having worked at nearly every phase of the newspaper's operation, edited *Soir-Républicain* throughout its brief career. Because of his criticism of government officials and of French colonial policies in Algeria, and because of his defiance of censorship regulations while editor of *Soir-Républicain,* Camus found himself after the paper's closure persona non grata in Algeria. In Paris, through the efforts of Pascal Pia, he found a job with *Paris-Soir.*

Camus had been active in left-wing literary circles in Algiers for some time before he started to work as a journalist. In 1935 he had organized the Théâtre du Travail, an experiment in collective

3

theater. In 1937 he had published his first group of essays, *L'Envers et l'endroit,* followed by *Noces* in 1939. It was probably by way of these activities that he first came in contact with Pia. Their association was to continue throughout the years of the Nazi occupation of France, when they worked together on *Combat,* until in 1947, because of financial difficulties, they relinquished its control.

The articles that Camus wrote for the two Algerian newspapers are, along with his notebooks, a valuable record of his early career, especially insofar as his ideas on social and political questions are concerned. Many of the ideas that were later to attract international attention were formulated during this period. Some of them, such as his views on the Franco regime in Spain, are less thoroughly developed than others; to the status of the Moslems in Algeria, for example, he devoted a considerable number of articles.

On the whole, the journalistic writings of this period tend to show that Camus, in his mid-twenties, had already arrived at the basic points of view that were to guide his involvement in political issues throughout his career. Although his outlook was naturally to undergo certain changes as his experience widened and the course of history brought about new developments, the principles that had fostered that outlook were to remain deeply rooted in the early years of his experience in Algeria. These were years of international upheaval and of internal unrest in France and in Algeria itself, where the clash between supporters of the Popular Front and the right-wing conservatives was especially violent. During this period of unrest Camus was also to form certain of his ideas on what journalism should be.

Camus's political activities began in earnest in 1934, when he was twenty-one and still a student. Two events that year were to have a decisive influence on his political thought and career as a writer and intellectual. In February the Stavisky scandal erupted into the riots and counterdemonstrations that ultimately resulted in the rise to power of the Popular Front, the first legally constituted Socialist government France had ever known.[1]

That same year Camus joined the Communist party. Quite probably the two events were connected. The riots of 6 February were mainly inspired by the followers of Colonel de la Rocque's Fascist Croix de Feu, although the Communists also took part in them. This development alarmed many Frenchmen who had been uneasily watching the growth of Fascism in Germany and Italy. Under the impetus of these threats, and because of other complex factors such as France's continuing failure to solve her fiscal and unemployment problems, the Radical, Socialist, and Communist parties were able to join together with the backing of the Confédération Générale du Travail, France's most influential labor union, to form an effective left-to-center coalition.

At the same time, French intellectuals also were rallying to the anti-Fascist cause. During this period many of them joined or actively supported left-wing political parties, in a movement referred to as *adhésion*. Camus himself later remarked that "the great movement toward adhésion dates from February 1934";[2] he presumably did his part by adhering to the Algerian Communist party. This movement among the intellectuals was paralleled by a similar one among French workers: in 1934–36 the ranks of the C.G.T. swelled from 1,300,000 to 5,000,000 members.

The Popular Front carried the general election of May 1936; and Léon Blum, leader of the center wing of the Socialist party, assumed the premiership. The Popular Front sponsored an ambitious legislative program calling for a forty-hour work week, nationalization of the railways and the munitions industry, partial nationalization of the Bank of France, and extensive social welfare measures. Blum was for the most part successful in having this program enacted, but he was not able to steady the French economy sufficiently to absorb the increased costs of the program. Plagued by financial problems, openly opposed by banking interests, and harried by disagreements within the coalition, Blum was toppled from power when the Senate, in June 1936, refused to grant him plenary powers in order to deal with a financial crisis.

Although Camus continued to support the basic principles for which the Popular Front stood, his membership in the Communist party seems not to have outlasted the Popular Front itself. On at least two occasions he asserted that he had left the party at the time of Pierre Laval's visit to Moscow in May 1935.[3] As a result of that visit and the signing of the Franco-Soviet pact, the Algerian Communist party's official attitude of hostility toward French colonial policies was softened, presumably on orders from Moscow. Camus, who in 1934 had been assigned the job of disseminating Communist party propaganda among the Moslems, later gave as his reason for leaving the party his feeling of disgust at this cynical reversal of policy.[4]

Some of his associates during the period maintain, however, that Camus held his party card until 1937, when he was expelled for having supported Messali Hadj's allegation that the Communists had been responsible for repressive measures taken against his Etoile Nord-Africaine.[5] The fact that Camus continued to direct the Communist-sponsored Maison de la Culture in Algiers until 1937 would seem to support this later date.[6] Actually, whether he left the Communist party in 1935, as he himself declared, or in 1937 is not too important. In either case the break came about because the party seemed to him to be exploiting the Moslems' misery for purely political ends. As Roger Quilliot points out: "Since a certain preference for the living human being inclined him toward the living Arab of today rather than toward the Arabs of the century to come, he decided that the Communist method was not the most desirable one."[7]

Camus did not definitively condemn either the Communist party or the U.S.S.R. until the time of the controversy sparked by *L'Homme révolté*. In spite of his own disenchantment with the party, he realized that the Communists enjoyed the confidence of large numbers of workers. He continued to look upon the Communist party as a source of hope for the working class and considered the Soviet Union's experiment in socialism a portentous one which, if certain grave faults were corrected, could become a positive force in promoting the cause of international socialism that he espoused. It is interesting to note that Jean-Paul Sartre was to take a similar position, but not until ten years later.

Camus himself did not entirely give up hope for a revival of the Popular Front or the creation of a similar working agreement that would bring together all the forces of the left, including the Communists, in a cohesive and effective political movement. Just such a synthesis he hoped would develop out of the Resistance movement after World War II.

Camus actually had little occasion to comment on Communist doctrine during the initial period in his newspaper career. However, he reviewed a number of books that touched on the question of revolutionary action. Among these were Albert Ollivier's *La Commune,* Jorge Amado's *Bahia de tous les saints,* and Paul Nizan's *La Conspiration.* His reviews contain a few random comments that are significant. They show that despite his hope for signs of improvement in the Communist camp Camus was already thinking along lines he was to develop in *L'Homme révolté.* He expressed doubts concerning the effectiveness of violent revolution, except perhaps as a means to some sort of personal fulfillment. He hesitated to accept Amado's conclusion that "the only valid and satisfying form of revolt is revolution" (*AR,* 9-4-39, p. 5). While admitting that such an attitude had a ring of psychological truth when considered in relation to the main character of Amado's novel, a South American Negro boxer, he questioned whether this individual case had a broader application where political group action was concerned.

He was intrigued by the concept of an individual and nonviolent form of revolution suggested by Giono in the *Lettre aux paysans sur la pauvreté et la paix.* He did not know, he said, if such a revolution were possible, "but I know that none is possible if it has not taken form in the hearts and in the minds of those who intend to carry it out. The failure of so many revolutions is perhaps related to that idea" (*AR,* 3-1-39, p. 3).* This reservation concerning the

* French texts of starred passages may be found in Appendix A.

motives that inspire the revolutionary is similar to that expressed by Camus's scrupulous murderers in *L'Homme révolté* and *Les Justes.*

Ollivier's description in *La Commune* of the ideal preparation for the would-be revolutionary also impressed Camus:

. . . Albert Ollivier thinks that that preparation should take place far from tumult and lies, and that it requires time, which is nothing, but that it also requires men of insight and intelligence, which is everything. . . . the book ends with a few lines that should be pondered . . . : "The true revolutionary must . . . avoid the heat of political controversy. . . . He must resist the temptation, strong as it may be, to take immediate action, and for him to do this, one will agree, he must have a great deal of humility and a great deal of pride" (*AR,* 4-7-39, p. 3).*

By 1939 Camus had come to the conclusion that the Bolshevik Revolution had turned out to be something less than an unqualified success. He felt that Nicholas Berdyaev's works did much to elucidate "the religious essence of Russian communism," as well as "the Soviet mystique," two facets of Soviet communism that he was later to treat in *L'Homme révolté* (*AR,* 25-6-39, p. 3). And in a review of Hélène Isvolski's study, *Femmes soviétiques,* he remarked: ". . . it will be to everyone's interest (even the Communists') to read a moving and at the same time well-documented book that remains lucid even in its hostility toward the Soviet regime. The greatest harm to the U.S.S.R., in fact, is done, not by those who criticize it in good faith, but . . . by overzealous admirers who present it as the paradise of mankind" (*AR,* 18-2-39, p. 5).*

It thus seems possible that Camus would have arrived earlier at the position he was to take in *L'Homme révolté* if his experience in the Resistance and Russia's belated entry into World War II on the side of the Allies had not given him new hope that an understanding might be reached among left-wing factions. As it was, his attitude toward the Communists and the Soviet Union was to remain ambivalent for some years after he dissociated himself from the Communist party.[8]

Significantly, after he left the Communist party, Camus did not join any other political party. He was working for a newspaper that expressed the *frontiste* point of view; but the Popular Front, not a political party in itself, was merely a working rapprochement among left-of-center groups that, ideally at least, crossed party lines. Camus remained loyal to the basic concept and the fundamental principles of the Popular Front, particularly insofar as they reflected the aims of international socialism. An article in *Soir-Républicain* endorsed the ideals of international socialism but suggested that the French Socialist party had strayed too far from these ideals.[9] The article, signed "Alius," may well have been written by Camus; it does express certain criticisms of the French Socialist party, criticisms that Camus was to develop in more detail in 1945. Nonetheless, as a journalist, after his involvement with the Communist party had come to an end Camus remained independent of party ties. He only once publicly supported a political candidate, personally endorsing Pierre Mendès-France and the Front Républicain in 1955.

Camus's experience with the Communist party undoubtedly accounts in part for his tendency to shy away from close party affiliations. It is also possible that the failure of the Blum government to intervene in the Spanish Civil War on the side of the Spanish Republicans reinforced this tendency. Camus felt almost personally involved in that war. His mother was of Spanish descent, and he often referred to his "espagnolisme." In 1935 he had coauthored a play, *Révolte dans les Asturies,* which dealt with the 1934 revolt of Spanish intellectuals and coal miners.[10] This play leaves no doubt as to the author's strong sympathy for the Spanish people.

Camus was certainly among the many French intellectuals who were disappointed in Blum's failure to aid the Spanish Republicans. It may be true, as John T. Marcus asserts, that "Blum *could not* have taken a strong stand [on the Spanish Civil War] in 1937, given the *de facto* attitudes of those groups among the Radicals and in his own party whose support he *had* to have in order to govern at all."[11]

Nevertheless, as premier in 1937, Blum was responsible for the nonintervention policy. Camus may well have seen in this policy an example of the kind of "political realism" he so detested.

Yet Camus, in *Alger-Républicain,* wrote relatively little about Spain, possibly because under the circumstances it would have proved embarrassing for a frontiste paper to print the kind of articles he might have wished to write. He did refer to the Spanish Civil War as "an unjust and bloody war," in an article reporting the hijacking of a French ship by the Falangist Navy (*AR,* 26-11-38, p. 2). He also replied with a blistering editorial to an article in the conservative daily, *La Dépêche algérienne,* which had described returning members of the International Brigade as a sorry-looking lot of adventurers. He suggested in his reply that those who did not admire or agree with the ideals that had led these men to join the Brigade could at least have the decency to keep silent and avoid insulting the returning volunteers in their moment of defeat (*AR,* 19-11-38, p. 1). In this editorial, however, he did not bring up the subject of France's failure to intervene in the war.

Camus's bitterness at this failure is nonetheless apparent in his review of a collection of articles and speeches by Dolores Ibarruri, the Spanish militant known as "La Passionaria":

Some people do not clearly understand that what makes so many of us loyal to the Spanish Republicans is not vain political affinities but the irrepressible feeling that they have with them the Spanish people, this people so like their land with their ingrained nobility and their ardent love of life. . . . But why insist? Nothing now can change the stupid game of hatred. The methodical murder of the Spanish people continues. We can take pride in it: we have done all that was necessary to that end . . . (*AR,* 18-2-39, p. 5).*

The intensity of his feelings concerning the repression of the Spanish Republicans makes it quite unlikely that he was ready to condone Blum's policy of abstention, whatever the political considerations involved. Just such compromises caused him to mistrust political party membership as a valid form of commitment for intellectuals. Even before the defeat of France in 1940, Camus's political experience, brief as it was, had led him to reconsider the whole question of adhésion to a political party.

The problem of just how deeply the intellectual's commitment should involve him in political affairs occupied a place in Camus's thoughts for some time after his break with the Communists—if we assume that there was at least some kind of preliminary break as early as 1935. In March 1936 he wrote: "Grenier, concerning communism: 'The entire question is this: in the name of an ideal of justice, must one subscribe to all sorts of nonsense?' To answer, 'yes,' is beautiful: to answer, 'no,' is honest."[12] Very early, then, he rejected the bravura gesture. Having come from a proletarian background, he had none of the sense of guilt that often seems to compel some French bourgeois intellectuals to seek "absolution" by adhering to the Communist party in one way or another.

At the same time he considered, although quite briefly, the sometimes conflicting responsibilities of the artist and the intellectual. He had decided at the age of seventeen that he would be a writer.[13] By the mid-1930's he had decided that dedication to his art came before all else. From his point of view it was a question of "To create or not to create," as he wrote in his notebook on 10 October 1937. "In the first case, everything is justified. Everything without exception. In the second case, one is faced with complete absurdity. It only remains to choose the most esthetic form of suicide: marriage plus forty hours a week or a revolver."[14] But he had also decided with equal firmness to accept the role of intellectual: "Intellectual? Yes. And never deny it. . . . I despise the intellect means in reality, 'I cannot face my own doubts.' I prefer to keep my eyes open."[15] Neither the artist whose supreme dedication is to his art—which to Camus meant dedication to the truth above all else—nor the intellectual who cultivates his doubts and prefers to "keep his eyes open" is likely to adapt very easily to the restrictions imposed by political party discipline.

Camus's continuing preoccupation with this conflict between the writer's commitment to his own sense of the truth and adherence to a party line is evident in a one-line entry jotted in his notebook in

1937: "The intellectual and the question of adhésion (fragment)."[16] A number of remarks taken from his book reviews in *Alger-Républicain* indicate that he subsequently came to some sort of conclusion on this difficult subject. He had definitely decided by the late 1930's that a form of commitment was unavoidable for the artist, at least in the present period of history. In a review of Armand Guibert's *Périple des îles tunisiennes* (*AR,* 5-3-39, p. 5), he noted that Guibert had come face to face with the signs of "the European tragedy," even in the remote islands off Tunisia. For the twentieth-century artist, Camus noted, "there are no more islands." The poet may try to refuse this fact, but to no avail: "It is the social problem that confronts Guibert and forces him to the wall. The artist today must, in one way or another, find a solution. That is at once his servitude and his greatness."*

But this servitude should not entail unquestioning acceptance of a ready-made political or social system. In 1934 Camus, like many other intellectuals, had felt it his duty to become a militant party member. In 1939, looking back at the events of five years earlier, he was inclined to think that, at that particular moment, "there was created in France an atmosphere of hatred which increased in everyone a sense of responsibility that was perhaps illusory" (*AR,* 23-5-39, p. 2). His association with the Communist party had ended in disillusionment, and he now thought the artist could better serve the revolutionary cause by submitting to the discipline of his art instead of to political party discipline.

The writer who placed his talent at the service of a political party, Camus believed, often had to subordinate the demands of his art to the demands of political necessity. When this happened, there was a danger of the writer's yielding to what Malraux called the "will to prove" and writing mere propaganda. But, Camus insisted, even for the militant artist-intellectual: ". . . there can be no revolutionary work without artistic quality. This may seem paradoxical. But I believe that if this age teaches us anything in that respect it is that revolutionary art cannot be deprived of artistic greatness without sinking back into the most abject forms of thought" (*AR,* 23-5-39, p. 2).* Moreover, to judge an author's work on the basis of his political involvement was inadmissible:

> For some years much has been said and written about adhésion. But, all things considered, the question is as futile as that of immortality, a matter that a man settles with himself and upon which others cannot base judgment. One adheres as one marries. And with a writer it is on the basis of his works that one may judge the effects of adhésion.
>
> Malraux, who adheres, is a great writer. One would like to be able to say as much for Aragon. . . . Montherlant, who rejects all forms of regimentation, remains one of the most astonishing prose writers of the century (*AR,* 11-11-38, p. 5).*

When an author does speak out on current political issues, Camus had said earlier, it should not be assumed that he is some sort of oracle who cannot err. Citing Gide as an example, he declared: ". . . the furor over Gide's political views is the result of an error in perspective. Gide's opinion on social problems has NO MORE importance than that of any other cultivated, compassionate and reasonably idealistic Frenchman" (*AR,* 23-10-38, p. 5).* Thus, by 1939, while personally accepting commitment as unavoidable for the artist, Camus's views on the subject were far from rigid. He seems to have already preferred to remain independent of political party ties and to have rejected as a writer the role of Vates *à la Hugo,* so frequently assumed by French intellectuals.

As a newsman, Camus was to remain faithful to his personal concept of commitment. "It is not for a political party that this is written, but for men," he wrote of his report on the Kabylia famine in June 1939.[17] The same statement can be applied to nearly everything he wrote in newspaper columns. Even in his attacks on national and local government officials he was motivated more by concern for the victims of oppression or threats to democratic institutions than by a desire "to score points" for any party in a partisan political battle. At the end of an article in which he gave a detailed step-by-step account of the arbitrary and illegal prosecution of an innocent man in an out-of-the-way Algerian village, he concluded:

. . . let no one think that we point out all these illegal procedures for the sake of scoring points for our side. . . . But a profound act of injustice is always revealed in details. . . . And, moreover, one can assess the state of mind of an innocent man, unjustly accused, treated arbitrarily, all his human feelings defiled, and defenseless against the unlimited authority that is invested in men who are inferior to their office. It is that man who is scoring points here (*AR*, 4-2-39, p. 2).*

Camus was interested in political questions only in the most fundamental sense of the word political: of the citizens. As Brée points out: "For Camus . . . political problems were of interest only in so far as they touched one of his major preoccupations, that is, the daily life of human beings, their freedom and the human justice meted out to them on this earth. He consistently refused to refer to the abstract universe of systematic ideologies and always stubbornly based his arguments on the individual universe of everyday living in relation to the general principles of freedom and justice."[18]

He was, in fact, already primarily concerned with maintaining the delicate equilibrium between freedom and justice. His own tenuous existence in a beautiful but indifferent universe had convinced him that men need and should have all the freedom possible in order to grasp whatever happiness they can. But when in the struggle for happiness some men impose on others a brutish existence and even deprive others of the only life they know, justice that limits this abusive form of freedom is mandatory. The problem that most concerned Camus at the very outset of his career was how to define the limits of both freedom and justice so that the precise balance, the tension between the two, could be determined and maintained.

The extent to which this problem obsessed him in these early years is dramatically demonstrated in an article entitled "Those

Men Who Are Struck from the List of the Living." The article, which appeared in *Alger-Républicain* on 1 December 1938, is a subjective account of a visit Camus had made to the *Martinière,* a convict ship that docked in Algeria on a stage of its voyage to a penal colony. He described the ship, its antiseptic cleanliness, the lugubrious silence of its officers and men, and its human cargo locked in cages in the hold of the ship. He was particularly moved by the sight of several Arab prisoners who, in an effort to catch a glimpse of Algeria, were clinging with their fingertips to the edges of portholes high above the deck.

He was deeply disturbed by this spectacle of men legally judged by their peers and condemned to remain in isolation from the rest of society. Justice had done its work. It had deprived these men of their freedom. So far as Camus knew, there was no question as to their guilt. But he could not shake off a sense of horror at the thought of these men.

It is not a question of pity here, but of something entirely different. There is no more abject spectacle than the sight of men reduced to a subhuman condition. It is this sentiment that we are dealing with here. . . . It is not for us to judge these men; others have done that. Nor to pity them; that would be puerile. But it was solely a matter here of describing that unique and definitive destiny whereby men are struck from the lists of the living. And it is perhaps the fact that this destiny is without appeal that creates all its horror (*AR,* 1-12-38, p. 2).*

The living death to which the prisoners aboard the *Martinière* were being subjected was for Camus a horror equaled only by death itself. Any act by which men were deprived of their lives or of their freedom, as were the convicts aboard the ship, was repugnant to him. This was one of many areas where justice and freedom needed to be defined and a means sought to maintain the proper balance between them. Camus set out to explore these areas in his novels, plays, and essays. But flagrant cases of injustice also occurred within already established definitions. To the victims in these cases too Camus was committed, for he believed it possible "in giving back his dignity to a single man, to bring a little more truth into a world where lies and hatred shall not always be able to triumph" (*AR,* 10-1-39, p. 1).

In his articles exposing inequities, Camus often gave expression to personal observations and concrete experiences that he was later to develop in more abstract form. And as the period between the two world wars came to a close, the course of political events in France and Algeria gave rise to situations in which he was to see many manifestations of injustice.

The hopes that many intellectuals, Camus among them, had placed in the Popular Front were soon dashed. After the fall of the Blum government, the Popular Front managed to carry on lamely under the administration of Camille Chautemps, who headed two cabinets between June 1937 and March 1938, when his second government fell. Blum was then called upon to form another ministry, which lasted only three weeks. Finally, on 10 April 1938, a new government was formed by Edouard Daladier, the Radical party leader.

Under the administration of this man who enjoyed the confidence of the right there was some return of the capital that had taken flight under Blum. Quotations on the Bourse rose. But war now seemed imminent. Faced with the problem of financing France's mobilization effort, Daladier and his finance minister, Paul Reynaud, set about curtailing by decree—Parliament had granted Daladier the plenary powers it had denied Blum—many of the gains labor had made under Blum's administration. Railroad workers were laid off to offset the national deficit. A 2 percent surtax was levied on all incomes, regardless of size, and a compulsory overtime statute was decreed that meant virtual abandonment of the forty-hour work week.

These measures met with wrathful opposition from the left. The C.G.T. called for a general strike on 30 November 1938, but the strike in full force never occurred. Daladier requisitioned the railroads and other public services. As a result, nearly all government workers were on the job. A few days earlier, Daladier had shown that he was quite willing to use force against striking employees. He had sent 10,000 riot police to the Renault automobile plant in order to clear it of workers engaged in a sit-down strike. The riot police accomplished their mission with the aid of tear gas. It was estimated that on 30 November no more than 50 percent of the workers in private industry stayed away from their jobs.

Bitterly disappointed, the backers of the Popular Front angrily denounced Daladier. Since most of the frontistes, like Camus, were pacifists or at least opponents of what they considered the all-or-nothing attitude of most of the right-wing parties, they were not inclined to accept Daladier's assertion that all these "sacrifices" were essential to the success of the mobilization effort and that the strike was an enemy-inspired attempt to sabotage France's rearmament. Camus himself, at this early point in his journalistic career, seems to have been less concerned with the international crisis than he was with the social aspects of local political problems, probably because in Algeria local political quarrels overshadowed the conflict that was creating a stir in the capitals of Europe.

Camus, however, assailed Daladier's repressive actions against the workers. He was always to feel great sympathy for the working class. His two early ventures in the theater, Le Théâtre du Travail in 1935 and Le Théâtre de l'Equipe in 1938, were attempts to interest the workers in the theater, both as spectators and as participants. While in Saint-Etienne in 1943, he wrote: "French workers —the only people with whom I feel truly at ease, whom I desire to know and whose lives I wish to share. They are like me."[19] In 1945 he was to declare that France's future was synonymous with that of her working class, a statement expressing equally well his point of view in the late 1930's.[20] He felt the defeat of the 1938 strikers in a very personal way. In an article entitled "Dialogue between a Premier and a Worker Earning 1,200 Francs a Month," he attacked Daladier on two grounds: his circumvention of democratic processes and his repression of the workers. In order to carry out his policies, Camus charged, Daladier had had to depend on "those instruments of democracy called troops, militia and councils of war" (*AR,* 3-12-38, p. 1).

In so doing, Daladier, though he was proud of being a baker's son, had shown a total ignorance of the basic human feelings of the workers and of their desire for dignity: ". . . politicians have no idea how difficult it is to be simply a man. To live, without being unjust, a life filled with inequities, on 1,200 francs a month, with a wife, a child and the certainty of dying without being inscribed in the textbooks of history."* Daladier could no doubt explain his actions, but what he called his devotion to duty and to the national interest appeared to the worker as "above all, layoffs, factory shutdowns, the loss of my 1,200 francs . . ." (*AR,* 3-12-38, p. 1).

This particular failure to understand that the workers' claims were motivated by a desire to free themselves from the unjust living conditions imposed upon them by a highly industrialized society was, in Camus's opinion, only one aspect of the general mediocrity and lack of imagination that characterized the leaders of the Third Republic. In 1944, after the liberation of France, he again emphasized this failing on the part of the country's political leaders.

Daladier's policies had found a staunch supporter in Mayor Rozis of Algiers, whom Camus accused of having learned his "lessons in orthodoxy from Maurras."[21] The mayor was only too ready to follow the tough line toward the workers as laid down by the premier after the general strike. Even before the proposed date of the strike, Rozis had fired a municipal employee for having engaged in trade union activities. After the abortive strike came more firings and layoffs, countered by protest meetings of the employees. Since the strike of municipal employees had never really taken place, the sole explanation that Camus could find for Rozis's actions was a desire for vengeance and a despicable "perseverance in acts of hatred." He attributed them to Rozis's mediocre intelligence and his incapacity to understand the motives behind the workers' demands and protests (*AR,* 7-2-39, p. 1).

Rozis refused to budge from his position or to reconsider his actions, in spite of the fact that the Departmental Council had heard the workers' case and had decided in their favor. He bragged that every means, including an appeal to his generosity, had been used to force him to bend. Camus retorted in disgust that Rozis had little claim to the virtue of generosity, since "generosity is a virtue of noble men. No one would have thought of asking that of him. . . . we shall not try to make M. Rozis 'bend.' It is now a question of defending the bread of our comrades. Resentment has no legal basis, and a decision as arbitrary as this one is unacceptable. The employees who have been dismissed will take their case to the Prefectural Council" (*AR*, 7-2-39, p. 1).*

Appeal to the prefectural authorities may seem anticlimactic after such a strong denunciation of Rozis's actions. It is indicative, however, of the approach Camus was to take most often in dealing with the cases of injustice that came to his attention while he was a reporter for *Alger-Républicain*. Although a matter of principle was involved in the case of the municipal employees, and the situation might well have served as pretext for a press campaign waged on the basis of the very wide divergence of political opinion between Rozis and *Alger-Républicain,* Camus did not overlook the more immediate necessity for defending "the bread of our comrades." He refused to lose sight of the actual hardships imposed upon the workers by the loss of their jobs. The fact that these men and their families would suffer if prompt action were not taken to reinstate them in their jobs outweighed any abstract political considerations.

It can be argued, of course, that Camus and *Alger-Républicain* were hoping that in the long run their practical approach would convert more people to their way of thinking politically. This is undoubtedly true. Camus was not so naive as to think that one could avoid party politics altogether. But he was convinced that human beings come first, and that, if given a reasonable amount of intelligent leadership and support, most people could make a sound political choice without having to be coerced into following a hard-and-fast political line. On these convictions he based his view of the dual role of a free press: that of a "bad conscience" that brings to public attention any miscarriage of justice in whatever form, no matter where the responsibility lies; and that of a well-balanced and intelligently partisan source of information.

Camus in the late 1930's already considered the press one of the most important forces in the struggle to revise the social order. He regarded control of the French press by moneyed interests as one of the right wing's most formidable weapons: "In our time the press constitutes a terrible weapon in the hands of those who control it. It makes or unmakes public opinion, directs it, curbs it, or exasperates it . . ." (*SR,* 6-12-39, p. 1).* To the inevitable objection that the press was only giving the public what it wanted, that is, sensational headlines and *faits divers* instead of well-balanced, intelligent reporting of the news, Camus replied: ". . . the deadly power of the press is explained as much by the corruption of those who run it as by the lack of critical judgment of those who read it" (*SR,* 6-12-39, p. 1).*

Camus believed a newspaper should not be simply an organ of political propaganda. The duty of the press, as he saw it, was both to reflect and to form public opinion. During the investigation of a mysterious explosion in Algiers, the cause of which might have been negligence on the part of a private utility company, Camus insisted that the press represented "one of the parties involved, that is to say, the public . . ." (*AR,* 30-12-38, p. 1). In several carefully detailed reports written for *Alger-Républicain,* he alluded again and again to the importance of enlisting the support of public opinion. ". . . we appeal to public opinion and to all honest people so that their indignant protests may prevent the consummation of such a scandal," he wrote in the course of one investigation (*AR,* 5-3-39, p. 3). On another occasion, condemning the use of torture by the police to obtain confessions, he insisted: "It is not enough to protest. It is necessary to arouse protest and to inform public opinion of an unacceptable and profoundly revolting situation" (*AR,* 25-7-39, p. 1).

This approach to news reporting does not at all imply that the press should not take a strong stand on certain issues. But it does require that a newspaper support its stand with an intelligent and reasonably objective presentation of facts and that, above all, it print the truth insofar as it is ascertainable. Camus maintained that "the expression of the truth, no matter how painful or bitter that truth may be, can only strengthen and stimulate our energies" (*SR,* 15-9-39, p. 1).

He followed his own criteria very closely as a reporter for *Alger-Républicain,* where he seems to have had a relatively free hand to report the news as he saw fit. As editor of *Soir-Républicain,* he established a policy of printing news from multiple sources and of informing his readers of the reliability of each source. Conclusions were drawn only after careful evaluation of all reliable facts available. If there were not enough facts to warrant taking a precise stand, judgment was deferred until there were enough. Where local issues were concerned, Camus preferred a detailed on-the-spot investigation. This view of journalism, which Camus expounded further in 1945, when he called it "Le Journalisme critique,"[22] enabled him to remain true to his concept of commitment while becoming actively involved in controversial social and political issues.

Having gained experience as a reporter and literary critic for *Alger-Républicain,* Camus began more and more to specialize in exposés and press campaigns on behalf of individual or collective victims of administrative injustice. His defense of Michel Hodent is an example of a spectacular success in the defense by a journalist of individual civil rights. Hodent, a government grain agent at Trézel, had been accused of defrauding Moslem farmers of part of their grain stored in the government cooperative warehouse of which he was in charge. The local judge, Garaud, had handled the case in a very high-handed manner: he had kept Hodent in jail for four months during an investigation of the charges, leaving Madame Hodent, who was pregnant, with only the revenue from a small flock of sheep of which Hodent was part owner. When an inventory of the warehouse revealed a surplus of grain, the judge arrogantly stated that this proved Hodent's guilt. He then confiscated the flock of sheep, Madame Hodent's last source of income.

Camus's attention was drawn to this situation by a letter to *Alger-Républicain* from Hodent himself. After careful investigation by the newspaper, it was found that the judge, the local *colons* or planters, and the *caïds,* Moslem leaders appointed by the French, were all involved in an attempt to discredit a government grain-price-support program enacted into law under the Blum administration. In a letter to the governor-general of Algeria, Camus made an appeal for Hodent's release from prison so that he might at least make arrangements to defend himself. Camus refused to believe, he said in the letter, that "injustice is so easily consummated" (*AR,* 10-1-39, p. 1).

As a result of the appeal Hodent was released, and a change of venue was granted so that he could be tried in Tiaret instead of Trézel. In the course of the pretrial investigation and during the trial itself, various organizations rallied to Hodent's cause. The Association des Anciens Elèves de l'Institut Agricole came to his defense, pointing out that the administration of the grain program was so badly organized that any grain agent could have been arrested on similar charges and would have found it almost impossible to defend himself. The Ligue des Droits de l'Homme provided Hodent with defense counsel.

Camus followed the investigations and the trial closely. He warned that the government must not use the trial, which involved a man's honor and reputation, as a means of glossing over the corruption that had come to light in connection with the affair: "We say that it is not a matter of saving appearances, that it is not a matter of a condemnation for the sake of principle. If Justice has erred, let Justice recognize the fact. . . . And paradoxical as it may seem, it is well for Justice that judges sometimes be confounded" (*AR,* 5-3-39, p. 3).*

As if to demonstrate this point, the judges who finally tried the case, in spite of Judge Garaud's protest that he had been made the victim of an invidious press campaign, delivered a verdict of not guilty for Hodent, his warehouse foreman, and several Moslem workers who had been inculpated with him. The court also ordered the state to pay the trial costs.

Camus, who had gone to Tiaret to cover the trial for *Alger-Républicain,* reported exultantly that the verdict was even more brilliant than he had expected. As ready to praise as to condemn when the occasion demanded, he remarked: "One must praise impartiality just as strongly as one denounces prejudice. . . . let us thank the judges of Tiaret for having been able to render complete justice in a case that was at once so obvious and so delicate" (*AR,* 23-3-39, p. 1).* Though this was a moment of heady success for a young reporter, Camus did not forget to point out that an acquittal could never completely remedy the suffering caused those unjustly accused: "Let us only hope that the decision of the court will help. And at the end of this long campaign, when justice that we recognize as such has been achieved, it is not congratulations that we offer to Michel Hodent. He has no use for them" (*AR,* 23-3-39, p. 2).*

Although tempered by this reservation, the jubilant tone of Camus's account of Hodent's acquittal tends to bear out Thody's assertion that "Camus's success in securing the acquittal of Michel Hodent also showed him that although the social system in Algeria stood in need of far-reaching reforms, a remedy to individual acts of injustice could be found in the due process of law."[23] This assertion is further supported by the contrast in tone between the report of the acquittal and the open letter to the governor-general written six weeks earlier. The letter had been hopeful, but somewhat skeptical of obtaining results. In concluding it, Camus had remarked: "I do not know if you will read this letter. You must read it however. . . . we know that from behind the mask of high office a man with human feelings may appear. . . . It is that man whom we wish to reach. . . . in this last moment, we want to think only of that inexplicable hope that we place in you—of that solitary and tenacious hope that a human appeal will suffice to bring about a human decision" (*AR,* 10-1-39, p. 1).*

Whether or not the letter succeeded in touching the human being behind the governor-general's façade, the resulting publicity brought the weight of public opinion to bear on the case and achieved very satisfactory results. This undoubtedly had some bearing on the manner in which Camus conducted two subsequent press campaigns, both of which dealt with French policy in relation to the Moslems, beginning what was to become a lifelong concern with the most burning political issue in his native land.

Camus's apprenticeship in journalism was nearly over. He had entered the political arena in a time of turmoil; his views on the political events of those years reveal a young man of great courage and integrity who felt that political action was not an end in itself but a means to attaining and safeguarding freedom and justice for those who suffer from flagrant inequities in the social system. His youthful enthusiasm may have sometimes resulted in overconfidence on his part, but his genuine compassion for afflicted human beings more than compensated for this failing. This compassion opened his eyes to the sufferings of the Algerian Moslems, a state of affairs to which many of his fellow countrymen seemed blind.

2

"Greece in Rags" and the Young Barbarians

ALGERIA, ITS land and its peoples, presented Camus with a paradox. In the rugged landscape, brilliantly lit by the sun and kissed by the sea, he found a potent source of imagery. In the youth of Algiers he saw a pagan innocence and a self-assured acceptance of nature that to him contrasted significantly with the fear-ridden youth of Europe who, deprived of the traditional moral guidance of Christianity, sought a substitute for it in one or another of the sociopolitical doctrines prevalent in the 1930's. So certain was Camus of the salubrity of the way of life represented by these "young barbarians" that he saw it as the potential source of a renaissance of which, in some ways, he was to become the prophet.

But in contrast to the exultant youth on the beaches of Algiers, the Moslem masses lived in poverty and subjugation. In the mountainous area between Algiers and Constantine, Kabylia in 1939 lay gripped by a murderous famine. Against a backdrop of savage natural beauty, men ate the roots of wild plants in order not to starve to death. "Greece in rags" Camus called the Kabylia he saw that summer. Aware of this tragic contrast in his homeland, Camus, along with a few others, tried desperately to bring about badly needed changes.

One hundred years of French rule in Algeria had seen only minimal improvement in the Moslems' social status and living conditions. This was particularly the case in the far-flung rural areas where administration was largely left to the military, to minor

25

civil servants who were easily influenced by the *gros colons,* and to caïds.[1]

The failure to correct the many inequities of French rule, in spite of the efforts of numerous well-intentioned French and Moslem leaders, had led to the rise of nationalist groups that began to gain strength during the period between the two world wars. By the mid-1930's the nationalist movements were fairly widespread, although the government made frequent attempts to hold them in check. Camus and other intellectuals in Algeria repeatedly protested against repressive measures taken against the nationalists and came to the defense of the persecuted Moslems.[2] These European Algerians felt that many of the nationalists' claims were justified, and that the government in Paris should long since have taken steps to correct the abuses on which the claims were based.

The main bone of contention in Algeria was the status of the indigenous populations. The gros colons, who were mostly planters owning large holdings of land, did not want to see the Moslems integrated or "assimilated" into the European community with full rights as French citizens. They rigidly opposed every effort to introduce educational and suffrage reforms that would eventually enable the Moslems to play an influential role in local government.

In the early days of the Third Republic it had been decided that the Moslems should be considered French subjects. As such they were permitted to retain their "personal status," under which they were subject to Koranic law. A Moslem was accorded citizenship only if he renounced his personal status, since this status was held incompatible with many of the statutes of French civil law. The arrangement attracted few Moslems. First, and most important, Moslem religious leaders considered it a form of apostasy. Secondly, the colons saw to it that the statutes regulating the granting of citizenship on this basis should not provide for the Moslems all the civil rights enjoyed by French citizens. A few French leaders like Clémenceau had had the courage to defy the colon pressure groups. In 1919 the "Tiger," out of gratitude for Moslem loyalty to

France during World War I, granted extended voting rights and the right to greater participation in local government to those Moslems who were classed as subjects. The effectiveness of even such relatively mild measures was often nullified by outright refusal on the part of local officials to administer the measures according to the provisions of the law.

Although during the period between the two wars France came to look upon Algeria as part of France, little effort was made to follow Clémenceau's lead. Not until 1937 did the Popular Front propose a plan, the Blum-Violette Project, which provided for the admission to full French citizenship of 21,000 Moslems—out of an indigenous population of seven to eight million. These Moslems were also to retain their personal status. The plan provided as well for increased offers of citizenship over a number of years. Once again colon opposition brought about defeat of the measure, and no new plan was devised until after World War II, when new proposals, based on the Blum-Violette Project and presented by General Catroux, fared no better.

While the French government failed to take any strong or decisive action on the problem of civil rights for the Moslems, it did take steps to improve living conditions among the indigenous populations. France's effort to combat disease and death in Algeria brought about a sharp increase in population. Ironically, overpopulation in turn nullified the hoped-for benefits of these efforts: the land could not produce enough food for the increased number of people. As Brace remarks, "Without the marvel of penicillin, disease and death would have kept the population in check."[3]

France was justly proud of her successful efforts to introduce modern industry into Algeria in order to complement a predominantly agricultural economy. Algiers and Oran had become bustling cities under French rule. Schooling was provided, often in spite of extremely difficult conditions, for Moslem children living in rural areas. While these measures were inadequate, had France not been there to subsidize the Algerian economy such measures might well have been nonexistent. Algeria today is as dependent as ever on outside help from France and other nations, and in the opinion of most authorities will be so for years to come.

Had these been the only aspects of the question, a settlement still might have been reached. But the presence in Algeria of approximately 1,200,000 European Algerians placed the problem of Algerian independence in an altogether different light. The bulk of these European Algerians were members of the middle, lower-middle, and working classes. They were professional people, tradesmen, white-collar workers, skilled and unskilled laborers. They were not wealthy and owned practically no land. Many of them came from families long established in Algeria, and they considered themselves first and foremost Algerians. These people, along with the Moslem masses, were caught between the Scylla and Charybdis of the archconservative gros colons and the nationalist extremists. They, along with the Moslem masses themselves, were to pay dearly for the colons' blind refusal to grant the nationalists' just demands and for the vacillations of successive French governments.

Camus was one of the small group of Algerians of European origin who were astute enough to realize that a radical change in French policy was urgently needed if a clash in Algeria were to be avoided. He had no patience with the arguments of those who used the Moslems' alleged backwardness as an excuse for holding them in subjugation. Castigating those who claimed that the Moslems' needs were not the same as those of Europeans, he wrote: "If they had no such needs before, we should have created those needs in them long ago. . . . The truth is that we rub elbows daily with a people who live three centuries behind the times, and we are the only ones who are insensitive to this incredible anachronism."[4]

This statement was made in the eyewitness report, "Misère de la Kabylie," that Camus wrote for *Alger-Républicain* during a tour of that famine-stricken area in June 1939.[5] A remarkable document, it provides a good overall view of Camus's attitude toward the plight of the Moslems. But this was not the first time he had pointed out the grave faults of French colonial policy and the need to apply measures other than temporary if the inequities that produced poverty and illiteracy among the masses of the Moslem populations were to be corrected. Along with other intellectuals he had signed a petition calling for implementation of the Blum-Violette Project as a minimal measure. He had approached the problem in *Alger-Républicain* for the first time on the occasion of the 1939 New Year's Day distribution of *couscous,* a wheat cereal preparation, to the Moslem poor of Algiers. This traditional observance had been established a few years earlier. Madame Chapouton, daughter of the governor-general, officiated.

Camus described the ceremonies that took place in front of the mosque and in the apartments of the Imam. He then switched to the cemeteries of the Casbah and Belcourt where the actual distribution of the couscous took place. The day was clear, the sky very blue, and the cemeteries filled with blossoming flowers. Against this background Camus described the mass of half-starved people in rags greedily eating the food doled out to them: "300 kilos of couscous, ten sheep, 300 kilos of figs and 40 kilos of butter will have sufficed to ease the hunger of hundreds of sufferers for one day only. . . . far too many children were present. I saw little Moorish girls hide beneath their veils the pieces of meat handed out to them. That says a great deal concerning the prosperity of their homes" (*AR,* 14-1-39, p. 4).*

In spite of the compassion he felt for these people, Camus refrained from making any remarks that might have been inflammatory. The facts, he no doubt thought, spoke for themselves. He did stress, however, the inadequacy of the measures taken to relieve the wretched living conditions of the Moslems. Complimenting Madame Chapouton on the gracious manner in which she had played her "woman's role," Camus noted that men too had a role to play, not in simply alleviating poverty but in eliminating it and thereby making such acts of charity unnecessary. "I know very well," he continued, "that this is not easy to do, and I don't think it possible to eliminate poverty in one day. But I must also say that I

* French texts of starred passages may be found in Appendix A.

have never seen a European population as wretched as this Arab population—and that must indicate something. We must set ourselves the task of doing away with this disproportion and this excess of poverty. It cannot be said, at least, that this is a utopian aim" (*AR,* 14-1-39, p. 4).*

Many Frenchmen too were in straits in the late 1930's. The French economy often hovered near bankruptcy. Devaluation of the franc always came too late to stabilize France's position in the world market. Unemployment ran high. However, conditions among the Moslem populations of Algeria, as Camus indicated, were much worse; they had reached the crisis stage by 1939.

Moslem workers had inevitably been the first victims of layoffs in factories in metropolitan France where many of them, especially the Kabylians, had emigrated. The layoffs had a direct bearing on the living standard of these workers' families in Algeria. During the period of relative prosperity in the early 1930's the post office in the *arrondissement* of Tizi-Ouzou had paid forty millions of francs in postal money orders in one month. The economic crisis in metropolitan France also resulted in a tightening of immigration laws so that Moslems seeking employment were prevented from going there. Thus not only was a source of income cut off, but overcrowded Algeria now had no effective outlet for its brimming population.

In April 1939 a side aspect of this situation came to light. It was symptomatic of the overall plight of the Moslems and effectively dramatized their status as "second-class citizens." Camus once again intervened, writing a series of articles that appeared in *Alger-Républicain* from 20 to 30 April. He brought to light the following facts: a physician for the Caisse d'Assurances Sociales in the Paris region had reported that in carrying out his official duties he had come into contact with large numbers of Moslem workers. Twenty percent of them, he had found, were afflicted with tuberculosis. Although they were required to contribute to the social security medical insurance plan that had been enacted into law in 1928, most had failed to benefit from this coverage. The law provided for payment of 93 percent of a worker's medical expenses, the worker himself paying the remaining 7 percent.

Most Moslem workers were unable to make even this small expenditure, since they were usually supporting relatives in Algeria. Those who became too ill to work generally returned to Algeria, a contingency not included under the provisions of the law; thus they and their families were cut off from any assistance other than that provided under Algeria's own public health program. Physicians under this program provided treatment free of charge, but in some areas there was only one doctor for sixty thousand inhabitants spread over a very wide area.

As a result workers returning from metropolitan France became a burden on families who no longer received the supplementary income that had provided them a bare subsistence level of living. In addition the returning workers spread disease in a region where medical care on a large scale was virtually impossible. The crowning irony, Camus pointed out, was that the law had made special provisions for Corsicans and even for foreigners working in France but residing in neighboring countries. Thus, he noted, "the Kabylian worker once again sees for himself that a French subject is not necessarily treated as a French citizen" (*AR*, 4-4-39, p. 2).

Camus launched an investigation into this situation for *Alger-Républicain*. Feeling himself unqualified to make a definitive judgment, he sent questionnaires to labor union leaders, the Algerian Medical Association, the dean of the medical school of the University of Algiers, and to various government officials. All groups except the Medical Association were in favor of extending the social security law to cover Algeria. The government already had the problem under study and was actually drafting proposals to correct the situation. In the light of this effort, for which Camus congratulated those involved, *Alger-Républicain* chose to defer further investigation and announced that it felt a conclusive judgment to be premature at that time (*AR*, 30-4-39, p. 2).

On 5 June appeared the first article in the more important series entitled "Misère de la Kabylie," based on Camus's survey during the famine. By comparison with what this report revealed, the inequities of the medical insurance law appear of minor significance. The fundamental problem was, in simplest terms, overpopulation and underproduction. The chief products of Kabylia were figs and olives; the staple in the Kabylian diet was grain. Figs and olives did not produce sufficient income to buy enough grain to feed the burgeoning population.

Beneath this deceivingly simple economic imbalance lay abject misery and human degradation whose causes were deeply rooted in colonial exploitation, official corruption, and the compounded results of years of sometimes well-meaning but badly administered rule. All added up to appalling social injustice that was reflected in the hunger-wracked faces of the Kabylian peasants.

Camus's profound shock and compassion were expressed in restrained prose charged with a mixture of anger, sympathy, and desperate appeal. The human suffering seemed all the more cruel to him, played out as it was against a ruggedly beautiful countryside that reminded him of Greece. He entitled the first article "Greece in Rags," but he assured his readers that the resemblance to Greece was restricted to the land only, for ". . . Greece irresistibly evokes a certain glory of the human body and its wonders. And in no country that I know have I seen the human body more humiliated than it is in Kabylia. It must be said without further delay: the suffering in this country is horrifying. . . . I clearly felt . . . that nothing mattered for these men—neither universe, nor world war, nor any of the concerns of the moment—as against the atrocious suffering that disfigures the faces of so many Kabylians" (*AR,* 5-6-39, p. 8).*

The detailed recounting of horrors and injustice that followed may still shock readers today, after an intervening quarter century during which planned, mechanized horror and injustice have become well known, if not commonplace: overcrowded huts reeking of human excrement, old women dying after walking thirty kilometers to receive a scant dole of grain, whole villages subsisting on roots and vines, and children dead from having eaten poisonous roots.

Not only was public grain distribution—the only form of relief provided in most areas—inadequate and badly administered, but the Moslems' ration was only one-fifth that allotted to the indigent whites. In the few areas where public works programs had been instituted to deal with the problem, the government withheld back taxes from the workers' pay. Once again Camus insisted that charity, public or private, was treating symptoms and not causes. If public works programs kept people from starving to death they had some justification, but "if their end result is to put to work, while continuing to let them starve, those who were already starving without working, they amount to an intolerable exploitation of misery."[6]

There are eleven articles in the series. About half are given over to a description of conditions in Kabylia and to a discussion of the prejudices and exploitation that were their basic cause; the rest are devoted to proposals for improving these conditions. In overall impact the articles are comparable to such protests against social injustice as Swift's *A Modest Proposal*. Quilliot compares them to La Bruyère's and Bossuet's descriptions of French peasants during the famines of the seventeenth century.[7] Even statistics take on vividness when presented in Camus's terse, emotionally charged style.

His proposals for alleviating the suffering of the Kabylians and for correcting the conditions that had brought it about are set forth with great urgency. They suggest what can only be termed sweeping reforms: complete political reorganization of Kabylia in order to provide realistic measures of self-government for the Kabylians, minimum-wage legislation for agricultural workers, the opening of government-owned lands to Kabylian peasants for development, the building of numerous small schools more easily accessible to more Moslem children than the "palaces in the deserts," which were impressive showplaces but too few. and too far apart. In addition Camus called for extension of the farm-price-support program, which applied only to cereal grains, to cover figs and olives; and the immediate liberalization of immigration laws to permit Moslems to emigrate to metropolitan France and thereby alleviate Algeria's and particularly Kabylia's overpopulation problem.[8]

He placed the responsibility for dealing with the situation squarely on the French nation as a whole. Metropolitan France, he insisted, should take steps to bring about the necessary reforms. He doubted the likelihood of any improvement in conditions being initiated by the colons. On the other hand, action coming from metropolitan France would have the twofold value of alleviating poverty among the Moslems and of bringing France and Algeria closer together in a common effort. "And," he asserted, "the day that the interests [of France and Algeria] are united into a single interest, one can be sure that unity of hearts and minds will soon be forthcoming."[9] Unfortunately, fifteen years and a war later, when metropolitan France came around to an awareness of its responsibility, the situation had too far deteriorated. It was then that French and foreign intellectuals reproached Camus for his silence with regard to his native land.

In none of Camus's articles is his wish to avoid an ideological battle on political grounds more evident than in "Misère de la Kabylie." He was concerned only with bringing to the attention of his readers the plight of the Kabylians. He refused to fall into the easy trap of exploiting human misery in order to launch political broadsides against his opponents. His experience with the Communist party had already shown him that this was all too often an easy way of salving one's conscience while actually doing nothing to correct the abuses against which one cries out. In the concluding article he made it clear that he was not looking for scapegoats on whom he could place the blame for conditions in Kabylia: "I have no liking for the role of accuser. . . . I know too well . . . what the economic crisis has done to further the distress of the Kabylians, to seek absurdly to hold a few victims responsible for that distress."[10]

Whatever attempts may have been made to prevent the economic collapse that had produced the crisis—and there had been some efforts made in that direction—they had been insufficient. In the light of that fact, Camus contended, no Frenchman could excuse himself on the grounds merely that the attempt had been made. The problem had gone beyond the stage of being a purely political one, and Camus felt that "some progress is realized any time that a political problem is replaced by a human problem."[11] The Kabylian crisis had clearly reached this stage. What mattered most was immediate relief followed by efforts to solve the entire problem.

Camus realized not only that making the responsibility for the Kabylian famine a political issue would, if anything, have hampered the prompt relief measures that were urgently needed, but also that any attempt to correct the generic causes could not effectively be made at the local level. Past attempts had been met with such determined opposition by the gros colons and local government officials that they had had to be abandoned. Camus's seeming conciliatoriness did not stem from any naive belief that a soft approach would gain the cooperation of local authorities, but from a practical realization that invective and a partisan political approach to the problem would carry less weight in high administrative circles in metropolitan France, from which source only, he well knew, any reform movement had to come.

One might question the soundness of Camus's judgment in this case, although it is hard to see what other alternative was possible; but it is an oversimplification to say, as Thody does, that the " 'conservatism' and 'timidity' of which numerous left-wing critics accused him in the nineteen-fifties are already visible" in these articles, and that Camus's attitude in this case amounted to "a refusal to attribute the situation in Kabylia to the evils of the colonial system set up by the French."[12]

In his closing remarks, at the end of the series of articles, Camus stated that if any excuse could ever be found for the colonial system, it would be the effort made by the conquerors to help the conquered retain their personalities.[13] His indictment of the colons' refusal to pay decent wages, and of their method of holding the Moslems in subservience by opposing and circumventing efforts to improve their lot as citizens and as human beings, amounts to a categorical condemnation of a system that had made such abuses possible.

Moreover, in the two months following the final article, Camus renewed his attack on official disregard for the basic civil rights of Moslems. Once again his attention was drawn to a trial in which there had been a flagrant breach of justice. A group of agricultural workers in the vicinity of Auribeau had been sentenced to from five to seven years at forced labor for having allegedly burned down several "buildings"—actually mud and straw huts—during a strike of agricultural workers in September 1937. Camus insisted that an example had been made of these workers because, at the time, the success of the Popular Front had caused right-wing elements to cry out that the foundations of society were being threatened by revolution. Confessions obtained by torture had later been repudiated by the accused, but to no avail. There is nothing conciliatory in Camus's denunciations of this outrage. In two successive articles he wrote:

At a time when so many voices that are important or are thought to be shout themselves hoarse in praise of all sorts of ignoble ideals, it is more than ever essential to make every effort to halt injustice whenever possible.

If democracy is to have any meaning, it will find it here and not in high-sounding phrases. And one might even hope that the recognized innocence of the condemned men of Auribeau may help it to regain the lost time and prestige that one-sided moral mobilization has already caused it to lose in this country (*AR,* 25-7-39, p. 2).*

No free man is assured of his dignity in the face of such procedures. And when base methods can lead to the imprisonment of men whose lives already were only a series of privations, then for all of us they amount to a kind of personal insult that it is impossible to bear (*AR,* 26-7-39, p. 2).*

Still another article, entitled "An Example of Ill-Conceived Arrests and Prosecution," related how three men, involved in demonstrations organized by the nationalist Parti du Peuple Algérien on 14 July 1939, had been charged with "reconstitution de ligue dissoute" (revival of an outlawed organization). In fact, two of the men were not even members of the P.P.A. Camus expressed stupefaction at the method by which these three victims had been selected for arrest and prosecution out of the three thousand who had taken part in the demonstrations. He concluded that they could only have been chosen by a toss of the coin. His patience at an end, he lashed out at the government:

This accusation would be laughable . . . if it were not fraught with malice. For that is what we must conclude. There was a desire to punish, to strike, to destroy the P.P.A. National defense demanded it, just as national defense excused the repudiations made by M. Daladier. But the answer is the same in both cases. For to defend democracy is first of all to strengthen it. If the demands of the P.P.A. so embarrass the Administration, the Administration should not furnish excuse for them. That is the only solution compatible with justice and freedom. . . . each time the P.P.A. has been attacked, its prestige has increased a little more. The rise of Algerian nationalism has grown out of the persecutions inflicted upon the P.P.A. And I can say without paradox that the widespread and deep-seated respect that this political party now finds among the masses is entirely the work of the high-ranking officials in this country (*AR*, 18-8-39, p. 1).*

A more clearly defined indictment of French colonial rule as it then existed is hard to imagine. The last sentence of the article reads: ". . . the only way to wipe out Algerian nationalism is to eliminate the injustices that gave birth to it" (*AR*, 18-8-39, p. 1).* This was the last article Camus wrote on colonial policies until May 1945, when *Combat* printed his analysis of the causes of a rebellion at Sétif.

It is clear that Camus tended to view discrimination against the Moslems primarily as a matter of degree, an extreme example of more widespread forms of social injustice. The Algerians of European origin, the workers, tradesmen, and small shopkeepers, suffered from the same injustices only to a lesser degree. The French Revolution had won for all these groups, in principle, certain rights that Camus wished to see extended and applied to all Algerians,

Moslem and European alike. He had grown up in close contact with the Moslems of Algiers in the popular quarter of Belcourt, and he had none of the prejudices of the "poor white." In his eyes all of his country's inhabitants were Algerians, and he refused to see any distinction among them insofar as social justice was concerned.

When the Algiers Municipal Council, under the leadership of Rozis, voted an unrealistic city budget for 1939, with cavalier disregard for the protests of the minority councilmen representing the workers and the Moslems of the city, Camus affirmed the right of the citizen to pronounce judgment on his civic leaders. He then went on to say with characteristic firmness and irony: "We pronounce judgment here, and with us the entire Moslem and working-class populations. . . . The gracious spectacle presented by the Municipal Council is a very slight compensation for the fiscal burden that is going to overwhelm us" (*AR*, 24-12-38, p. 3).*

This tendency to intermingle the claims of the Moslems with those of the working class had its limitations. The discrepancy between the living conditions and the social status of the Moslems and the workers, as Camus knew, rendered a comparison between them almost impossible. Poverty-stricken as Camus's own childhood had been, the Moslem poor lived in far worse conditions. The working class had at least gained relatively widespread recognition of its demands; and some of them, under the Popular Front, had been granted.

Had the Popular Front endured and been more effective, it might eventually have arrived at a peaceful and equitable solution of the Algerian dilemma. Its legislative program included provisions for reforms that would have benefited all Algerians, in some cases the Moslems in particular. It had enacted the grain-price-support program on which Camus based his proposal for subsidizing the fig- and olive-growing industries in Kabylia. The Blum-Violette Project had set forth proposals for taking definite steps, timid as they may now seem, toward making a reality of the long-talked-about policy of assimilation.

Hence Camus's view that the lots of the workers and of the Moslems could be improved simultaneously was not without some basis in fact. Even after the war, Camus's editorials indicated that he had not lost hope for the resurgence of a Popular Front type of government. In such a government, he felt, lay the hope for the future not only of metropolitan France but also of Algeria and the whole empire as well.

It is not difficult, of course, to make a case against Camus's attitude as stemming from the "white man's burden" philosophy of colonialism. But this would be to ignore the peculiar circumstances of the situation in Algeria where, as we have already pointed out, the European segment of the population was made up not of military or colonial office functionaries but of over one million people many of whom had been established in Algeria for two or more generations. Camus's grandfather had come there in 1871. Many of these Algerians had never set foot in metropolitan France; their ties with Algeria were as strong or stronger than their ties with France. Although Camus's outlook was somewhat more cosmopolitan, he shared his countrymen's sense of dual nationality.

In his biographical and critical study of Camus, Thody asserts that Camus's consistent refusal to consider the possibility of Algeria's completely breaking its ties with France was based on economic considerations rather than on national pride.[14] Camus did feel that Algeria could not stand alone economically as an independent nation. And if the term national pride implies blind, sentimental patriotism, Thody's assertion is certainly correct. In face of the hatred and intolerance that the French had permitted to grow in Algeria, Camus felt little pride in being French; he spoke of France's role in Algeria as "a work of which we are not proud today."[15]

But Camus had a definite personal sense of pride in being Algerian. That pride could cause him to rebel against what he considered an affront to the Algerian entity. He reproached Jules Romains, for example, for having shown, in a lecture, a lack of respect for the intelligence of his Algerian audience. This con-

descension, Camus felt, was inexcusable on the part of so distinguished a personage. "And I persist in the belief," Camus maintained, "that the Algerian public, young, interested in everything,
new in so many respects, and always receptive, deserves that a
writer who speaks before 1500 *Algérois* make an effort to live up to
his own capabilities" (*AR,* 15-1-39, p. 2).

Camus's interest in newly emerging North African writers was
keen. A wide open field, he felt, lay before them, for "This new
race, whose psychology no one has yet attempted to explore (except perhaps Montherlant in his 'Images d'Alger'), needs a new
language and a new literature. It has forged the former for its own
personal use. It is waiting for someone to give it the latter"
(*AR,* 22-11-38, p. 3).* Throughout his life he continued to help
young North African writers of merit to establish themselves and
reach a public. He joined with Gabriel Audisio and Emmanuel
Roblès in organizing the review *Rivages,* and wrote the preface to
the first issue. One of the aims of the Théâtre de l'Equipe, as stated
in its manifesto, was to give to Algiers "a theatrical season that suits
it. A youthful city, Algiers deserves to have a youthful theater"
(*AR,* 21-1-39, p. 5).

This sense of being a vital part of a developing culture might of
course be attributed to an excess of youthful enthusiasm were not
the youth and vigor of Algiers closely associated with the Mediterranean imagery of sunlight and sea so conspicuous in Camus's work
throughout his lifetime. The contrast between the sunny climate of
Algeria and the wintry grayness of northern Europe is fundamental
to Camus's imagery. The fortuitous combination of French culture
with the neopagan world view, a combination which Gide and
Montherlant had also sought and found on the shores of North
Africa, seemed to Camus to open the way to a new renaissance at
the moment when the Judeo-Christian civilization had reached an
advanced stage of decay. In the preface to *Rivages* he reveals his
admiration for the new culture:

At a time when doctrinaire attitudes would separate us from the
world, it is well for young men in a young land to proclaim their

attachment to those few essential and perishable possessions that give meaning to our lives: the sun, the sea and women in the sunlight. They are the riches of the living culture, everything else being the dead civilization that we repudiate. If it is true that true culture is inseparable from a certain barbarianism, nothing that is barbaric can be alien to us.[16]*

It is evident that Camus was using the term barbarian in the Greek sense of one who lives outside the pale of established civilization. In the notebooks, among the entries Camus made while reading Spengler and Cecil Rhodes, the following notation occurs under the heading "Civilization versus culture":

Culture: the cry of men in the face of their destiny. Civilization, its decadence: desire of men for wealth. Blindness.

Concerning a political theory based on the Mediterranean. "I speak of what I know."[17]

Camus, then, was associating the Algerian Man described in *Noces* and in *L'Envers et l'endroit,* essays in which the contrast between the joys of physical existence and man's ignominious destiny is sharply drawn, with a new and burgeoning culture in which we can hear "the cry of men in the face of their destiny."

Europe, by contrast gray and dim in its decadence, is the dead civilization that the young barbarians, representatives of the new culture, repudiate. In *Noces* Camus speaks of these barbarians as embodying "the unreasoned hope that, without their knowledge, perhaps they are modeling the visage of a new culture where man will find at last his own true image."[18] Once again it was from the shores of the Mediterranean that a renaissance was to come.

But Camus recognized a weakness in this nascent civilization. He saw that "a certain intensity of life goes hand in hand with injustice,"[19] and that "thought inspired by the play of sunlight and of the sea can be unjust in its judgments. . . ."[20] The Algerian Man, like all barbarians, possessed a kind of wild innocence. This innocence, as Jean Bloch-Michel points out, knows no moral code or limitations: "it reigns over happy bodies that are preoccupied only with themselves. It is situated outside of history, since it suspends the passage of time and restores to the world the freshness of its first mornings."[21] Camus had been tempted by the appeal inherent in this kind of innocence. He realized, however, that such innocence is fatal, and he decided that he could not remain outside history. His criticism of French colonialism was at once an acceptance of human solidarity within history and an attempt to warn his fellow Algerians that their blind innocence was a trap set for their self-destruction.

The bronzed youths on the Algerian beaches had grasped a fundamental truth of human existence, and Camus would not, like the jury that condemns Meursault, judge them guilty. But he did realize that this truth was only a point of departure, not an end in itself. If one did not go beyond that truth, one ran the risk of annihilation by one of the many manifestations of the absurd: by a jury that does not understand that love of life is more important than a vain show of sorrow, or by the forces of history that descend like a plague on the unwary. Nowhere did the absurd manifest itself more clearly than in Algeria. Camus's Algerian Man rejected any hope of immortality and clung with ardor to this life. But he loved life perhaps too much and too selfishly. This Camus knew: ". . . I do not delude myself. There is not much love in the lives I speak of," he wrote in *Noces*.[22] From this point of view, Camus's first novel, *L'Etranger,* throws a good deal of light on his evaluation of the European Algerians' unpreparedness to face the reality of their situation.

Like Meursault, who is his prototype, the Algerian Man does not hope, does not lie, does not love. In addition, as Germaine Brée says, Meursault "fails to ask any question and thereby gravely errs. In *L'Etranger* Camus thus suggests that in the face of the absurd no man can afford passively just to exist. To fail to question the meaning of the spectacle of life is to condemn both ourselves, as individuals, and the whole world to nothingness."[23] Thus Meursault falls into the trap of his own innocence. Many critics have failed to understand Camus's assertion that Meursault was innocent. Thody, for example, while admiring Meursault's refusal to lie in order to save his own life, finds it difficult to accept Meursault's innocence in face of the latter's involvement with Raymond Sintès.[24] But that involvement is the direct result of Meursault's unquestioning acceptance of his world as it exists. Although Thody points out certain resemblances between *Noces* and *L'Etranger,* he fails to note that among this "childlike people" "Two men do not attack a lone adversary because 'that's playing dirty.' "[25] This is undoubtedly one of the reasons why Camus said to Gaëton Picon, a metropolitan Frenchman, "Naturally you can understand Meursault, but an Algerian will enter more easily and more deeply into an understanding of him."[26]

Guilt, and with it a sense of responsibility, only comes into play when one begins to reflect on the possible implications of one's acts. This Meursault does not do before he murders the Arab. In the Camusian universe, Jean Bloch-Michel points out, "there comes a day when a man begins to reflect, that is to say, he enters at one and the same time into the problem of moral values and into History; at the same instant he loses his innocence."[27] Meursault does not consciously reach this stage until after his trial when, in prison awaiting execution, he admits his guilt.

Louis Rossi feels that one best resolves the question of Meursault's innocence or guilt by approaching the problem on a metaphysical level.[28] This is true up to a certain point, but it obliges one to separate the myth from the narrative in *L'Etranger,* a misleading process since both myth and narrative are firmly grounded in Camus's Algeria. The problem of Meursault's innocence is closely related to the problem of the innocence of the European Algerians who asked no questions and who failed to see a manifestation of the absurd in the face of a starving Moslem. They, like Camus and like Meursault, loved the sun and the sea and the sight of women in the sunlight. For the majority of European Algerians, however, the presence of so much physical beauty shut out all other preoccupations. Only a few realized as Camus had realized, when watching a sunset from a mountainside overlooking a Kabylian village, "that it would have been pleasant to abandon oneself to an evening so surprising and so grandiose, but that the suffering whose flames burned red before us imposed a kind of ban on the beauty of the world."[29]

This kind of examination of *L'Etranger* adds perspective to Camus's view of the Algerian problem: under the circumstances, he could not possibly have seen it in purely political terms. This is, however, only a limited aspect of the novel. Any attempt to judge Camus's literary works solely on the basis of his involvement with the Algerian problem would, of course, be questionable. In much the same way, to use his literary works as the only means of gaining insight into his position on the social and political aspects of the Algerian problem is misleading. Yet there has been a recent tendency on the part of certain French critics to use *L'Etranger* as a document to prove that Camus's attitude toward the Algerian War was simply that of a "poor white."

Henri Kréa, a leftist critic, declared in an article written in 1961 that when Meursault kills the Arab on the beach he is killing a racial entity into which he fears he will be absorbed, so that his act is actually "the subconscious realization of the obscure and puerile dream of the 'poor white' that Camus never ceased to be. . . ."[30] In a slightly more sympathetic interpretation, Pierre Nora, who has written on the Algerian conflict, suggests that *L'Etranger* is the first work of Algerian literature to deal with the psychological relationship between the Arab and the European Algerian. Nora too maintains that Camus was aware of the problem only on a subconscious level, the only level on which Nora thinks the European Algerians, "consciously frozen in historical immobility," are able to confront the problem at all. Thus, he believes, the entire novel, and Meursault's trial in particular, is a "disturbing admission of historical guilt and takes on the aspect of a tragic anticipation."[31]

To assume that Camus could only treat the Algerian question on a subconscious level or that he was otherwise incapable of coming to terms with it merely reveals either Kréa's and Nora's ignorance of a large part of Camus's journalistic writings or their intention deliberately to disregard them. Camus was clearly aware of the deeply rooted resistance of the European Algerians to any policy that prepared the way for assimilation of the Moslem population in Algeria. In 1939, as we have seen, fifteen years before Algerian independence became a burning international issue, he attempted to warn metropolitan Frenchmen that they must take the responsibility for lifting the yoke of oppression from the shoulders of the Moslems, since the initiative would never come from the European minority in Algeria itself. He was to repeat this warning in 1945, when, as editor of *Combat*, he spoke directly to an audience of metropolitan Frenchmen. *L'Etranger* is in no way a disguised rationalization of the "poor white's" fear of losing his identity. It is rather a statement, in artistic form, of the need for awareness of a human solidarity that transcends national and racial differences.

So long as the inequitable status of the Moslems in Algeria existed, it continued to be offensive to Camus's profound sense of justice. Moreover, it would have been difficult for him to have proposed his Algerian Man, even symbolically, as an exemplary prototype of a new "renaissance man" while the European Algerians went on tolerating social injustice. Thus, the effort to correct the evident imbalance in the Algerian social order was also, in a sense, an effort to render his artistic universe more coherent. But, in the late summer of 1939, his preoccupation with Algeria and its problems was relegated to a secondary position. Camus was about to "enter history" in a way that he probably had never imagined.

3
The Plague Years

IN MARCH 1939 Hitler annexed Czechoslovakia. The threat of war hung over Europe all during the summer of that year. On 3 September war was declared. In Algeria as elsewhere interest in the war became paramount. *Soir-Républicain* was born out of the need for fuller coverage of the war news than *Alger-Républicain* alone could give. Its brief life of less than four months was a tumultuous one. Camus outlined the paper's policy in the lead editorial of the first issue:

> In this war where their very lives are committed, where each hour that passes can decide their fate, the public hungers for truthful news and information.
> This paper brings it to them. It will do so without excess or vain boasting.
> A just cause can do without abject and useless "brainwashing."
> The rule of cold reason alone will prevail here.
> No other consideration will make us deviate from our course. In being faithful to our ideal, we will be faithful to the truth (*SR*, 15-9-39, p. 1).*

Camus was to remain faithful to this ideal, but in so doing he ran head on into official censorship regulations. He used every means at his disposal, including humor, to needle and circumvent the censors; on one occasion the entire lower half of page two was left blank except for a brief announcement which read: "The abundance of material obliges us to postpone until tomorrow our serial, 'La Chartreuse de Parme,' by Stendhal" (*SR*, 22-10-39, p. 2).

He had a knack too for pointing out, with ironic understatement,

* French texts of starred passages may be found in Appendix A.

46

the similarities between the conduct of the Daladier government and that of those totalitarian states against which it claimed to be defending democracy. In one article, after having declared that the League of Nations should be a society of peoples instead of a society of governments who merely carried their bellicose attitudes to the conference table, he commented: "People will say to me that governments represent their peoples. But we read every day in the papers that this is not true of certain countries. As for the others, you will allow me to smile discreetly" (SR, 15-12-39, p. 2).*

One of Camus's most notable targets in the war with the censors was Jean Giraudoux, at that time minister of information, whose office was responsible for press and radio censorship. Camus cared little for Giraudoux's works. He had earlier referred to them as typifying "a certain tradition in our present-day literature that has specialized in the genre known as 'superior product of civiliza- tion' " (AR, 9-4-39, p. 5).* After Giraudoux's appointment to the Ministry of Information, Camus suggested that it only remained for the censors to suppress La Guerre de Troie n'aura pas lieu: "M. Giraudoux will be the first to rejoice over it. His past suppressed, he will be more at ease in his new functions" (SR, 27-11-39, p. 2).* This stinging remark was undoubtedly in part evoked by the diffi- culties that Camus was having at the time with local censors in Algiers.

In spite of harassment by the censors, Camus was able to put into effect techniques of news reporting that he was to use more exten- sively in Combat after World War II. A full page was devoted to a review of news from diverse sources such as foreign press, news agencies, national press and radio, etc., printed under the collective title "In the Spotlight of War." Each item was presented with a comment on the reliability of the source and its political affiliations, if any, as well as a reference to other sources that corroborated or contradicted the news or point of view expressed. All items re- ferring to a specific subject were grouped together and were fol- lowed by editorial comments written by Camus or other members of the staff.

Soir-Républicain's editorial line followed closely the pacifist point of view formulated by Léon Blum. Essentially this meant a policy of seeking every means to arrive at a truce which would lead to discussion of grievances by the Allies and the Axis powers. As far as Camus and his paper were concerned, Germany did have certain just grievances, and other European nations were not without responsibility for the conditions that had led to war. In reviewing a lecture entitled "Against Imperialism," Camus, in April 1939, had written:

I think it takes a certain courage today to dare to say that imperialism is *also* a trait of the democracies. Many of us knew it. Most have forgotten it. However, the destinies of the world's peoples are inseparable, and we can be sure that the desire for power engenders the desire for power, hatred breeds hatred, imperialism gives birth to imperialism, and that the Treaty of Versailles is, in its spirit, the ancestor of the Munich Agreements (*AR,* 25-4-39, p. 4).*

Since all the peoples of Europe, including those of the democracies, would suffer enormously from a war conducted on the basis of a policy of total victory, he felt it mandatory to try every possible means to avoid such a war. In a front page editorial on 6 November 1939, Camus outlined a policy of "peace in wartime." He reiterated earlier statements to the effect that the democracies shared in the responsibility for the situation as it then existed. He pointed out that over the previous few years Hitler had presented, along with demands that were outrageous, some that were justified. The Allies had seemed bent on granting the outrageous claims while refusing to consider those that were justified. This policy had led ultimately to German aggression. Since Hitler had committed overt acts of war, armed resistance was unavoidable. But Camus believed it still possible to avert full-scale war; an energetic and honest effort to reestablish peace on a sound basis had to be carried on simultaneously with deterrent military action. He insisted, however, that what he and his paper advocated was not a lenient policy toward Hitler:

We were the first to repudiate a regime under which human dignity counted for nothing and freedom became an object of scorn. But we continued to say at the same time that such excessive bestiality found its source in the despair of a nation. Nations in this respect are like individuals. It is in the depths of suffering that they forge their will for power (*SR,* 6-11-39, p. 1).*

He went on to list briefly the steps he felt were necessary to halt the war and to begin the work of establishing a permanent peace.¹ Then he continued:

We believe . . . there is only one kind of inevitability in history, that which we create. We believe that this conflict could have been avoided and that it can still be stopped to the satisfaction of all involved. We believe that if but one possibility of doing so still existed, it would be forbidden to despair before having tried it (*SR,* 6-11-39, p. 1).*

In spite of his insistence that disarmament and an attempt at negotiating European unity be tried in an effort, as Caesonia says in the play *Caligula,* "to give the possible a chance,"² Camus seems to have realized that the possibility of averting a full-scale war was slight. On 17 September 1939, the page one headline in *Soir-Républicain* read: "Soviet Troops Attack Poland." Also on page one was a brief editorial by Camus entitled "The War." In it he wrote:

Never perhaps have left-wing militants had so many reasons to despair. Many beliefs have collapsed along with this war. And amid all the contradictions that the world flounders in, forced to see things clearly, we are led then to deny everything.

We understand. We understand everything. And we even understand very well. Many of us had failed to understand the men of 1914. We are closer to them now, for we now know that a man may go to war without consenting to war. We know that at a certain extremity of despair indifference becomes overwhelming, and with it comes a sense of the inevitable and a taste for fatalism.*

In 1914, he continued, there had at least been the hope that men were fighting "the war to end all wars." The men of 1914 had been able to place their hopes in "a reaction of the peoples." But so many hopes for peace and so much faith placed in mankind had only ended in another collapse and in new carnage. After the war trees would once more burst into flower. The world in the long run always survives the ravages of history. But if there were still men alive to look at trees in bloom, their only certainty would be that another day would surely come when they would be called upon once more to give up their lives.

Probably Camus never wrote more despairingly than in this editorial. His only act that compares with it is his determined silence after he had spoken his last word on the Algerian War in 1958. There must have seemed little hope left for the liberalization of the "transitional" dictatorship in Russia, when the only established Socialist nation in the world had just joined Adolph Hitler in order to crush Poland. There was even less hope that the peoples of Europe would at last demand the justice they had so long been denied rather than resign themselves once more to slaughter.

But in spite of his shaken faith in humanity, Camus did not give up hope of the war's somehow being stopped. *Soir-Républicain* pointed out that as late as December 1939 Blum still dared to advocate disarmament in *Le Populaire,* although he was nearly drowned out by strident voices demanding that Germany be crushed and dismembered. In a review of the Parisian press, the paper quoted M. Elie-J. Bois, who had declared in answer to Blum's disarmament proposals that France needed another Richelieu who could impose on Germany another treaty of Westphalia (*SR,* 14-12-39, p. 2). While noting, "We are not always in agreement with the Socialist leader," Camus wrote a defense of Blum's disarmament proposals and condemned Elie-J. Bois's position. ". . . all experiments have been tried except for [Blum's proposals]," he wrote of disarmament. "And all these experiments have brought us war. One should say that intellectual honesty requires at least that the ultimate attempt be made before deciding upon the inevitable nature of wars" (*SR,* 14-12-39, p. 2).*

As the new year began, in a moving editorial simply entitled "1940"—one of the last Camus was to write for *Soir-Républicain* —he restated his belief in man's ultimate ability to control his destiny:

We have precise, generous, and ardent New Year's wishes to formulate. We desire and we summon forth with all our strength a new world and a life in which mankind may have its chance at dignity. Our readers know very well what we want and hope for. Then let them think as we do that it is vain to wish this a happy year but that it is essential to work in order to construct a happy year. Wish for nothing, but accomplish. Do not expect from a destiny made entirely by others what is still in your own hands. *Soir-Républicain* does not wish you happiness since we know that you are wounded in your flesh and in your hopes. But from the bottom of the heart we wish that you may keep the strength and the lucidity necessary to forge for your-selves your happiness and your dignity (*SR*, 1-1-40, p. 1).*

Camus's notebooks reflect on a more personal note his despair at the catastrophe that struck Europe in 1939. His attempts to cope with the reality of the war he so detested created a crisis in his thought. It ultimately resulted in a somewhat altered outlook marked by a kind of maturity that had tended to tone down the enthusiastic optimism which reached its high point at the time of Michel Hodent's acquittal. Camus had never looked upon the task of bringing about social progress as an easy one, but he now realized that right and good intentions did not automatically assure that the masses would follow those who championed their cause.

Like many intellectuals who were inclined toward internation-alism and pacifism, Camus was not prepared to assimilate the fact of full-scale war into his thinking. In a review of Montherlant's *Equinoxe de septembre* (*AR*, 5-2-39, p. 7), he expressed admira-tion for Montherlant's acceptance of the war as "one of the im-placable faces of destiny," and continued: "Montherlant doesn't ask how to prevent or to cure, but seeks only the way to undergo the scourge of war. And what other problem confronts honest minds in our country at this hour?"* But if he was willing to admit that the question imposed itself, Camus was not convinced that Montherlant's example was one he himself should follow. For Camus and many other intellectuals, to flaunt one's indifference in the face of destiny did not provide a satisfactory answer: "We are divided today into two clans, according to whether we choose slavery or death. But there are many of us who refuse to accept this dilemma, who do not want to choose, who admire those who have deliberately ceased to act. Montherlant is not among these" (*AR,* 5-2-39, p. 7).*

Nonetheless there was a strain of the hidalgo in Camus, and he did see in Montherlant's point of view a certain stoical nobility that appealed to him. Once war becomes a reality, he noted, Montherlant "will accept it as a sickness and try still to find in its midst reason for living. There is perhaps in our literature no more virile and more bitter passage than the one where Montherlant states that he will fight without believing, with no ideal but that of being the equal of a destiny that has come without being called."* As Brée points out, Camus was to use similar arguments to justify his own attempts to enlist in the French Army in September 1939.[3] He was turned down because of poor health, the result of tuberculosis which had stricken him at the age of eighteen and from whose aftereffects he suffered throughout his life. Had the army accepted him it is still doubtful that Camus, who was so sensitive to the suffering of others, would have been content to accept the war with stoical indifference. Camus was to treat the war as a sickness in *La Peste,* the symbolic chronicle of the Resistance and the Nazi occupation written in 1946; but for Montherlant's aristocratic aloofness he was to substitute the lucid attitude of Rieux, who struggles against the plague while knowing that the battle is in the long run futile: the microbe inevitably returns to a dormant state, only to become active again at a later time.

This view of war, or of any other social evil, as a recurring malady was eventually to replace the somewhat facile view of human progress that characterized Camus's political outlook up until 1939. But in the autumn of that year he tended to see in the war a negation of all that he had thought possible in the way of human progress. In the faces around him he saw only bestiality. "One meets only wild beasts, the beast-like faces of Europeans," he wrote in his notebook in a September entry of about the date of "The War" editorial.[4] This was the most pessimistic phase in Camus's attitude toward the war. He was depressed by the complete collapse of all efforts to avert the conflict. The resigned acceptance of its inevitability, not only by people in general but also by political and intellectual leaders, appeared to him as a betrayal: "All are guilty of betrayal, those who demanded resistance and those who spoke of peace. They are there, as meek and as guilty as the others. And never has the individual been more alone in the face of the lie-making machine."[5]

It seemed to Camus that if the masses had failed to act or to re-act against being slaughtered it was the fault more of the leaders who now stood stricken silent and resigned before the onrush of the Wehrmacht than of the people themselves. He was not to forget this point of view in 1944 when the time came for France to assume once more her role as a sovereign, independent nation. It was also on the political and intellectual leaders that Camus was to lay the prime responsibility for the political anarchy of the French nation under the Fourth Republic.

Like Rambert in *La Peste,* Camus in 1939 felt the temptation to ignore the whole affair. Algeria was far from the conflict, and the rhythm of the seasons went on with the promise of happiness; the almond trees still bloomed in the Valley of the Consuls. But he knew that an *homme absurde* could not ignore the war, which only generalized the absurdity of life. It had to be faced and taken into consideration in the formulation of one's judgments. In September 1939 he wrote: "From the moment the war 'is,' any judgment that does not embrace it is false."[6] Being unable to remain detached from it, one could only choose between collaboration in its stupidity and cruelty, and an attempt to fight against it.

Acceptance of the war as one manifestation of the absurdity of the human condition finally prevailed over resignation and despair in Camus's mind. The "Letter to a Man in Despair,"[7] set down in his notebook in November 1939, expressed his understanding and sympathy for the feeling of despair experienced by an imaginary correspondent, an intellectual overwhelmed with disgust at the war. But, he asserted, despair could not be an end in itself. Despair was a transient, not a permanent, condition. It had to give way to a more lucid view of things. Only if a person could say that he had personally done everything possible to prevent war could he claim that war was inevitable. Even if every effort to avert war had been made and had failed, no one could be justified in withdrawing into his own ivory tower of despair. The individual human being, while he might despair of ever finding meaning in life in general, could still shape and give meaning to history. One must accept the fact "that war is waged as much with the enthusiasm of those who desire it as with the despair of those who repudiate it with all their soul."[8]

In this letter, actually written to himself, Camus seems to have come to terms with his doubts and questions. The war, like sickness and death, had become a fact of existence. If one could not prevent it one could struggle against its encroachment on human life. The opportunity to join the struggle was not to come until three years later when, during a trip to the continent, he made contact with the Resistance movement, which had become a well-organized network by 1942.

After *Soir-Républicain* was forced to cease publication in January 1940, Camus left Algiers for Oran, where he spent the month of February. In March he went to Paris; Pascal Pia had found a position for him with *Paris-Soir*. He worked as a rewrite man, not wishing to contribute as writer to a paper which did not allow him full freedom of expression. During this short period he wrote only two articles, which appeared in the left-wing weekly, *La Lumière*. He seems to have concentrated mainly on his literary works; *L'Etranger* was completed in May 1940.

That same month the German Army started the Battle of France. The French press moved out of Paris before the German advance and fell back to Clermont-Ferrand. Camus went to Clermont, then Bordeaux, and finally to Lyon with the paper. In Lyon he married Francine Faure in December 1940.[9] Shortly afterward the couple returned to Oran, where Camus taught in a private school. He divided his time between teaching, writing, and visits to Algiers. In

Algiers he briefly revived the Théâtre de l'Equipe and produced *Hamlet*. "Les Amandiers" and "Le Minotaure" were written during this period (1940), and *Le Mythe de Sisyphe* was completed in February 1941.

France fell in June 1940. The French Parliament turned over the government to Marshal Pétain who, along with Pierre Laval, negotiated an armistice with Germany which left France "free" south of the Loire. Vichy became Pétain's capital, and for a short time a number of the French felt relieved. Total disaster, it seemed, had been averted. Pétain was of course unacceptable to many others, particularly the left-wing intellectuals. Instead of looking upon him as the savior of France he claimed to be, they considered him an opportunist who had chosen France's moment of humiliation in order to concentrate power in the hands of reactionary elements. While underground resistance to the Germans was being organized in the North, small underground groups began to form in the South in opposition to the Pétain-Laval government at Vichy.[10] Resistance began on an almost individual level, often in the form of publication of clandestine tracts, pamphlets, and newspapers attacking the *maréchalistes*. The network that Camus was later to join grew out of the efforts of Henri Frenay, who began in the spring of 1941 to publish a small newspaper titled *Les Petites Ailes de la France*. This paper later became known as *Vérités* and finally as *Combat*. The first issue bearing the name *Combat* appeared in December 1941.[11] As the newspaper's operation expanded, Frenay enlarged his editorial staff; among his chief assistants was Claude Bourdet, a journalist who became a leading figure in the Resistance organization. Pascal Pia was a member of the network, also known as Combat, which published the paper. It was probably through him that Camus established contact with the network sometime in the fall of 1942. Because of the very nature of clandestine activity, it is not easy to follow Camus during these years. An examination must be made here of some facets of the Resistance operation, or many of Camus's subsequent political positions will remain somewhat obscure.

The history of the French Resistance movement is a complicated one. Many of the contradictions and myths surrounding both it and its members may never be cleared up entirely. Since the need for secrecy in many cases precluded keeping written records, attempts to write the history of the movement have had to depend on personal accounts that often conflict. However, some salient features do emerge from studies published so far.

In the beginning, there were literally hundreds of small Resistance groups. They were generally initiated by intellectuals, working either as individuals or in small groups. Late in 1940 and early in 1941 they began to publish pamphlets and newsheets such as Frenay's *Petites Ailes*. In time contact was established among some of the larger groups, and some kind of cohesive action became possible. By 1942 Combat, Libération, and Franc-Tireur, along with the Communist "Front National," were the major Resistance networks. Each of the first three put out a major publication which bore the name of its respective network; the Front National was represented in the clandestine press by *Humanité*. By March 1942 the Combat and Libération networks had joined to form the M.U.R. (Mouvements Unis de la Résistance). On the fringe of the M.U.R. groups was Father Chaillet's *Témoignage Chrétien*, a Catholic clandestine publication. Father Chaillet had originally been associated with Frenay and the Combat network; but it was decided that *Combat,* the newspaper, should avoid sectarian leanings and that Father Chaillet should publish his Catholic paper separately.[12]

The M.U.R. encompassed an extensive cross-section of political ideas. It included men of liberal Catholic persuasion, such as René Leynaud and Father Chaillet, as well as men of the non-Communist left like Claude Bourdet and Emmanuel d'Astier de la Vigerie. Some Communists also belonged to this group, having joined before the Front National became active. The Communists on the whole were rather late in organizing cohesive Resistance cells, mainly because of their propaganda and policies at the time of the Germano-Soviet pact. Moscow's failure to warn the French Com-

munists of the change in policy had left them in an almost untenable position since the official party line, up until the announcement of the signing of the pact, had been one of hostility toward the
Fascists. Germany's attack on Russia in June 1941, however, set
things right once more, and the Communists then went ahead with
officially organized resistance against the Nazis.

In England as head of the government in exile, de Gaulle had to
convince the Americans and British that the entire French nation
was behind him. In May 1943 he sent Jean Moulin to France to
help organize the Conseil National de la Résistance (C.N.R.).
Representatives of the major Resistance networks included in the
M.U.R.—eight altogether by this time—two trade union representatives, and six representatives from the major prewar political
parties comprised the membership.

According to Claude Bourdet, the M.U.R. was reluctant to see
itself superseded by the C.N.R., particularly because of the mistrust
M.U.R. members felt toward the prewar political factions.[13] The
M.U.R. had already published a manifesto calling for a revolution
in France after the war. In the opinion of many résistants such a
revolution could be accomplished only by abolishing the political
factions of the Third Republic and by eliminating the Vichyites and
the French Nazis led by Doriot, Déat, and Darnand. In September
1942 *Combat* along with the other clandestine papers had published the manifesto of the M.U.R. "Our task will not end with the
liberation of our territory. Beyond that we want to rebuild France.
We want to support the necessary contribution of France to the
restoration of Europe and of the world."[14]

The manifesto also demanded that the Provisional Government,
which was to be set up after the Nazis were driven out of France, be
ready to assure the material well-being of all Frenchmen, punish
the Vichy traitors and collaborators, and abolish the unjust and
degrading laws promulgated by the Vichy regime. Moreover, the
manifesto declared, the Resistance believed that a revolution for
France was a necessity. This would not be a class revolution but "a
revolution of all Frenchmen for all Frenchmen." The Resistance, it

continued, was living proof that all classes and creeds could work together for the good of the French nation. Out of the "crucible" of the Resistance the revolution, Socialist in form, was to come. The men of the Resistance carried within them "the dawn of a new civilization." This civilization was to include a United States of Europe in which the peoples of Europe would at long last receive the benefits of an economy that had remained too long in the hands of a powerful oligarchy (*Com. cl.,* 9-42, p. 1).

After it was organized, the C.N.R. immediately drew up a charter based on almost identical goals. Unfortunately, however, the C.N.R. suffered from internal difficulties. Even before its founding it had been decided that the Communists should have a voice in establishing the new order in France. In spite of their early wavering, the Communists were among the most valiant of the résistants, and they were, after all, Frenchmen. They were also bearing the brunt of the punishment meted out to captured résistants, since both Vichy and the Nazis hated them with equal fury. In December 1943 *Combat* made clear its stand on Communist participation in the postwar government. A similar stand was taken by the C.N.R. and the Congrès de Combat in Algiers in March 1944. *Combat* stated that "The dialogue between Communists and non-Communists is necessary"; without it there could be no hope of founding a true democracy (p. 1). So far as can be determined, Camus did not write this article, nor the M.U.R. manifesto. However, as editor of the postliberation *Combat* he was to subscribe to the principles expressed in it and in the M.U.R. manifesto.

In working within the C.N.R., the Communists did not prove to be so cordial as had been hoped. They represented only a minority on the organization's sixteen-man executive committee, but that committee was too cumbersome to meet often. Of the five-man steering committee that did the actual administrative work they were able to gain control. They also secured majorities on a number of local liberation committees that had been set up in Paris and in the provinces. They had plans for merging the rest of the Resistance

groups with the Front National after the war, and they did everything possible to prevent the reverse from happening.

According to Robert Aron, the Communists were instrumental
in having Georges Bidault elected president of the C.N.R. because
they considered him the most manageable of the possible candi-
dates.[15] Bourdet asserts that Bidault actually helped the Communists gain control of the C.N.R. in return for their support of his
nomination as president, a position that could later allow him to
split his Catholic group off from the C.N.R. in order to form the
M.R.P. party and launch his own political career.[16] Whatever the
case, Bidault's election as president of the C.N.R. did not augur
well for the effectiveness of the role that more liberal elements of
the Resistance hoped the movement would play in France's postwar political affairs.

Little concrete information is available about Camus's part in the
Resistance. He consistently refused to talk about it, insisting that
"the ex-soldier's role is not for me. . . ."[17] In early criticism of
Camus's works, much was made of the alleged contradiction between the hedonistic pessimist of *L'Etranger* and *Le Mythe de
Sisyphe,* and the dedicated résistant. Thody finds it hard to reconcile the Camus of the early essays with the Camus who defended
Michel Hodent and wrote the passionate appeal on behalf of the
Kabylians.[18] However, I think Camus's early career as a journalist
and the citations from the *Carnets* earlier in this chapter make it
quite clear that the contradictions discovered by the critics resulted
more from a distorted view of Camus and his works than from any
schizophrenic tendencies in Camus himself.

Once Camus had acknowledged that he could not remain detached from the war, it became inevitable that when the opportunity presented itself he should join the Resistance. Camus himself
said much later, in 1948, that the question of motivation was
pointless. "I didn't think of myself as being elsewhere, that is all
there is to it." The death of Gabriel Péri, the brilliant Communist

deputy and journalist shot by the Gestapo on 19 December 1941, definitely decided him to join the Resistance.[19]

In the spring of 1942 he suffered from a recurrence of tuberculosis. In an effort to conquer the disease he went to France in August 1942 and spent the remainder of that year on a farm in the village of Mazet-Saint-Voy. It was probably here that he first established contact with the Combat network. He traveled back and forth to Saint-Etienne and Lyon and seems to have been engaged in some sort of propaganda work among the miners of Saint-Etienne. In any case, Camus's role in the Resistance was relatively far removed from the level of intrigue and political maneuvering that was characteristic of the directing committees of various movements. To this fact Bourdet, with some justification, later attributed what he considered Camus's overly idealistic political outlook during the immediate postwar period.

Camus's journalistic activities in the Resistance seem to have been stepped up during the summer of 1943: in July he wrote the first letter to a German friend, which appeared in the clandestine *Revue libre* that December. Whether he was actually contributing articles to clandestine *Combat* by the summer of 1943 is not certain; it seems unlikely, since Camus himself told Germaine Brée that he was called to work for *Combat* in the latter part of 1943. Mlle. Jacqueline Bernard, secretary of the Combat network, also states in a letter to Madame Camus that Camus's association with the newspaper was established that fall.

According to Marie Granet, Frenay and Bourdet decided to move the center of the network's operations to Paris in August 1943. The fact that the printing press had to remain in Lyon made it difficult to coordinate the work of the editorial staff in Paris with that of the printers in Lyon. Pascal Pia, as a professional journalist, was asked to take over as editor of the paper and to supervise this operation. Pia soon found himself busy with other activities and asked Camus to assume the responsibilities of editorship.[20]

Bourdet, on the other hand, claims that he first met Camus in February 1944 at the home of Maximilien Vox, and that Pia was only asked to take over the position of editor that March, shortly before Bourdet's arrest on 25 March. It was then, according to Bourdet, that Pia, finding himself short-handed because of the arrest of several of *Combat*'s regular contributors, asked Camus to assist him in editing the paper.[21]

Only two articles in the clandestine issues of *Combat* have been conclusively identified as by Camus. Granet states that he composed the June 1944 issue almost singlehandedly.[22] Unable to obtain the printed copies from Lyon, Camus made up and distributed a mimeographed issue for that month. I have so far been unable to locate a copy. There seems to be little in the clandestine issues that can add greatly to an assessment of Camus's attitude toward the intellectual's involvement in the war. His views on this subject could hardly have differed much from those he expressed in his notebooks or in his editorials in postliberation *Combat*. Most of the articles and editorials in the clandestine papers were of necessity devoted to reports of Nazi atrocities, to messages from de Gaulle, to corrections of news printed in the collaborationist press, and to political condemnation of the Vichy government. Many of the articles are impressive for their style and bear out the claim made by Camus and other résistants that the struggle the Resistance waged against the Nazis was unmarked by poisonous hatred and vicious propaganda.[23]

Because the Gestapo had arrested so many of the Resistance leaders during the last months of the occupation, by August 1944 Camus found himself editor-in-chief of *Combat* and spokesman for a large segment of the non-Communist résistants. He wholeheartedly endorsed the Resistance demands for a revolution. He shared the faith of the majority of Resistance leaders who saw the movement as a source of fresh and forward-looking political leaders for postwar France.

This latter aspect of the Resistance program was of great importance for Camus. He had learned from his experiences during World War II that social reform was not likely to be initiated by the masses. It could only be brought about by leaders dedicated to democratic ideals more than to party platforms and personal ambitions. In late 1941 or early 1942 he had come to the conclusion that the people were able to exercise effective political power only when, as in ancient Athens, they had the leisure to devote their time and thought to political problems. A government of workers by workers seemed to him to be a contradictory ideal in the twentieth century: ". . . it is at the time when the proletarization of the European is at its most advanced stage that the ideal of popular sovereignty has become strongest: that is impossible."[24]

Camus had watched with disgust the peoples of Europe put their lives in the hands of political leaders who did not hesitate to abandon their responsibilities when faced with the reality of defeat. He knew that the misery and frustration of human beings who felt themselves inextricably caught up in an unjust existence favored this kind of mass surrender to a leader. He had noted in 1938 how "Many young men, in Germany and elsewhere, thought they had found relief from their suffering by putting themselves entirely in someone else's hands" (*AR*, 24-1-39, p. 3).* The German people, by merging their individual identities into a single national entity embodied in Hitler, had put themselves squarely on the side of death, violence, and injustice.

The peoples of the occupied nations of Europe had become their victims, but it had taken the defeat of 1940 to shock these conquered peoples and their intellectual leaders into a realization that, as Camus stated in *Lettres à un ami allemand*, "We had much to overcome: perhaps to begin with the ever-present temptation in us to resemble [the German people]."[25] That resemblance had been manifest in the all-or-nothing attitude of French politicians and in the indifference of the masses toward political matters. As early as August 1937 Camus had been disturbed by the hollowness of the pronouncements of French political leaders. He was equally disturbed by the complacency with which peoples accepted corrupt leaders and governments. He saw such complacency as a willingness to play a deadly game with their very lives.[26]

In *La Peste* Camus deliberately chose the Oranais to represent the peoples of Europe, and Oran for him was a city where "people work from morning till night and then choose to waste the time left them to live in playing cards, in drinking and in gossiping."[27] It was also a city where "people make up their minds only when forced to do so."[28] While the people of Oran gossiped and played cards, the plague swept down upon them unawares. There had been warnings: the rats, carriers of the plague, had come into the streets to die, first one or two, then in ever-increasing numbers. But these warnings went unheeded. No preventive measures were taken. Within a few weeks Oran had become a hotbed of pestilence. Thousands of Oranais suffered and died, but only a few men, like Dr. Rieux, Tarrou, and Rambert threw all their strength, knowledge, and talents into the struggle against the disease. Like the Oranais of *La Peste,* the majority of Frenchmen had suffered from the plague, the Nazi plague. World War II had come, and the French people had paid dearly for the weakness of their leaders and for their own failure to accept political responsibility. Most of them had suffered in silence, neither collaborating nor resisting. It had actually been a dedicated few—the Rieux, the Ramberts, and the Tarrous—who had redeemed France's shameful defeat. These same dedicated men, those of them who still remained, were now faced with the task of rebuilding a France and a Europe in which liberty and justice would be assured for all Frenchmen and for all Europeans. Not that Camus had come to advocate an oligarchical form of government or a benevolent despotism: the editorials of postliberation *Combat* show that he still firmly believed an informed public under a government that embodied truly democratic principles was capable of self-government. But in the transitional period between war and peace only the men of the Resistance, a tested elite, would be in a position of sufficient authority and respect to institute really democratic political procedures.

Lettres à un ami allemand expresses Camus's conviction that the peoples of Europe, and particularly the intellectuals, had learned a lesson from their defeat by the Nazis. The confrontation with death and violence, the general suffering caused by the separation from loved ones, were the dreadful price paid for yielding to resignation and despair. From awareness of the costliness of violence, Camus hoped that France and all Europe, under the continuing dedicated leadership of its Resistance movements, would find the strength to build a federation of nations in which man would give "justice, of which he alone is able to conceive, its chance."[29] It therefore was imperative that institutions guaranteeing the right of self-government be built or rebuilt; this was to be the ultimate objective of the revolution that the Resistance advocated.

By August 1944 the Allied armies had reached the outskirts of Paris. The Parisians rebelled against the occupiers on the night of August 20. With the city still in a state of insurrection *Combat* printed a front page editorial by Camus outlining the aims of the Resistance. Using as a title the motto of clandestine *Combat,* "From Resistance to Revolution," he pointed out that the Resistance had been not only a military organization but a political one as well. Out of it had come a new political force: "Having had only a faith in 1940, they [the résistants] have a political creed, in the nobler sense of the word, in 1944." On 1 September 1944 another editorial spoke of the new sense of fraternity and solidarity that had been born out of the struggle against the Nazis. Men of all religious and political creeds had joined together to combat a common evil.

The battle was not ended, however, with the withdrawal of the Germans. Those responsible for the debacle of 1940 had yet to be uprooted and punished. The Resistance, Camus insisted, was well qualified to carry out this task by virtue of its members' recent experience. When France fell, the résistants had been faced with a choice between shame or action. They had chosen action, and out of that action they had evolved a new concept of political conduct. The "conniving solidarity" of the politicians of the Third Republic was no longer to be tolerated: "It is truly a new order that has been founded. . . . Politics is no longer dissociated from individuals. It is the forthright address of one man to other men."[30]*

Political issues in the past had too often been decided on a basis of party loyalties or of personal ambitions rather than on the needs and wishes of the electorate. The election of 1936 had indicated that the French people were weary of the old political party control of government, yet a complicated electoral system and the powerful ultraconservative interests had prevented any change in the then existing political institutions. The ability of the Resistance movement to carry out the reforms the Resistance envisaged, once the unifying influence of the occupation was removed, appeared questionable even in 1944. Nonetheless the situation in France at the time of the liberation presented the résistants with an opportunity to renovate France's outworn political habits; it must have seemed to them a calculated risk well worth taking.

In the 1950's Camus was accused of having fostered, during the late 1940's, a mystique of the Resistance that was quite unrealistic. Yet a survey of the opinions of many former résistants, conducted by *L'Observateur* in 1952, showed that most of them, although they expressed bitter disillusionment at the time of the survey, had thought immediately after the war that something constructive would come out of the movement.[31] Others, it is true, felt that from the outset the Resistance had been essentially an anti-German movement and that it could not sustain the positive role demanded of it by Camus and some others in 1944.

Camus's hope that the Resistance would prove able to bring about changes in French political institutions lasted longer than most. But it is essential to note that in the late 1940's those who abandoned hope in the Resistance movement tended to move either to the right, as did Bidault, Pia, and Albert Ollivier, or to the left, like Bourdet, d'Astier, and Sartre. Camus, as we have seen, had an insurmountable aversion to the right and to its leaders. His doubts with regard to communism were also solidly established even before World War II. The Communists did little to allay his mistrust in the period immediately following the liberation; they were in fact instrumental in undermining the C.N.R. Although Camus made every effort to cooperate with the Communists, he consistently refused to join them, even if only on a quasi-official basis as did Sartre.

Politically speaking, then, Camus's postwar espousal of the Resistance cause was based largely on practical considerations. The Resistance represented an almost desperate hope that much-needed reforms could be brought about without resort to violent revolution. It was for him the only acceptable means at hand to achieve a renovation that France badly needed and that the Fourth Republic was to fail so glaringly to accomplish. But he had a deeper reason for refusing to abandon his hopes. He had joined the Resistance knowing that in the last analysis there were only two sides, and to have remained silent or to have avoided participation in the struggle would have amounted to being on the side of the executioners. In order to act, however, he and other résistants like himself had had to conquer a basic repugnance toward killing and violence: "None of us liked war. . . . We had no taste for hatred and we believed in justice. That is why we asked ourselves then if justice were with us. And while we were asking that question, lightning struck us and knocked us down into the dust" (*Com.,* 12-9-44, p. 1).*

The men of the Resistance had learned to look upon the face of death without flinching. In an article in clandestine *Combat* Camus tells how the sight of disfigured faces and of slaughtered innocents had reinforced the résistants' sense of revolt. That sense of revolt had given them the determination to carry on the struggle against oppression. But after a time men had lost sight of the reasons for struggling, as the daily horror of the struggle itself became routine (*Com. cl.,* 5-44, p. 1). Having looked upon so many innocent faces in death, the men of the Resistance could no longer feel revulsion at the execution of a man like Pierre Pucheu, the Vichy minister of the interior who had turned over thousands of Frenchmen as hostages or as deportees for the German labor camps.

Pucheu, on a mission to the Darlan government in Algiers, had been caught there by the Allied invasion of North Africa in November 1942. He was tried, condemned, and executed by the French

Provisional Government in Algiers in May 1944. His death left the résistants "at the same time without hate and without compassion," Camus wrote in an article in the clandestine *Lettres françaises;* he keynoted there the campaign that *Combat* would later wage in favor of a purge of collaborationists and traitors: "We know now that in the world where we live there is one thing that is tantamount to death and that is the lack of imagination." Too many good and loyal men had died as a result of that lack of imagination on the part of many Frenchmen for the surviving résistants to yield to the temptation to forgive: "It is in the full light of the imagination that we learn . . . to admit without any sense of revolt that a man can be struck from the lists of the living."[32]

Camus felt with deep conviction that the surviving résistants were responsible to those who had lost their lives during the struggle. If the living had not carried on beyond the day of liberation the common struggle against injustice and tyranny, the suffering and sacrifices of the war years would have appeared as derisive irony. Therefore a return to the ways of the Third Republic, that "caricature of a democracy" in the eyes of most résistants, was out of the question. The men of the Resistance had tacitly sworn an oath that this would not happen. Camus gave verbal expression to that vow when he wrote: ". . . this oath that we never swore except deep within ourselves was sworn to our dead comrades; we will keep it to the end" (*Com.,* 22-8-44, p. 1).* In many cases those in France whom Camus held responsible for the defeat of 1940 had been responsible, before the war, for the repression of working class and minority groups, a fact that was to fortify his indictment of them. His insistence that these men be punished, by death if necessary, was to involve him in a drawn-out dispute with François Mauriac. If Camus, during the last months of the occupation and the first few months that followed the liberation, resembled Saint-Just in his unbending attitude, it was precisely because he felt that the country "does not need a Talleyrand. . . . It needs a Saint-Just" (*Com.,* 11-9-44, p. 1).*

Thus toward the end of the war Camus had come to feel that,

given the executioners' uncompromising will to destroy human life and its values, there were occasions when a rebel was justified in taking up the weapons of the executioner and in using them against him. In 1944 he had not yet come to admit that revolt imposed upon itself its own limits. As the war drew to its close and the moment neared when the victims would overpower their judges and executioners, the victims knew that they would soon be strong enough to judge their judges. Camus called upon them to do so "without hatred, but without pity."[33]

That commitment might take the violent form required by the Resistance had certainly been far from Camus's mind in 1938 and 1939. He later wrote: "I began the war of 1939 as a pacifist and I finished it as a résistant. That inconsistency . . . has rendered me more modest."[34] Commitment to human life and happiness had, by a catastrophic stroke of history, become simultaneously a commitment to death. In the four and one-half years since his visit to the convict ship in the harbor of Algiers, Camus's thinking concerning the sanctity of human life had come full cycle. He now admitted that one could watch without pity or compassion a human being struck irrevocably from the lists of the living. He could even condone its being done.

It is not difficult to see that so diametric an opposition in Camus's thought could not long endure. The equilibrium he had sought to maintain was close to being destroyed. Once he had condoned the death of Pucheu and other traitors, it would have taken only a few more steps to the admission, on dialectical grounds at least, that violence with a worthy end in view can be justified. It is not surprising, therefore, that murder was to replace suicide as Camus's major philosophical preoccupation in the years following 1944. Out of the contradictions to which the war and the divisions among Frenchmen had given rise, Camus was eventually to develop a revised concept of commitment and revolt, but only after he had experienced at first hand the nihilism of his times.

In August 1944 the former victims, as Camus had foreseen,

suddenly became the judges and, logically, the executioners as well. For the first time Camus found himself a judge, with a measure of power enabling him to enforce his decisions. He had become concomitantly an accomplice of the executioner. He was not to find the position comfortable.

4

Men of Justice
"To Err Is Human . . ."

T HAT DURING the occupation years Camus had come
to accept violence as inevitable reveals how fundamentally his
choice of a given course of action depended on personal experience
and observation rather than on a doctrine or ideology. Between
1939 and 1941 he had had ample opportunity to reflect upon the
nature and meaning of war and violence. But in 1944 when, at the
age of thirty-one, he suddenly found himself becoming one of the
major spokesmen for the Resistance and its revolution, events were
moving much faster. During the four years of the occupation,
violence and death had come to be accepted almost as routine. This
now made it perhaps too easy for the Resistance groups to demand
unflinchingly the death of those who might stand in the way of the
projected revolution.

Camus, as we have seen, believed in a revolution that would
bring about long-denied social justice in France. He plunged headlong into the postwar revolutionary movement, fully concurring in
the Resistance demands for a "purification" of the corrupt and
reactionary elements in France. This position soon led him to
condone revolutionary "justice" and the death penalty for traitors
and collaborators, a clear departure from his prewar attitudes.

Had the men of the Resistance lived up to the principles they had
formulated during the war years, it is quite possible that Camus
would have continued to defend the consequences of their acts
whatever his own personal misgivings. However, with the removal
of the unifying Nazi presence, the former résistants began to differ

among themselves as to how the revolution should be carried out. Some of them proved just as ready as their prewar political predecessors had been to place personal ambition above the national interest. The Communists' failure to cooperate with the non-Communist groups within the movement further weakened the Resistance from the inside. The ruthless tactics of some Communist-dominated provincial liberation committees rapidly damaged the public image of the entire Resistance movement, particularly with respect to the national purge which the Resistance championed.

Camus's concern for the way in which the future revolution was to be conducted can be traced through the editorials he wrote during the first six months after the liberation. From August to October 1944 the editorials in *Combat* were marked by hopeful enthusiasm for the revolution. From October to December a growing uneasiness accompanied his continuing demands for reform; the editorials written in defense of the much-criticized purge trials soon turned into an uncomfortable polemical exchange between Camus and François Mauriac. Finally, in January 1945, Camus realized that the hoped-for revolution had become a myth and that the Provisional Government, moving off on a new tack, had abandoned the Resistance. On 9 February 1945, in his *Combat* editorial, Camus reaffirmed his faith in the principles that had inspired the résistants in the early weeks after the liberation: "No, nothing has changed except perhaps the aims of the government" (p. 1). The failure of the revolution had become all too evident, however, and the path of failure was strewn with corpses.

In the light of this experience, Camus returned to the doubts and questions concerning revolution that he had raised in 1938–39. He had now truly lived and breathed the nihilistic atmosphere of his time. Out of this experience several works were to come—"Ni victimes ni bourreaux," *L'Homme révolté, Les Justes*—all of them bearing on the validity and the effectiveness of violent revolution. The same preoccupation was also to be reflected in *La Peste, L'Exil et le royaume, La Chute, Les Possédés,* and in fact in nearly everything Camus wrote after 1947. Therefore, in terms of the long-range effect on his thought, the brief period in Camus's career that began on 21 August 1944 assumes all-important proportions.

As the Allied armies neared Paris in late August, insurrection broke out in the still-occupied city. In all parts of Paris, with the exception of Passy, Auteuil, and the Champs-Elysées district, barricades were thrown up in the streets. The Resistance leaders and the people seemed determined to welcome de Gaulle and the Allied armies to a liberated city. There was talk of a Communist plot to seize power during the insurrection, but such a plot never materialized sufficiently to prove a serious threat. This would have almost certainly resulted in the institution of a military occupation government by the British and the Americans. The Communists knew this as well as anyone else, and they had more reason for wanting to avoid it.[1]

For the Parisian population the insurrection was also release of pent-up tensions. As Alexander Werth remarks, the barricades were relatively ineffective as far as actual defense of insurrectionist positions was concerned, "Yet it 'felt good' to be on the barricades; and out of their poor homes men and women and children dragged cupboards and mattresses."[2] Camus himself perhaps better described the feelings of the Parisians when he wrote on 23 August, as the Germans fled the city: "Peoples who wish to live do not wait for someone to bring them their freedom. They take it" (p. 1).*

Another reason behind the insurrection was the determination of the Resistance to demonstrate that its demands for a revolution were serious. The uprising of the people of Paris was an action symbolic of their hopes and expectations. On the day before the official Allied entry into Paris, Camus warned that those who thought the insurrection was a mere gesture failed to understand its full import. The people of Paris were determined to make known the demands of all Frenchmen for long overdue freedom and

* French texts of starred passages may be found in Appendix A.

justice. In short, the insurrection in the streets of Paris was "the birth of a revolution."[3]

Thus for Camus and many of his fellow résistants, the insurrection of 21 August represented not only an end to the Nazi occupation and the reestablishment of France as a free nation but the beginning of a new era which was to be characterized by a clean break with the old "forces of resignation and injustice." But in spite of their high hopes and the threat of the barricades, the meaning of which could not have failed to penetrate the consciousness of most Frenchmen, there were numerous unpredictable elements upon which the future course of the revolution depended. Not the least of them was de Gaulle himself. Although the Resistance had recognized him as its chief and as the legitimate head of the Provisional Government, many résistants were not certain they could trust him. De Gaulle's summary treatment of Georges Bidault, president of the C.N.R., on the day of the triumphal entry into Paris, did little to ease these misgivings.

Furthermore, the elements that traditionally resist revolutionary action, the peasants, the bourgeoisie, and the old political parties, might prove stronger or more hostile than expected. Most important of all, there was a war to be fought and won. France was now host to the Allied forces, and any action tending to hamper military operations would have been unthinkable. The Resistance press, however, insisted that the war and the revolution could and had to be carried on simultaneously. All the Resistance newspapers called upon Frenchmen to rise to this new effort.

What was this revolution that loomed monumental in the minds of the résistants? Certainly the word "revolution" did little to reassure more conservative elements of the French population. After four years of occupation by a foreign power, the thought of a revolution could not have been appealing to the vast majority of Frenchmen. But the Resistance groups, or at least that segment that Camus represented, were not thinking of a revolution in the sense of a massive popular uprising. This was to be "a revolution within the law." Camus had hastened to assure his readers that, in spite of the determination shown by the people of Paris on the barricades, it was probable that the revolution could be accomplished without violence. On 21 August he stated the aims of the Resistance as follows:

We wish to realize without delay a true people's and workers' democracy . . . , a Constitution under which freedom and justice recover all their guarantees, profound structural reforms without which a policy of freedom is a mockery, the pitiless destruction of trusts and of vested financial interests, the definition of a foreign policy based on honor and loyalty to all our allies without exception. In the present state of affairs this is a revolution; it is probable that it can be carried out in a calm and orderly fashion. In any case, it is only at this price that France will once again be able to assume that pure countenance that we have loved and defended above all else (*Com.*, 21-8-44, p. 1).*

On 19 September 1944 he stated: "Revolution does not inevitably mean the guillotine and machine guns; rather it means machine guns when necessary" (*Com.*, p. 2).* This statement is characteristic of the balance between threats and reassurances that Camus tried to achieve in his editorials touching upon the revolution, during the first three months after the liberation. He implied that the revolution of 1944 need not be patterned after the bloody revolutions of 1789 in France and 1917 in Russia; but that the principles that would inspire it were important enough, and the need to implement them sufficiently great, to warrant the use of force if that should prove necessary. On one occasion when Pierre-Henri Teitgen, minister of information, imposed what Camus considered an unjust ruling on the allocation of newsprint, Camus warned that French journalists had had lengthy experience in dealing with such tactics, and that if necessary they would resort once more to clandestine publication (*Com.*, 30-11-44, pp. 1–2).

These threats, made during the winter of 1944, were probably due more to a sense of frustration than to any solid determination to foment an uprising. Any attempt at a popular rebellion was out of the question. Too many conditions opposed such action. German resistance was stiffening as Allied troops reached German soil.

Paris was suffering from the food and coal shortage in France. And there was the ever-present danger of a take-over either by Allied Military Government for Occupied Territories or by the Communists if any dissension got out of hand. As Raymond Aron points out, in the winter of 1944 most Frenchmen were *gaullistes,* some "out of enthusiasm and others out of resignation. Behind the lofty figure of the liberator the shadow of Maurice Thorez was discernible."⁴ Under these circumstances, the revolution was dependent on the goodwill of de Gaulle, of the Provisional Government in general, and on the willingness of the population to bring about an effective overhaul of France's entire political, economic, and social structures. There was, of course, always the possibility of joining the Communists, with all the risks that such a move would have entailed, in demanding a sweeping revolution then and there. But the Communist stand was probably more a pose than a firm position. In any case, Camus was determinedly non-Communist— although not anti-Communist—and he felt that no matter how mandatory the need for a revolution it had to be carried out on a democratic basis. "If tomorrow the people of France, called upon to express themselves freely, repudiated the policies of the Resistance, the Resistance would yield . . . ," he wrote on 8 October 1944 (*Com.,* p. 2).*

Camus recognized, perhaps somewhat unwillingly, that one of the more serious flaws in the revolutionary movement was the lack of a clearly defined program. The clandestine press and the C.N.R. charter had called for a Socialist form of government with nationalization of key industries, broad economic and social reforms, and punishment for those responsible for the collapse of 1940 as well as for those who had taken advantage of it. With France now actively engaged in the war against Germany, an energetic and sharply outlined program was imperative if a revolution was to be effected without resort to force. Camus admitted that the majority of the members of the M.L.N., or Mouvement de Libération Nationale,⁵ an inchoate movement still split within itself, had no precise idea of the form the revolution should take. Its members "spoke in the name of an inner force, greater than themselves, which carried them through four years, and which, in certain circumstances, could take its true form tomorrow. . . . What carried the Resistance for four years was a sense of revolt. That is, the complete, obstinate refusal—almost blind in the beginning—to accept an order that sought to bring men to their knees. Revolt is first of all courage."*

The desire for revolution, he continued, is born when the sense of revolt "passes into the mind where the feeling becomes an idea, where the spontaneous élan culminates in concerted action" (*Com.*, 19-9-44, p. 1).* In this analysis of the transition from revolt to revolution, which he was to take up again and develop in *L'Homme révolté,* Camus defined the process by which many résistants had come to feel the need for a revolution. Of the aims of the revolution itself he spoke now in even more general terms than he had used in his editorial of 21 August: "We do not believe here in definitive revolutions. All human effort is relative. The unjust law of history is that man must make immense sacrifices to obtain often ridiculously small results. But however slight man's progress toward his own truth may be, we think that it always justifies such sacrifices. To be exact, we believe in relative revolutions" (*Com.*, 19-9-44, p. 2).*

Camus was apparently not yet seriously concerned that the concerted movement which had coalesced in opposition to the Vichy regime and to the Nazis was already showing signs of disintegrating as a result of partisan disagreements over basic political issues. The disagreements made it momentarily impossible to draw up a definite program that would prove acceptable to all parties. Also a general feeling prevailed that nothing in the way of political change could be finally accomplished before the return of the war prisoners from Germany. Doubtless Camus still felt throughout the autumn of 1944 that the will for reform was strong enough to overcome any friction among members of the M.L.N. The revolution was to be democratic, so it was of prime importance for all parties to be heard before a definite program was decided upon.

Camus's reference to the relativity of all revolutions provides further evidence of his conviction that the Resistance pointed the way toward a revolution that would not be a murderous break with the past. It would bring rather the relatively peaceful establishment of a new political order more relevant to the needs of a proletariat-oriented society than the old order based on the ideals of liberal capitalism had been. By admitting that the proposed revolution was flexible and open to suggestion, Camus showed his willingness to compromise within certain limits. But if he was willing to postpone the formulation of a hard-and-fast program of reforms, he was intransigent in his insistence that no progress toward a new order could be realized so long as the representatives of the old order of compromise and opportunism, symbolized by the Vichy regime, still existed.

Camus demanded a purge of the political leaders of the Third Republic, the traitors of Vichy, and collaborationists. For the politicians of the Third Republic who had not been compromised by association with the Vichy regime or the Nazis, he required only retirement from active political life. For traitors and collaborationists, particularly those involved in political and economic dealings with either the Vichyites or the Nazis, he demanded more severe punishment.

Almost immediately after the liberation, the Socialist party had put forward a proposal by which the Provisional Government would be made up of a combination of prewar leaders, who would be able to assure continuity of the Republic, and of new men, whose presence in the government would assure the country's revitalization. Camus categorically rejected this proposal. Acceptance of it, he was sure, would mean the return to an order characterized by cowardice, abdication of responsibility, conniving parliamentarians, and personal ambitions, an order that was merely disorder.

The Fourth Republic, he maintained, would have no use for such men as Daladier, Reynaud, and Herriot. These and others like them, "who no longer inspire anything but indifference or scorn, can always busy themselves with the preparation of memoirs destined never to be read" (*Com.*, 2-9-44, p. 2).* Continuing in the same vein two days later, he announced: "we have decided to suppress politics in order to replace it with ethics."* He reiterated his conviction that "it would be contrary to justice if men whom the French people had already condemned reappeared on the political scene with smiles of innocence."* The prewar parliamentarians must be declared ineligible to enter their names on ballots in future elections (*Com.*, 4-9-44, p. 1).

Two days later Camus extended this proscription from active participation in French political affairs to cover the bourgeoisie. The violent tone of this editorial is rather surprising, coming from Camus. Very rarely does class hatred as such enter into his political writings. Attacks against the bourgeoisie as a class are in fact conspicuous by their absence. In February 1938 he had indicated that he considered "tyrants and bourgeois bugbears" little more than excuses for revolutions that were in reality protests against the human condition itself.[6] And in his review of Renaud de Jouvenel's *Commune Mesure*, written in 1939, he had declared: ". . . the average reader like ourselves can only despise these bourgeois milieux that Jouvenel hates for so many reasons. Thus we do not join the author in his hatred because he, rightly or wrongly, considers it necessary to judge these milieux, whereas we consider them already judged. . . . To call M. Renault 'a great exploiter of the French workers' is somewhat like breaking down a door that is already open" (*AR*, 3-1-39, p. 3).* For a left-wing intellectual the tone here is relatively moderate. This is no longer the case in 1944.

Camus began the 6-9-44 editorial by saying that the bourgeoisie feared "the people" and that "the Vichy regime was a form of vengeance for the events of 1936." These assertions, together with the reference to Renault, make it likely that he was speaking of the bourgeoisie in the somewhat limited sense of the legendary "one hundre ' families" whose immense financial holdings enable them to wield great political power. This extremely wealthy minority had long controlled the Bank of France; they had been responsible for the flight of capital out of France at the time of the Popular Front. Whereas some of these men were as powerful as "economic collaborators" like the well-known automobile magnate, Louis Renault, they were protected by stockholders' anonymity, an advantage the directors of large corporations did not share.

A later editorial, which Thody attributes to Camus, corroborates the idea that Camus was equating bourgeoisie and "anonymous wealth."[7] This editorial approves the Provisional Government's decision to go ahead with requisitioning the Renault holdings in spite of Renault's recent death. By so doing, the editorialist believed, the government was involving not Renault himself so much as his company's stockholders and, through them, money in its most abstract form. The writer emphasized that he did not envy wealthy people or object to the possession of wealth in itself, but was rather condemning the tendency of the moneyed class to abdicate its patriotic responsibilities in order to protect its holdings (*Com.,* 16-11-44, pp. 1–2).

Whether Camus wrote this editorial or not, it is safe to say, I think, that by "bourgeoisie" he meant that highest, upper-class strata of French society—*la grande bourgeoisie*—whose financial holdings would almost automatically create a "conflict of interests" whenever they participated personally in political affairs. It is unlikely that he meant the term to encompass the entire middle class, which in its broadest definition would include small shopkeepers, professionals, white-collar workers, and even small stockholders.

Camus also accused the bourgeoisie of having yielded without a struggle before the German onslaught. While he admitted that some members of this class had fought honorably in the army and in the Resistance, the bourgeoisie as a whole, he claimed, had failed to accept its responsibilities. The moment had come when the bourgeoisie would have to accept the fact that its privileged place in French society had been lost in 1940. Its political representatives had but one duty left: "to hear and to understand that enormous

voice of the people that speaks of the future" (*Com.*, 6-9-44, p. 1).
Camus was in no way advocating a class purge: "We know now
that French lives are irreplaceable. But [the bourgeoisie] must
understand that they must leave us alone after having wearied us so
much. And that after having been so devoid of courage and compassion they must not be lacking in that fundamental intelligence
that would permit them still to be the witnesses of a grandeur they
were unable to achieve" (p. 2).*

Behind this attack there may have been another motivation: the
desire on Camus's part to prepare the public for the campaign in
favor of the purge trials, which were to begin in mid-September
1944. In any case, only his supreme confidence in the strength of
the Resistance movement and in the determination of the masses to
assert themselves at last could have made Camus think that the
politicians and moneyed interests would accept such banishment
from public life. His attitude bears out an assertion made later by
Claude Bourdet: that Camus considered in 1944–45 that the era of
liberal capitalism had come to an end and that the revolution was
inevitable. Bourdet, however, oversimplifies the position Camus
took after the Resistance-backed revolution failed to materialize;
he interprets Camus's subsequent refusal to accept Communist
revolutionary leadership as a tacit recognition of the meaninglessness of history.[8] Camus certainly thought in 1944 that the revolution was already under way: "Our conviction is not that [the
revolution] will take place, but that it is taking place today," he
wrote on 24 August 1944.[9] For the first three months after the
liberation he refused to take seriously, in print at least, the possibility that it might not succeed. Since he felt that its success
depended on a purge of what the Resistance considered the more
corrupt of France's political, economic, and intellectual leaders, he
was not so lenient in his demands for the punishment of collaborators and traitors as he had been with non-Vichyite politicians
and the bourgeoisie.

Essentially, the accusation that Camus leveled against all these
groups was the same: lack of imagination. This may seem an

innocuous charge, but in Camus's eyes it had resulted in cowardice and defeatism on the one hand and in treasonous repression and murder on the other. In 1938–39 Camus had accused Daladier and Rozis of a similar lack of imagination. In their cases it had led to the lack of compassion that caused them to treat in purely political terms the workers' protests against social injustice. Pierre Pucheu, Camus thought, had also shown a lack of imagination when he accepted the Pétain and Darlan governments simply as governments equivalent to any other. This had prevented Pucheu from seeing that the laws and decrees he signed daily caused untold suffering for thousands of human beings.[10] The men of the Resistance, on the other hand, had not lacked imagination: "We had the necessary imagination when confronted with the thousands of reports of our arrested, deported, massacred or tortured brethren. For four years we carried within ourselves those dead children who were kicked into their coffins. Now we remember. We do not act from hatred. But we must be men of justice" (Com., 22-8-44, p. 1).*

Whatever moral force stood behind Camus's indictments of the leading representatives of the old order, these indictments had at best a questionable juridical basis, especially when it came to deciding what punishment such offenses deserved. Was Gaston Bergery, who had merely been a political apologist for the Vichy government, as guilty as Pétain or Pucheu? Was the guilt of René Gérin, the pacifist literary critic for L'Oeuvre, who had accepted French defeat without seeking to take political advantage of it, equal to that of Stéphane Lauzanne, a writer for the pro-Nazi Matin, who had openly cooperated with the Germans?[11] And were the civil servants who had followed Pétain out of sheer habit or the workers who had voluntarily gone to work in German factories as guilty as Laval or Renault? Camus saw at once that "our difficult task is to judge in the name of a truth that has not yet taken legal form" (Com., 27-9-44, p. 1).*

In the Renault case, the first major case to come up for trial, the defense argued that Renault, like other industrialists, had been forced by the Armistice of 1940 to produce for the Germans, that he had turned over his profits to the Resistance, and that he had sabotaged production as much as possible. "What have we," Camus asked, "to oppose to that argument? The simple intuition that one of the most sacred duties of a man and a citizen has been violated. . . . We must . . . , if we wish to condemn, give meaning to our accusation. . . . We must not be ashamed to say that that accusation is a moral one, and that it is without appeal. In a word, the problem lies in the area of responsibility. . . . Men must bear the responsibility inherent in their privileges" (*Com.*, 26-9-44, pp. 1–2).*

It was clear, Camus declared, that the responsibility of a Pucheu or a Renault was far greater than that of a civil servant or an émigré worker who had not been in a position fully to understand the best interests of France; in most cases these last two groups had blindly followed the lead of those whom they had always considered their superiors. Those who deserved relentless prosecution were the men who had held high government positions, the leaders of the press and of the industrial and banking communities. These men shared the responsibility of leading the nation and of setting an example. They had been responsible for the weakness and vacillations of the Third Republic; their collaboration with the Nazis, whether open or tacit, had done the greatest moral and physical damage to the country. The object of the purge was to eliminate this corrupt core of national leaders; therefore, "it is not a question of purging a great deal, but of purging well" (*Com.*, 18-10-44, p. 1).*

It is not surprising that the name of Saint-Just appeared frequently in *Combat*'s editorial columns during 1944–45; and inevitably the comparison, although it was only superficially valid, was made between Camus and the revolutionary leader of 1792. But Camus never failed to question the grave implications of his demands for a purge, and his uneasiness in the role of judge and prosecutor became more and more evident as the purge trials picked up momentum.

Almost with relief Camus announced on 8 September 1944 that Louis Renault had been sentenced to *l'indignité nationale*, that is, deprived of his civil rights and his property; the court had instructed the Provisional Government to start proceedings for requisitioning the Renault factories. This sentence appeared to Camus to be just since it met the stringent demand that the personal freedom even of the enemy be respected. Renault's person had remained inviolate.

In the Renault case open collaboration was not involved; but by late October the court was taking up the cases of Stéphane Lauzanne, Suarez, Brasillach, and the French Gestapo chiefs, Bony and Laffont.[12] It was a foregone conclusion that in these cases the prosecutor would ask for the death penalty, and Camus made a noticeable effort to steel himself intellectually against his own feelings on the subject of capital punishment. On 21 October 1944 he approached the problem in *Combat*. France's problem as he saw it was that she had to carry on a war and a revolution at the same time. So serious an undertaking could not be taken lightly. It was essential that those responsible for the working of justice should sometimes doubt their own wisdom and revaluate their motives and their methods. But self-criticism and doubt could not be allowed to stifle action:

. . . at the extremity of doubt there must be resolution. We are well aware that the day the first death sentence is executed in Paris we will feel repugnance. But we must think then of so many other death sentences that struck innocent men, of beloved faces lying in the dust and of hands that we loved to grasp. When we are tempted to prefer the generous sacrifices of war to the black chores of justice, we shall need our memories of the dead and the unbearable recollection of those of us whom torture turned into traitors. Hard as it may be, we will know then that there are impossible pardons and necessary revolutions (p. 1).*

This article started a now famous controversy. François Mauriac wrote a rebuttal in *Le Figaro*.[13] While he recognized the guilt of the collaborationists, he made an appeal for clemency in the name of Christian charity and questioned the impartiality of human justice under the existing circumstances. Camus replied immediately on 25 October. He agreed that Mauriac had raised the central issue involved in the trials: the possibility of error in human justice. But, he maintained, "the problem of justice consists essentially in silencing the compassion of which M. Mauriac speaks, when the truth of the entire nation is at stake." He was not, he assured Mauriac, speaking lightly, for their exchange of opinions was taking place while the guillotine awaited its first victim. The preceding Monday the first death sentence had been pronounced in Paris: "Will we or will we not approve that sentence? There is the entire problem, and it is frightening."

It was possible for Mauriac, a Christian, to refuse to condemn, since for him there was always the final appeal to divine justice. A non-Christian like Camus, however, could only count on human justice with all its fallibility; therefore, the non-Christian had to assume all the frightening consequences that human justice implied, repulsive as its "black chores" might be. Camus had "no taste for murder," but there existed in France a minority that had placed self-interest and personal ambition above the good of the country. The existence of this minority, "men of treason and injustice," posed an obstacle to the attainment of justice for the entire nation. Repugnant as the death sentence itself was to him, Camus found it mandatory to dispel personal doubts and to accept the destruction of that minority. In so doing he and other résistants had "chosen to assume the burden of human justice with all its terrible imperfections, careful only to correct them through a desperately maintained sense of honesty" (*Com.*, 25-10-44, pp. 1–2).

The Resistance, Camus pointed out, had never asked for a mass purge but only for the trial and punishment of those in high positions of responsibility who had failed in the exercise of their responsibilities. The Resistance would not relinquish its position on this point even though to maintain it "meant speaking against oneself." After all, he asked, was his language so terrible as Mauriac seemed to think? It was not charitable language, but it was the language of men who, recognizing no god, loved humanity and were resolved to do all in their power to ameliorate its suffering. These men lived in a tragic epoch and they were willing to assume the burden of its consequences. For them it was their only chance "to prevent France and Europe from becoming a desert of silence and mediocrity where we no longer wish to live" (*Com.*, 25-10-44, p. 2).

At the time Camus wrote this editorial the purge trials had not yet degenerated into the degrading circus that culminated in the Laval trial in 1945. I have already noted how carefully Camus had distinguished between the conduct of the Resistance-led revolution of 1944 and the bloody uprisings of 1789 and 1917. He was even more careful in his attempts to keep the purge in hand. He insisted that the judges and prosecutors charged with carrying it out should keep full knowledge of their own fallibility in mind, acting always with meticulous respect for human life and liberty. The leaders of the revolution, he felt, had in a sense heeded Albert Ollivier's exhortation to plan their actions at a distance from public strife and turmoil. The résistants had had four years in which to plan; they had learned to combat injustice without losing sight of the enemy's fundamental right to life and liberty.

The C.N.R. had requested that judges drawn from the ranks of the Resistance sit in the special courts set up to try collaborationists; this request had been denied. But the Renault trial seemed to Camus to have established a wholesome precedent both in its conduct and in the sentence pronounced; it had been very different from trials generally associated with revolutionary tribunals that condemned without deliberation: "This is not the way we have chosen; we maintain freedom to the advantage even of those who have always opposed it" (*Com.*, 26-9-44, p. 1).*

The Resistance leaders were certain that reactionary forces in France had cynically used the country's defeat to regain political control lost under the Popular Front. Camus and others were convinced that progress was possible only if these forces of reaction were completely uprooted. There was disagreement within the Resistance movement itself on the methods to be used—the Communists would have preferred more direct and faster action—but there was agreement at least on the necessity of the revolution.

Whether sentencing to death such men as Brasillach, Lauzanne, and Henri Béraud,[14] or even Pétain and Laval, was necessary or sufficient to guarantee future progress and reform is certainly open to question. But given the circumstances—the undermining of the Popular Front in 1937, the collapse of France in 1940, the unenviable record of the Vichy government, and above all the great sacrifices the men of the Resistance had made—the hostile attitude of the résistants toward prewar ruling cliques is understandable.

All of the complex developments that ultimately resulted in the failure of the revolution and the mismanagement of the purge trials do not alter the basic problem of whether or not Camus and others were justified in demanding the lives of those found guilty. This question was to become a major issue for Camus within a few weeks after the exchange of editorials with Mauriac in late October 1944. It was eventually to affect the whole course of his political thought. First signs of his misgivings concerning the future course of the revolution began to appear in November 1944.

The Provisional Government, with de Gaulle at its head, had begun to function with increasing authority. The Consultative Assembly was to start deliberation in early November.[15] *Combat* gave its qualified approval to the government's financial policies in two editorials (author unknown) on 17 and 18 November 1944. The editorialist expressed some concern over the timidity of certain proposals made by René Pleven, the finance minister. *Combat* favored the more radical proposals of Pierre Mendès-France, minister of the national economy; however, it was soon clear that the government intended to follow Pleven's policies. Criticism of the Resistance grew more vocal as news of the high-handed actions of many of the provincial liberation committees became known. Some of the former résistants who had been taken into de Gaulle's cabinet were showing a disquieting tendency to shed their Resistance loyalties once they had portfolios. Moreover, the old political parties were beginning to regroup and to take an ever-increasing part in political affairs.

On the day the Consultative Assembly opened, Camus, in a dour mood, warned that too often in French politics uncompromising warfare between right- and left-wing extremists had replaced honest debate on questions of national interest. This had been the prime cause of political stagnation in the period between the two wars. He cautioned Frenchmen not to forget so soon the lesson in unity they had learned during the four oppressive years of the occupation. In calling for a balance between the all-or-nothing political extremes, he described the frustration of those who were attempting to bring about progress, as they found themselves once more caught between two opposing and irreconcilable political factions while their only defense was "the ineffectual weapons of scrupulous language and stubbornly maintained objectivity" (*Com.*, 8-11-44, p. 1). This statement shows that if Camus's approach to politics was "idealistic" rather than "practical," as many of his critics have since maintained, he knew only too well that integrity and objectivity were weak weapons against the intransigence of extremists, but he chose to continue using them all the same.

Camus showed that he too could be intransigent in his own way. On 11 November he announced that *Combat* was not satisfied with the Provisional Government's recent record. The paper had every intention of continuing to attack in any quarter where it saw a failure to live up to the high level of political action and official responsibility it demanded. Freedom had been returned to France through the stubbornness and intransigeance of her patriots. Justice, still a distant ideal, could be obtained only in the same way. There could be no lies, no talk of a political revolution while reactionary measures were being proposed: " . . . we must call things by their names. . . . it is not possible to add silence to the lies that still are met with in France" (*Com.,* 11-11-44, p. 2). A little more apologetically, on 22 November 1944, he admitted that, being determined to accept only the best course of political action, *Combat* sometimes too severely criticized what was merely less good. The line between "morality" and "moralizing" is a narrow one and "it happens through fatigue or forgetfulness that one oversteps it."[16] Nevertheless Camus was becoming more and more concerned with what some were beginning to see as *Combat*'s disregard for political realities.

One point of criticism with which he had long been faced was the paper's failure to adopt a definite political line or to formulate in concrete terms a political program. As early as 1 October 1944, in answer to the persistent question from readers, "What do you want?" Camus had written, "For France we want a collectivist economy and a liberal political structure." He viewed collectivism as the only way in which wealth would lose its privileged position. However, careful constitutional guarantees of political freedom were essential to prevent loss of human initiative and individual expression under a collectivist system. In this delicate balance between controlled economy and free political institutions resided "not human happiness, which is a different matter, but the necessary and adequate conditions under which each man may be solely responsible for his own happiness and his own destiny. It is simply a question of not adding a form of injustice that is fundamentally human to the profound suffering of our condition" (*Com.*, 1-10-44, p. 1).* This statement, reasonable though it is, was only slightly less general than previous ones concerning the revolutionary aims of the Resistance movement.

The need to find a political party that could translate these principles into action had become acute by the time of the opening of the Consultative Assembly on 8 November. It had become plain by then that hopes of forming a strictly Resistance party from the ranks of the M.L.N. were very slight. Therefore on 10 November Camus cautiously gave *Combat*'s qualified support to the Socialist party while at the same time refusing to compromise the paper's independent status. The program of the Socialist party, he declared, came closest to reflecting the ideal balance that he called the conciliation of liberty and justice. Still *Combat* was disturbed by the Socialists' past record and was, like many others, reluctant to give them an unqualified endorsement. The party's image was one of weakness and disarray. In the past it had been more lavish with words than with actions. Too often it had tended to confuse the realization of its program with simply obtaining a majority, by whatever means, in the National Assembly. Although aware that there was a tendency toward reform and a new, more energetic line of action within the party itself, Camus was not at all pleased with party chairman Félix Gouin's rather pompous manner and equivocal statements before the Assembly.

In subsequent editorials Camus noted a growing inclination of many Frenchmen to support the Socialist party. Even François Mauriac had shown an appreciation for the aims and ideals of socialism. But, Camus warned, there could be no half-hearted alignment; it was impossible to support the social ideals of the party while maintaining a more conservative outlook with regard to its economic principles (*Com.,* 23-11-44, pp. 1–2). On the other hand, he pointed out on 24 November, observers should not be surprised that many résistants, after so much effort to bring about innovations, should have arrived only at the conclusion that the long-established Socialist party best represented their views. The new for its own sake was not what they were seeking. Social justice had no need for an ingenious political philosophy but only for "energy, clear-sightedness and objectivity." As far as Camus was concerned, in politics to seek entirely new doctrines at any price was "to work for the year 2000."[17]

Unfortunately, he went on to say, socialism had become a political doctrine that used love for humanity to dispense with service to mankind, that talked of inevitable progress while passing over the issue of wages, and that championed world peace to avoid making necessary sacrifices. Adherence to Socialist doctrine, in fact, "had never committed those who professed it."[18] There was hope for a resurgence of strength in the Socialist party, however, since many of the résistants saw in it a means of giving form to their political ideals. They would in turn bring new blood into the party.

The foregoing remarks reveal how little the basis of Camus's political thought had changed since 1939. Among the abstractions and arguments of daily political debate, it is easy to lose sight of Camus's essential purpose and to wonder why he clung so persistently to involvement in politics while refusing to make the compromises that political action almost inevitably entails. In 1939 he had been more interested in improving the lot of the Kabylians who were starving to death than in working within a party framework toward some highly problematical utopia in which unborn Kabylians might know a better life.

His primary aim in 1944 was to see that all Frenchmen shared in the benefits to be derived from the political and economic institutions of the new nation that he hoped would rise from the ashes of World War II. His involvement in politics had reached its deepest point by late 1944, yet it was still founded on the conviction that the oppressed classes of society needed spokesmen to represent them in the political forum. Not spokesmen such as representatives in Parliament had too often been, more interested in political maneuvers and in maintaining power balances than in the immediate alleviation of unnecessary human suffering, but spokesmen who understood that the primary aim of political action should be to safeguard those rights that permit the individual the maximum freedom compatible with justice, so that he may take advantage of all available potentialities for happiness.

In simplest terms, Camus thought that the chief aim of political and governmental organization was "to render freedom and justice compatible" (*Com.*, 1-10-44, p. 1). As Serge Doubrovsky points out, Camus seldom bothered to define such terms as liberty and justice.[19] He usually used these terms in their traditionally accepted meanings, which derive fundamentally from centuries of philosophical speculation concerning the problem of achieving a balance between freedom and necessity.

On one occasion at least, Camus did briefly define liberty and justice: "We shall call . . . justice a social state in which each individual receives every opportunity at the start, and in which the country's majority is not held in abject conditions by a privileged minority. And we shall call liberty a political climate in which the human being is respected for what he is as well as for what he expresses" (*Com.*, 1-10-44, p. 1).* But he insisted once again that the definition of principles was rudimentary, while the detailed work of incorporating the principles in a workable social-political-economic structure was endlessly complex.

It was precisely his view of an individual-oriented society that placed Camus at odds with the French intellectuals who increasingly during the late 1940's came to think in terms of a collectively oriented society. Camus was at a disadvantage since the basic principles he defended were hard to distinguish from those that the right claimed to be defending against the left. Thus he was in the difficult position of refusing to accept economic collectivization on Communist terms, while repudiating the right for having made a mockery of humanistic concepts of liberty and justice. When the Resistance movement disintegrated and the Socialist party failed to become a vital political force acceptable to many left-wing intellectuals, Camus was left without any firmly established political grouping to which he was willing to give public support.

While the Socialist party had yet to prove itself in Camus's eyes, it was becoming evident by late 1944 that the Resistance movement had suffered severe setbacks in the eyes of the French people, of the Provisional Government, and of the British and American leaders. In the provinces alleged collaborationists were often shot without benefit of trial; those who were tried were frequently brought before "kangaroo courts" set up by liberation committees, often though not always run by the Communists. Many executions appeared to be little more than political or even personal vendettas. Just how extensive this sort of activity was, however, is still a matter of controversy. In all likelihood the record of the Resistance in this respect, while it is far from spotless, is not so black as many of its critics claim.

Camus did not deny that injustices had been committed in the name of the Resistance, but he felt that they had been grossly exaggerated by the enemies of the movement. He sardonically described the detractors of the Resistance as those who clung to the status quo and whose hopes and ambitions went no further than a return "to their traditional menus, to their automobiles and to *Paris-Soir.*" Their motto was "May freedom quickly return and may we finally be powerful and mediocre at our leisure" (*Com.,* 1-12-44, p. 1). Camus still insisted that the Resistance demands not only were justified but were based on necessity. However, for the first time he spoke of the Resistance as "a force for rejuvenation" (*rénovation*). The word revolution was to appear less and less frequently in *Combat* after this date.

On 3 December 1944 Mauriac attacked the Resistance for the criminal deeds of some of its members.[20] Camus picked up the challenge. He admitted that many reprehensible acts had been committed in the name of the Resistance and that some résistants were not of the highest character. Still, he maintained, the Resistance had the right to be heard; the fact that all its members were not saints did not alter France's real need for the renovation that the movement espoused. The general tone of this editorial is far milder than that of any previous one on this subject.

Within the Resistance itself the strained relations between opposing factions had by now nearly reached the breaking point. The split was to be clearly manifested in late January 1945, when the Paris Regional Congress of the M.L.N. rejected a proposal adopted earlier by the Lyon Regional Congress calling for a merger of the M.L.N. with the Communist Front National. When the National Congress of the M.L.N. met in Paris 23–28 January 1945, it quickly became evident, as Werth points out, that the organization "was sharply divided into an 'anti-fusionist' majority and a 'fusionist' minority, the former gravitating towards the Socialist Party, the latter towards the Communists. . . . The split, though not official, was a fundamental one. . . ."[21]

There were other disquieting signs. The Consultative Assembly, whose membership included a number of former résistants and M.L.N. members, was showing a marked predilection for the very sort of parliamentary laxness for which Camus and other men in the Resistance had so often castigated the legislators of the Third Republic. On 14 December Camus angrily denounced absenteeism in the Assembly during the debate on formation of *comités d'entreprise*.[22] This was a dry subject, he granted, but an extremely important one. Once again the nation found itself represented in Paris by men who considered their work finished when they had received portfolios or mandates. Under these conditions, Camus remarked bitterly, "a revolution within the law" was not likely to be carried out. The unwillingness to make necessary sacrifices was apparent everywhere, he asserted, even among those who had earlier been the most ardent supporters of the Resistance movement. In spite of so many reasons for discouragement, since *Combat* had pledged itself to defend the Resistance to the end, Camus vowed, "We will never shrink from defending it against itself" (*Com.,* 5-12-44, p. 2).

The final blow, although Camus did not accept it as such at the time, came in January 1945, not from the split in the M.L.N. but from the fact that the whole process of the purge trials had gone awry. In spite of *Combat*'s earlier warnings that collaborationists should not be tried within the existing judicial framework, and that special judges should be appointed to hear these cases, the government had turned the special courts over to the regular magistracy. No real attempt had been made to define clearly the nature of the defendants' guilt outside the established legal code. As a result, such barely tenable situations arose as the appointment of Procureur-Général Mornet to preside at the trials of Pétain and Laval. Mornet, like most members of the magistracy, had sworn allegiance to Pétain in 1940 and had narrowly missed, through no fault of his own, being appointed to preside at the infamous Riom trials.[23]

By late 1944 the purge trials had begun to take on a very unsavory aspect. Many notorious collaborationists, particularly lesser known bankers and industrialists, had been given light sentences or not even been indicted. On the other hand minor journalists, a few second-rate entertainers, and other "small fry" had received stiff prison sentences or been executed. Stéphane Lauzanne, who had been openly pro-Nazi, was sentenced to twenty years at hard labor; while Henri Béraud, Anglophobe editor of the ultrarightist *Gringoire,* who had merely been tolerated by the Nazis, was sentenced to death. Later in the year one of Déat's assistants, Albertini, was to receive only five years at hard labor.[24]

Camus had become alarmed at the inequitable sentences being handed down by the courts and at the preferential treatment being given to influential suspects. On 5 January 1945, he stated that he still believed a new order could not be established in France until the country had rid itself of traitors. But he found himself unable to condone the flagrant abuses of justice that had come to characterize the purge trials. He concluded his editorial with a bitter warning: "A nation that fails in its purification is on the way to failing in its rejuvenation." What was needed was lucidity and firm devotion to integrity: "Without that, we are going to need hollow consolations. It is evident that M. Mauriac is right; we are going to need charity" (*Com.,* 5-1-45, p. 2).*

In a harshly worded article Mauriac took issue with Camus for having referred to charity as a "hollow consolation."[25] Camus retorted that Mauriac had not read the editorial in question very well if he thought that he, Camus, had had any sarcastic intent in speaking thus of the virtue of charity. If Mauriac did not want to add to the hatred that abounded in France, Camus himself did not wish to see that hatred compounded with lies. Citing the names of friends who had died during the occupation, he insisted that forgiveness and charity were unthinkable; they would only constitute an insult to these men's memories. Forgiveness, he felt, was not in his own hands but in the hands of the widows and parents of his murdered comrades.[26] Besides referring to these highly personal reasons for demanding the continuation of the purge trials, Camus repeated his contention that if traitors were not punished others might follow their example, and this was precisely what must be avoided if France were to survive as a democratic nation. Nor would Camus accept any plea in the name of "a divine charity that would deprive men of their right to justice" (11 January 1945).[27]

In spite of the defensive tone of this editorial, Camus undoubtedly still felt that there was some hope, however faint it might have become, of the revolution's succeeding. Everything was not lost; election of the Constituent Assembly had been postponed until the return of all French war prisoners, and it was still possible for the Resistance to regain the confidence of the public. But the war in Indochina, the cold war, the Marshall Plan, and other factors, none of which Camus could have foreseen in early 1945, were to channel France's internal policies in a different direction. Had this not been so, a constitution more nearly reflecting the ideals of the Resistance than the Constitution of the Fourth Republic might have come out of the political struggles of 1944–45. Camus might then have felt that the purge, no matter how badly botched, had perhaps been justified. In 1948 he admitted that, while "the heated passions of those years, the difficult memory of two or three assassinated friends" had led him to take issue with Mauriac in 1944–45, he had now come to think, after three years of reflection, that "on the precise point of our controversy" Mauriac had been right and he himself wrong.[28]

The precise point in Camus's running debate with Mauriac had been the fallibility of human justice, the right of one human being to take, directly or indirectly, the life of another. By November 1946, two years before he admitted that Mauriac was right, Camus had decided that there was no truth in the name of which he would ever again demand the life of another human being.[29] However limited it turned out to be, the revolution in which he had taken part had convinced him that revolution as a means to social progress often led to more harm than good. He never denied that in extreme cases a revolution might be justified, but the ethical conduct he was to demand of the revolutionist in *Les Justes* and *L'Homme révolté* was so stringent as to make revolution in our time nearly impossible. Thus, at the very moment when Sartre, d'Astier, Bourdet, and others were moving toward acceptance of the only live revolutionary doctrine of the mid-twentieth century, communism, Camus was beginning his search for a nonviolent method of achieving social reform.

The editorial of 11 January 1945 marked the end of a first phase in Camus's career as editor of *Combat*. Because of poor health he had to withdraw from the editorship for one month. He returned on 9 February, but seems to have taken a somewhat less active part in editing the paper. In the autumn of 1945 he took a year-long leave of absence. After the January editorial, his participation as an editorialist notably decreased. Nonetheless, as late as 30 August Camus was still defending the Resistance as well as the motives that had originally prompted the demands for a purge. But he openly admitted that the trials themselves had degenerated into a hollow mockery of justice.[30] It was not until 1946 that his revised ideas concerning justice and revolution began to take form, although the process of reappraisal certainly started in early 1945.

During the winter of 1944–45 the theme of revolution dominated *Combat*'s editorial columns, but Camus also dealt with other problems. He showed keen interest in international problems and devoted considerable attention to them. Trouble was also looming in Algeria. Now that the four years of occupation were over, Camus's outlook again took on a broader scope.

5

Out of the Valley of Death

OR FOUR years France had been shut off from the outer world. During those four years the struggle against the Nazis had occupied all the energies of the French intellectuals. Since the lines between the forces of freedom and the forces of tyranny had been so clearly drawn, partisan political opinions had become secondary. But by 1945 France's horizons expanded once more to include the entire world. Problems within the French Empire, and the growing mistrust between the United States and the Soviet Union, vied with domestic problems for public attention. That a dangerous state of unrest existed in Algeria was forcefully demonstrated in the rebellion and massacre at Sétif in March 1945.

Within France itself, the Resistance movement continued to lose ground. When the Constituent Assembly began deliberations in November 1945, as many old names stood on the rolls as new ones. The Constitution that was drafted and finally ratified in 1946, although it incorporated some token reforms based on Resistance demands, represented by and large a return to multiparty parliamentary rule much like that of the Third Republic. Disgusted and disappointed with the newborn Fourth Republic, most left-wing intellectuals began to seek a new and better organized organ of opposition. A few followed de Gaulle, some joined the Socialists, still others were attracted to the Communist party.

Camus shared his fellow intellectuals' disappointment in the newly created Fourth Republic, but the experience of the post-liberation years had made him wary of giving his unswerving loyalty to a particular party or movement simply because it claimed to speak in the name of this or that social entity or because it claimed that its ideals were "progressive." His was destined to become a lone voice: his warnings that a grave crisis was impending in the colonies went almost unheeded, while his criticism of fellow-traveling intellectuals and totalitarian ideologies earned him the scorn of many of his former friends and associates. Camus, who was happiest when working with a "team," was now to become a rather solitary figure on the French intellectual scene.

One of the first issues Camus raised in *Combat* (13-10-44, pp. 1–2) soon after the liberation was that of the French Empire. He reminded Frenchmen that they were indebted to the colonies, and that metropolitan France had too often taken the Empire for granted. Using North Africa as an example, he described the impasse that had been reached throughout the Empire: the peoples of Asia and Africa had long demanded reform measures only to find themselves opposed at every step by colons and overzealous civil servants for whom loyalty to France meant oppression of her colonial subjects.

In the case of Algeria, he pointed out, before any further effort was made to extend the civil rights of its indigenous populations, "it must be made known that the greatest obstacle lies . . . in the French population [of Algeria]." Moreover, he continued, "It would be stupid . . . to permit the country to remain ignorant of the fact that this population was largely sympathetic to the policies of Vichy." That sympathy in fact derived from the same reactionary conservatism which opposed any reforms that would benefit the indigenous population. The "colon mentality" had always resisted innovation, even that demanded by the most elementary requirements of justice. The government, in order to implement any policy of friendship and protection for the Moslems, would necessarily have to depend on the cooperation of the French Algerians.[1] Therefore it would be necessary as a first step "to reason away or reduce" the resistance of the European community. Once again Camus argued that it was the responsibility of the central government to seek a solution to the Algerian problem, since no efforts in that direction could be expected from the European community in Algeria itself.

Camus also specifically warned against any policy that would call for the use of force to maintain French rule, whether in Algeria or elsewhere in the Empire. The defeat of 1940 had led to a serious loss of prestige for France among the Moslems. Any attempt to regain that lost prestige by force would be disastrous: "No policy could be more blind. We shall find no real support in the colonies until the moment we have convinced them that their interests are ours and that we do not have two policies: one that would give justice to the people of France and another that would condone injustice with regard to the Empire" (*Com.*, 13-10-44, p. 2).*

On 28 October 1944 Camus took up the question of Algerian nationalism itself. The growth of the nationalistic Progressist party in Algeria, he wrote, was the consequence of France's refusal to consider seriously Moslem demands for full French citizenship. What, after all, he asked, had been the Progressist party's demand? Simply that the Moslem populations be allowed to accept the same duties and benefit from the same rights as Frenchmen: "We thus had the spectacle of an occupied nation (let us not indulge in idealism) dispossessed of its territory, finally accepting the civilization of the conqueror and asking to be completely integrated into it." But "tradition, blind psychology, the interests of a single class," had kept French leaders from recognizing the greatness of the task that lay before them. As a result, "They kept in their vocabulary the word assimilation, while they continued in practice to maintain a sometimes benevolent occupation" (*Com.*, 28-10-44, p. 1).²* Previously, simple common sense should have dictated the granting of Moslem demands; now Moslem loyalty to France during the war made reform mandatory. Time was growing short. The Catroux Plan, a revival and slightly extended version of the Blum-Violette Project, was a step in the right direction; but in relation to the immensity and the acuteness of the problem, it was painfully inadequate. Reinforcing the arguments on the side of

* French texts of starred passages may be found in Appendix A.

human justice were other practical considerations: for example, expanding world markets would inevitably bring about international agreements wherein France would be forced to surrender all or part of her trade monopoly in the colonies (*Com.*, 28-10-44, p. 2).

The winter of 1944–45 was a difficult one for France. There was a food and coal shortage, the black market was thriving, and France was trying to bear her share in the defeat of Germany while carrying on the much-discussed "revolution" at home. Little thought was given to colonial questions, although de Gaulle had promised the Algerian nationalists that their demands would be given high priority. The situation in North Africa was brought abruptly to the attention of metropolitan France, however, on 16 March 1945, when violence broke out at Sétif. In the rioting, which spread to other areas in Algeria, a number of European Algerians were massacred. The French press, particularly the right-wing element, demanded immediate and uncompromising reprisals against those responsible. Camus was alarmed by the flagrant display of ignorance concerning North African social and political problems apparent in the metropolitan press and in the reaction of the French public in general. He went on a three-week fact-finding tour of Algeria. On his return to Paris, he published in *Combat* a series of six informative articles on the Algerian crisis.[3]

There had been little change in the Moslems' living conditions since his investigation of the Kabylian famine five years earlier. Moslem unrest and nationalist demands, he explained to his metropolitan readers, derived from two basic sources. The first was the repeated failure of successive French governments, under pressure from colon interests, effectively to carry out the process of assimilation to which they paid continual lip service. Enlightened Moslem leaders such as Ferhat Abbas and Aziz Kessous now believed that Algeria's only hope lay in complete independence rather than in an assimilation that had so long remained an empty promise. The second main source of discontent was economic. The intolerable economic condition of the Moslem working class and peasants easily provided mass popular support for nationalist demands.

Once again Camus described the inequitable salaries and oppressive working conditions of the Moslems, graphically pointing out that a loaf of bread cost 120 francs whereas the average Moslem worker earned only 60 francs a day.[4] He agreed that the rebellion at Sétif had been the work of professional instigators. Their efforts, however, had been successful only because French misrule had created a discontented Moslem population. France's loss of prestige as a military power and the American landing in North Africa had added further fuel to the fires of nationalism. It was imperative that metropolitan Frenchmen realize that the nationalist movement had the sympathy of the Moslem masses: "I read in a morning paper that 80% of the Arabs desire to become French citizens. On the contrary, I shall sum up the present state of Algerian politics by saying that they in fact did desire it, but that they no longer desire it."[5]

In spite of the gravity of the situation in Algeria, it was not, Camus insisted, entirely hopeless. A concerted effort to supply the country with the food it needed, and the immediate implementation of an unequivocal policy aimed at correcting all abuses, could still save Algeria and keep it French. Camus had no illusions as to the difficulties involved in such a program. The economic and logistic problems alone were staggering. Moreover, such forces of hatred and resentment had been building up on both sides that any firm policy, no matter how energetically pursued, would encounter almost insurmountable obstacles. But since ignoring the situation in Algeria could only make it worse, means had to be found to avoid further incidents like the Sétif massacre. Violence would merely revive and accelerate the senseless cycle of massacre and repression, which served to increase already deeply entrenched hatreds.

In this series of articles there is not even a suggestion that Camus thought the problem might be solved by total French withdrawal from Algeria. For him the presence in Algeria of the European community was simply one of the given factors; to remove a part of the population, either Moslem or European, was no solution. The solution, as he envisaged it, would consist rather in providing an atmosphere in which the two groups could live together peacefully and eventually build on a firm foundation an Algeria where mutual respect and understanding could flourish.

How realistic was Camus's contention that an immediate, energetic move to remedy food shortages and to grant the claims of the Moslems would take the teeth out of nationalist demands? It is impossible to give a definite answer. Had the Provisional Government, plagued as it was with economic problems, adopted such a policy, it could only have been carried out through great effort and sacrifice on the part of metropolitan France. But more than nine years were to elapse between the time of Camus's summary of the causes of the Algerian crisis and the actual outbreak of organized rebellion in Algeria. During that nine-year period, under the Fourth Republic, successive governments repeatedly failed to initiate any new program. They continued to answer Moslem demands with reprisals and with the arrest of nationalist leaders, the very acts that Camus had branded sheer stupidity.[6] No energetic move was made to implement a policy of assimilation. Instead, the government favored efforts to build schools and to extend medical aid and other welfare measures, in the quixotic hope that these policies would win back the loyalty of the disaffected Moslem masses. These pitifully inadequate measures were outweighed by Moslem reaction to the rigged Algerian Assembly elections of 1948, which became an odious symbol of French colonial corruption and hypocrisy. Added to this was the increasing effectiveness of the widespread terrorism of the F.L.N., the Front de Libération Nationale, whose aim was to silence any Moslem voice that spoke out in favor of continued French presence in Algeria.[7]

Even in 1945 the most enlightened policy of assimilation might not have stemmed the nationalistic tide, but it certainly could not have been any more disastrous than the course of action followed by the Fourth Republic, and might have been far less costly in terms of money and human lives. In fairness to Camus, it must be admitted that of all possible courses of action open at the time, short of complete disengagement, his plan does seem to have been the best proposal the French had for averting the bitter war that finally broke out in Algeria in 1954. And certainly he had not, as later critics claimed, remained silent on the issue of French abuses in Algeria.

On the other hand, the May 1945 series of articles in *Combat* attracted little attention in the French press. Had intellectual and political groups, including the Communists, been less silent themselves between 1945 and 1954, they might not have been drawn to reproach Camus for his silence in the late 1950's. It should also be recalled that the Communists, the more vociferous of Camus's later accusers, played an active role during 1946–47 in the Tripartite Government of France, which made no realistic move to improve the situation in North Africa.

In the final article on the Algerian crisis, Camus decried the new outburst of hatred that was contaminating the "air that one thought had been cleared of its most terrible poison."[8] By late 1945, when he took a leave of absence from *Combat* in order to work on *La Peste,* he had begun to realize that it was not only in Algeria that the air was still filled with the ideological poison so many hoped had been eliminated. In the spring of 1946 he made a lecture tour of the United States and Canada. Speaking at Columbia University, he revealed a new trend in his thinking. He began by saying that since Hitler's disappearance several things had become clear. First of all, the poison of Hitlerism had not been eliminated. Some of it remained in all of us, and whoever spoke in terms of "historical tasks" was spreading that poison, and was thus potentially or in fact a murderer. For "if the problem of mankind boils down to a historical task, whatever that task may be, man is no longer anything but the raw material of history, and one can do with him what one wishes." Furthermore, it had become clear that it was impossible to accept any optimistic view of existence or any "happy ending" for mankind. On the other hand, to take a pessimistic view of the potentialities of human action with regard to the human race as a whole would be cowardice. Great care had to be exercised in choosing a course of action, however. Camus was axiomatically opposed to any form of human action dependent upon terror, whatever its final aim, since it posed the unavoidable choice of "kill or be killed, and rendered communication impossible. That is why we refuse any ideology that claims any jurisdiction over human lives."[9] These remarks were aimed not only at the proponents of historical determinism but also at the Western nations, some of which were already using the struggle against communism as an excuse to tighten their grip on colonial nations and to justify closer ties with such dubious allies as Franco.[10]

In Camus's view the nihilism that had helped bring the Nazis to power was thus being perpetuated after the Nazi defeat. World leaders seemed to have learned little from World War II. The Resistance-led revolution in France had been effectively sabotaged. The United States and the Soviet Union were demonstrating, as the Resistance movement had already demonstrated in France, that unity achieved in the face of a common threat was not sufficient to destroy deep-seated political mistrust and fundamental ideological differences. The veto power in the United Nations Security Council had reduced what Camus had hoped would at last be a "Society of Peoples" to little more than an idealistic debating society.[11] Camus had found it necessary to abandon many of his hopes. While one kept the goals of world federation and the ultimate conciliation of freedom and justice in mind, it was becoming more and more necessary, he felt, to defend from further encroachments the relative freedom and relative justice that did exist in democratic societies.

After nearly a year's absence, Camus returned to *Combat* in November 1946 with the series of articles, "Ni victimes ni bourreaux."[12] In these he did not yet take sides in the debate between East and West. Rather, he pointed out, in this "Century of Fear" both capitalism and Marxism had come to consider their respective political systems as a means toward social progress that would lead ultimately to the perfect social balance. Each side clung so uncompromisingly to its own system that the world was once more in danger of a war of mass annihilation. Camus did not question the sincerity of either protagonist, but he had decided, after the experiences of 1944–45, never again to assume a position that would require him, "directly or indirectly, to condemn a man to death. . . ."[13] Now the main problem of the committed artist, as he saw it, was to seek a means of averting the mass murder that would follow if the ideological war between East and West were to become a "hot" war. For Camus, murder had replaced suicide as the prime philosophical problem; at the same time it had become a major political problem.

Despite Camus's attempt at objectivity in "Ni victimes ni bourreaux," it is clear that he was more disturbed by Marxist doctrine and the Stalin regime in Russia than by the less absolute doctrines and governments of the West. He questioned the Marxist axiom, "the end justifies the means," and pointed out that the adherents of international socialism, including the extremists in the French Socialist party, had either to abandon Marxism as a rigid political philosophy or admit that terror and murder were legitimate political weapons.

It was no longer realistic, he said, to speak of national revolutions in terms of the Russian Revolution of 1917. Modern armaments and the existence of two superpowers representing diametrically opposed ideologies necessarily altered the conditions that had made possible the revolutions of the past. Any national revolution could flare up into a revolutionary war, ending in the victory of one of the two superpowers. Although Camus's conclusion has yet to be proved, there is abundant evidence that his basic premise was correct: the Hungarian rebellion, the Korean War, and the recurring upheavals in the Middle East and in Asia have made it clear that no country, not even remote Yemen, can entirely contain the effects of internal strife within its own borders.

Although a revolutionary war might have once appeared desirable to proponents of international revolution, World War II had shown, Camus believed, that another war, even if atomic weapons were outlawed, would be so mutilating to the human race as to be unthinkable. What was the way out? International democracy, Camus replied, replacing the international dictatorship which existed because the world had reached a point of necessary economic interdependence while nations still placed their respective interests and sovereignties above all else. A truly international code of law and a world parliament representing every segment of the world's population—Camus suggested that the United Nations itself might more closely resemble a world parliament if the Soviet delegates there represented the Russian people rather than a ruling clique of ministers—were the only means of avoiding a conflict that was too ruinous and too costly even to contemplate. Therefore it was imperative to work assiduously toward world peace while avoiding any means to that end that would contradict the end itself.[14]

Although Camus reproached both liberal capitalism and Marxism with being outdated concepts, his refusal to consider history as an absolute entity beyond the control of men placed him firmly in the ranks of the opponents of Marxism as it has come generally to be understood. He had declared in 1939 that there was no predetermined end to history other than that brought about by the actions of human beings. In "Ni victimes ni bourreaux" he wrote: "History is only the desperate effort of men to give substance to the most clairvoyant of their dreams."[15]

Like the series on Algeria, this series of articles attracted very little attention when it was first published in *Combat* in November of 1946. The articles, however, were reprinted in the November 1947 issue of *Caliban,* a leftist review.[16] During the interval there had been a shift to the left among certain French intellectuals; and this time the articles drew fire from the Communist convert, Emmanuel d'Astier.[17] Thus it was against "Ni victimes ni bourreaux," and not *L'Homme révolté,* that the first shots were fired in the ideological battle that was to reach the peak of its fury in 1952.

After the publication of "Ni victimes ni bourreaux," Camus seems to have devoted little time to his work as editor of *Combat* until the spring of 1947. At the time the paper was faced with a double crisis. A month-long printers' strike, which lasted from 14 February to 17 March 1947, crippled *Combat* financially. Up to that point, the paper had managed to continue publication on its income from sales and from its minimal advertising revenues. The strike was, of course, disastrous for a publication operating on such a marginal budget. Camus threw himself into the effort to save the paper, only to find himself ultimately confronted with the disintegration of the team that had kept it functioning for nearly three years.

Pia, Ollivier, and Raymond Aron wanted *Combat* to drop its independent line and back de Gaulle and the *gaulliste* Rassemblement du Peuple Français. Camus refused. In a letter to Ollivier, dated 22 April 1947, he denied Ollivier's request to print in *Combat* an editorial supporting de Gaulle and the R.P.F.[18] That same day, in a signed editorial, he once again restated *Combat*'s independent position and its determination to maintain it (*Com.*, 22-4-47, p. 1). But the break was beyond repair. With the financial situation worsening, Camus announced his resignation on 3 June 1947. The paper was bought by Henri Smadja, a Tunisian with Socialist leanings; and Claude Bourdet took over as editor-in-chief. Part of the old staff remained with the paper; but others, including Pia, Ollivier, and Aron, left, each to follow his own political path.

To many French intellectuals it appeared that when he abandoned *Combat* Camus also abandoned the struggle for social reform. Claude Bourdet later attributed Camus's resignation to poor health and to an "excess of fervor." According to Bourdet, the paper that Camus had once viewed as an "independent tribunal" had outlived its usefulness and was no longer capable of resolving any of the problems confronting France in 1947.[19]

Bourdet's statement is probably, in part, quite correct. Camus had made it clear in October 1944 that if it should become plain that the Resistance did not represent the will of the majority of Frenchmen, the résistants who had sought to continue the struggle beyond the end of the occupation would gladly return to "that private life and those easier pleasures from which they had been drawn for a moment, in the midst of defeat, by the then justified feeling that there was something to be done which could not be done without them" (*Com.,* 8-10-44, p. 2).* Camus's association with the Resistance had come about in a time of crisis. His conception of commitment, as he had expressed it in his notebooks and in *Alger-Républicain,* had made no provision for extensive involvement in political action on the part of the artist, and he had always considered himself an artist first of all. Once it was clear that the revolution had been completely misdirected and that there was no longer any hope, short of global war, of immediately changing the status quo, he was faced with the choice of abandoning his literary career and joining Sartre or of devoting himself primarily to his career as a writer, taking only a limited part in political controversies.[20]

The Catholic philosopher and novelist Jean Guitton judged that, in 1944–45, "Camus was constrained by circumstances to assume this role of prophet that was not in his nature." Guitton goes on to say that Camus, because of his genuine modesty, was always a bit surprised at the role of seer that had been almost forced upon him. "*Le Juste,*" said Guitton, is always tormented when involved in politics, "since on many occasions he must keep silent concerning injustice. . . ."[21] This statement would probably have come even closer to the truth had Guitton added that Le Juste, when he becomes involved in politics, must at times pronounce judgments founded on the presupposition of future results, results over which he has no actual control. When, in the name of a revolution that had proved to be abortive, Camus had demanded the death penalty for certain men, he had temporarily aligned himself with judges and executioners. His reaction to this experience baffled many of his contemporaries. In his subsequent refusal ever again to accept any political doctrine that condoned murder as a means to its ends, they saw only the protest of an idealist who recoiled at "dirtying his hands" and who refused to recognize the realities of political action.

The misunderstanding between Camus and men who, like Sartre, had been his friends was certainly due in part to the failure of many of Camus's critics to understand the full implications of his works and to see how deeply his whole experience and personality were involved in them. It was perhaps inevitable that in 1944–45 those around Camus should have interpreted his political attitude as being that of a nihilistic pagan who, in spite of his belief in the meaninglessness of life, had thrown himself impulsively and magnanimously into the struggle against the forces of oppression and injustice. But the contradiction that Camus consequently exemplified in Sartre's eyes did not exist as such.[22] Camus had never expressed any nihilistic point of view as being his own. On the contrary, from the outset his explicit intention had been to counteract in his works what he felt were the dangerous nihilistic tendencies of the twentieth century. The failure, after the liberation, of many critics and readers to perceive correctly Camus's intentions had repercussions in the political controversies that his political positions later inspired: in these controversies, by a curious interplay, the meanings read into his literary works were used to interpret his political points of view.

Le Mythe de Sisyphe had been the first major step in the search for positive values that could justify man's existence in a world rendered meaningless by the "death of God." That essay had proposed a solution on an individual basis; but before *Le Mythe de Sisyphe* was even completed Camus found himself faced with the seeming contradiction—although it was a contradiction on the surface only—of having to justify the taking of human lives in the name of a justice founded on the inviolability of human life. Camus's decision to join the Resistance seems to have come with the realization that when the forces unleashed by the nihilists inflict widespread death, the only answer is to kill in return. However, the real contradiction in his thought arose only when Camus sought to extend this extraordinary permission to kill beyond the Nazi defeat and attempted to apply it to the forces of defeatism and of political and economic oppression in France. He came to feel that he had then momentarily placed himself on the side of those political ni-hilists who declare that, since everything is permitted and there is no preexistent scale of moral values, human life can be justifiably expended as a means to the establishment of social order.

Many of Camus's friends did not see that if, in *Le Mythe de Sisyphe,* Camus had seemed to destroy, he had done so only in order to rebuild; his was more than a mere voice of protest bearing witness to the misery of the human condition. It was this error of perspective that led Bourdet to write in 1960 that Camus's political activities in the Resistance and as editor of *Combat* were in "evi-dent contradiction with a pessimistic doctrine leading generally to inactivity. . . ."[23] Most recent critics have emphasized that in 1945 the reading public had tended to seize upon the statement of the absurd itself in *Le Mythe de Sisyphe,* rather than upon the affirmation that Camus was seeking to express, using the experi-ence of the absurd as a point of departure only. This was due in part to the fact that Sartre's *La Nausée* had already aroused a great deal of interest and speculation concerning the experience of the absurd. The tendency to associate the two authors, in spite of Camus's objections, prevented many readers and critics from reaching a clearer understanding of Camus's intentions and of the full meaning of his works.

In 1938 Camus had already noted Sartre's failure in *La Nausée* to go beyond a mere recognition and a partial definition of the absurd:

. . . the error of a certain kind of literature lies in the belief that life is tragic because it is miserable. It can be overwhelming and magnifi-cent; therein is all its tragedy. Without beauty, love and danger, it would be almost easy to live. And M. Sartre's hero has perhaps not supplied the true meaning of his anguish when he insists on what he finds repugnant in man, instead of basing reasons for despair on cer-tain aspects of man's grandeur. To assert the absurdity of life cannot be an end in itself, but only a beginning. . . . It is not that discovery that interests us, but the consequences and the rules of action that one draws from it (*AR,* 20-10-38, p. 5).*

In 1946, in a letter to the editor of *La Nef,* Camus made his position even clearer. "The only book of ideas I have ever written, *Le Mythe de Sisyphe,*" he stated, "was directed precisely against the existentialist philosophers." His criticism of the existentialist position, in part at least, still applied to Sartre, he maintained.[24]

In *Le Mythe de Sisyphe,* with Cartesian precision, Camus sets out to tear down the false façades that thinkers had spent centuries building in order to protect man from the shattering recognition of the disparity between his own desire for coherence and the fundamental incoherence of the world in man's own terms. But he refuses to let man, thus shorn of his illusions, seek escape either by committing suicide or by retreating into the hope of a mystical prolongation of life after death. He takes away the little painted screen which the priest holds before the eyes of the condemned man,[25] not for the sadistic pleasure of subjecting the victim to the sight of the horrible end that awaits him, but so that the consciousness of death and of the finite length of his lifetime will render the victim aware of the only real value he can know with any certainty, his life.

Camus was thus affirming that human life, reduced to a measurable span of time, was a basic value in itself. At the time most of the essay was written, before 1940, he had felt that to affirm this fundamental value was enough without specifically stating that in itself it implied ethical and moral values. He was concerned primarily with establishing a point of departure for the individual in search of happiness. His emphasis on an individual "style of life," at a time when most people were thinking in terms of human solidarity in the face of horrible suffering, seemed to imply that history and social ethics were without meaning. Many readers were led to interpret the essay as a nihilistic or pessimistic statement of man's condition.

Camus's thought was in this incipient stage when World War II intervened and historical events catapulted him into personal involvements far ahead of his own thought. The war and the Resistance compelled him to recognize that in an extreme situation one is justified in denying the value of human life by destroying life. *Lettres à un ami allemand* was an attempt to deal with this problem on a more or less pragmatic basis. The conclusions he arrived at therein are valid insofar as they go, but they deal only with a very specific aspect of the problem: the Absurd Man's—or the rebel's—reaction when tyrannical forces resort to murder and terror to impose a social order of one kind or another. Having reached this point in his thinking, Camus next found himself using what had originally been an extraordinary justification for killing, in order to justify his condemnation of others in situations where the line between the forces of tyranny and the forces of justice was far less distinct.

Because they knew only the Camus of the Resistance and post-liberation periods, many left-wing intellectuals did not understand that, between 1946 and 1948, Camus had not so much changed his original position as returned to his earlier philosophical concerns. The social struggle was no less important to him then than it had been in 1938–39 or in 1944–45, but Camus was not prepared to go on fighting along lines that contradicted his fundamental thought. A human life, he was now sure, was priceless in itself, regardless of the political creed of its possessor.

Camus was aware that, should the enemy again resort to arms, there would be no choice but to meet violence with violence. He refused, nonetheless, to sanction any course of political action that threatened to destroy whole classes—or whole peoples, since it had come to that—in the name of an ideology based on doctrines that seemed to him to subordinate the one absolute value, human life, to abstractions. For Camus the abstractions in the name of which totalitarian governments held sway were far more dangerous and far more lethal than armies of men. Abstractions, as their survival after the Nazi defeat proved, were harder to destroy than human lives.

This was one of the reasons why Camus chose the plague to represent the Nazi forces of oppression. A disease, he thought, more closely symbolized the abstractions in the name of which the Nazis had waged their war. The German people and the Wehrmacht had merely allowed themselves to become the instruments that had translated the abstractions into action.

When Roland Barthes called *La Peste* a "refusal of history" and asked what Camus would do if faced with the destruction of human beings rather than with the destruction of microbes,[26] Camus replied that he and the other résistants had already answered that question. The résistants had admitted the necessity to take human lives, even though that admission had cost them dearly. He was sure that they would do it again if faced with any similar reign of terror. Indeed, he had not specifically named the Nazi terror in *La Peste* "in order to be better able to strike at all [kinds of terror]. Undoubtedly, it is precisely for this reason that I am being criticized, since *La Peste* can justify all forms of resistance against all forms of tyranny."[27]

That *La Peste* was aimed not only at the Nazi and the Communist ideologies but also at the all-or-nothing attitudes of French intellectuals and politicians is borne out by the article "Les Archives de la peste."[28] Again using the plague as a symbol, Camus warned the "doctors treating the plague victims" to take great precautions in treating the victims of the disease lest the "doctors" themselves become carriers. The warning was not directed at left-wing intellectuals alone. Those who sought to justify the Western democracies' tolerance of Franco had become, in Camus's opinion, carriers of the plague just as surely as those who supported the Soviet Union while it tightened its grip on Eastern Europe.

Nevertheless, it was to the left that Camus saw the greatest danger. In France many left-wing intellectuals, having despaired of the Resistance, were prophesying the death of European culture and declaring that communism remained the only acceptable form of involvement in political action. As for "dirtying one's hands" by accepting Communist methods, that was the price one had to pay. Camus saw such blind loyalty to an admittedly faulty system as incompatible with the intellectual's calling. He sought to warn the fellow-traveling intellectuals that they were only subscribing to a form of tyranny as violent as the one they had so recently fought to defeat. Instead of destroying the plague they were helping to spread its germs.

As a symbol of the committed intellectual, Camus now proposed the figure of the physician who treats illnesses on a day-to-day basis while remaining ever watchful for the initial signs of an epidemic, which he prevents if he can. When the epidemic strikes, as it inevitably must sooner or later, he puts his entire strength and talents at the service of the victims, never forgetting the rules of hygiene; he must not inadvertently spread the very disease he is fighting. For Camus, this availability to fight injustice in whatever form it may take had become the only viable form of commitment possible in an epoch when revolution was no longer feasible. He vehemently denied that such an attitude was in any way a refusal to accept the reality of history: ". . . in particular one cannot accuse me of rejecting history in *La Peste* except by declaring that the only means of entering history is to legitimize tyranny."[29]

That such critics as Roland Barthes, Jean Pouillon, and Etiemble saw *La Peste* not only as an oversimplification of the problem of commitment but also as a shift toward conservatism in Camus's thought once more demonstrates their failure to understand the meaning of *Le Mythe de Sisyphe*.[30] There are, of course, elements in Camus's works that might have been legitimately misleading. Ambiguities exist in all great works of art, and Camus's are no exception. But, from 1947 onward, much of the misunderstanding surrounding Camus's work was due to the fact that many commentators in France approached his writing with preconceived political notions. Etiemble's concluding remarks in his review of *La Peste* are one example of this tendency. He suggests that in the next confrontation with tyranny Rieux will not be able to indulge in his purifying swim in the Mediterranean because the Americans will have polluted the oceans with radioactive material.[31] This was written shortly before the announcement by the Russians in 1948 that they also had succeeded in developing an atomic bomb.

When Camus refused to be forced into thinking in conformity with the rest of the Parisian left-wing literary-intellectual Establishment, the Establishment rejected him. Sartre undoubtedly spoke sincerely when he suggested that Camus had once been exemplary and could be so again—provided, it was nonetheless implied, he behaved himself and joined Sartre.[32] But Sartre was also providing an example of the intellectual tyranny that many writers and critics in postwar France do not hesitate to use when attacking those who hold ideas contrary to their own. This was one of the forms of tyranny Camus had undertaken to fight.

Because Camus did refuse to conform, he was subjected to a barrage of insults, sometimes from the right but more often from the left. Until the end of 1947 he had kept his criticism of political affairs well balanced, dealing impartially with the opposing views of East and West. After 1948 this balance shifted in favor of the West, and Camus became the target of political attacks in the leftist press. Significantly, the first virulent criticism of his position came from the "progressists," the intellectual Marxists and neo-Marxists, who were usually "fellow travelers" rather than Communist party members. Their attacks probably did more in the long run to influence Camus's continued defense of Western democracy, with whatever faults and weaknesses it may have, than any other single factor except perhaps the crushing of the Hungarian revolt in 1956.

In two articles written in June and October 1948 in reply to d'Astier's attack against "Ni victimes ni bourreaux,"[33] Camus sharpened his criticism of the Soviet brand of authoritarian socialism and of the French progressists. He was at work on *L'Homme révolté,* which was to be at once an indictment of historical determinism and a search for a means of restoring to the revolutionary tradition the humanitarian spirit it had lost in the course of the nineteenth and twentieth centuries.

During 1948–51 Camus was again suffering from the aftereffects of tuberculosis; he took little part in political activities. One notable exception was his support of Garry Davis' Crusade for World

Federation.[34] On 3 December 1948 Camus spoke at a rally at the Salle Pleyel on behalf of Davis' movement. His answers to questions from the audience on this occasion appeared in *Combat* on 9 December.[35] In his remarks Camus once more denounced both Western and Soviet imperialism. He insisted that extremists from both sides, intentionally or not, were devoted to the destruction of the human race. Their unbending attitudes rendered "any historical future unforeseeable." Asked if he would choose capitulation rather than war, he answered: "I know that certain of those among you willingly accept the choice between hanging and the firing squad. That is their idea of human freedom. As for us, we are doing what we can to keep this choice from becoming inevitable. You are doing what is necessary to make this choice inevitable."* He then asked that both sides reexamine the political beliefs they held to be more inviolable than human life and attempt honestly to decide whether or not they were so certain of those beliefs that they were willing to risk, "even if there were only one chance in a thousand, bringing the danger of atomic war still closer."

Camus on 25 December again came to the defense of the Crusade for World Federation and its supporters after François Mauriac had criticized both. Camus defended Davis, insisting that the West and its spokesmen, Mauriac among them, who accepted Fascist regimes in Greece and Spain on the grounds that they were necessary allies in the cold war, were bogged down in an untenable contradiction. If any means whatsoever to defeat the Soviet Union was admissible, there was only one logical conclusion: immediately to launch a preventive war before Russia could reestablish her economy and develop atomic weapons of her own. The West, Camus thought, would not go so far, but whitewashing Fascist governments for strategic reasons was already a dangerous step in that direction.[36]

To envisage war on any terms was in itself unacceptable to Camus. In his reply to Mauriac he stated: "I know Paulhan[37] thinks it foolish to say that wars are baneful because they destroy human beings. I cling to that foolishness. . . ."* The intellectuals who supported Davis, Camus maintained, were trying to make it clear that the only hope for the future of the world lay in finding some compromise measure that would prevent the outbreak of atomic war. Neither they nor Davis claimed to bring truth to the world: "They know that their way lies elsewhere, as does their true vocation. They have only uttered a cry of alarm, in accordance with their abilities, and it is quite possible that this cry is uttered in the desert."[38]*

Two important points emerge from Camus's remarks at this time. First, he was not directing his criticism of the all-or-nothing political attitude specifically at the two great powers of the mid-twentieth century. He also had in mind the attitude of Western and mainly French intellectuals who, through their willingness to compromise on what Camus considered the most vital moral issues, were supporting the political traffic in human misery and death. Through his attacks upon them, he was aiming at the more general state of mind which allowed the ambitions of imperialistic nations to thrive.

Second, his reference to the "true vocation" of the intellectual indicates he no longer believed it possible for intellectuals to bring about sweeping changes in the status quo. He had already pointed out in October 1948: "I am aware that my role is to transform neither the world nor mankind."[39] Only when a significant opportunity to speak out arose, as in the case of Davis' crusade, or when some flagrant act of oppression was committed, would he enter the political arena, not as a spokesman for any political group but to bear witness to the injustices inherent in the historical aberrations of our time.

In 1950 in a letter to Jean-Paul Déron, a journalist for the independent *Paris-Normandie,* Camus set certain broad limits to the artist's participation in political affairs. In answer to Déron's question, "Why do you remain silent at the present time?" he spoke of the "true tasks" as being creation and the search for happiness. The world, he said, was governed by the nihilists and it was up to those who believed in the existence of certain values to affirm them and to give them form. However, "to spend all one's time shouting their existence at every crossroads" did not necessarily affirm those values. The struggle against nihilism was a battle against time; crying that time was too short was a waste of time, "But if we succeed during this time in defining what is opposed to nihilism, illustrate it, make others share it, then our chances of success will increase and we will gain more time." The true task of the artist, Camus insisted, was "to maintain amid outcries and violence our lucidity, our generosity and our will to live. . . ."[40] Camus had always tended to regard artistic creation as a form of commitment in itself, an attitude he made explicit in *Le Mythe de Sisyphe*.[41] He was further to develop this point of view, which harks back to earlier statements in *Alger-Républicain,* in *L'Homme révolté,* the major work written during 1948–51.

By 1950 the lines of battle between Camus and the progressist intellectuals were clearly drawn. The break with many of his friends and associates had already occurred. But it had not reached beyond the narrow circles of the Parisian literati. *L'Homme révolté,* which marks the climax in the evolution of Camus's political thought, was to explode like a bombshell over the rocky terrain of the Parisian political and intellectual battleground, and make the break irreparable.

6

In Search of a
New Prometheus

THE POLITICAL attitudes prevalent in many French
left-wing intellectual circles at the time of the quarrel over
L'Homme révolté had begun to take form as early as 1944. At that
time, in spite of the friendly attitude of the non-Communist résistants toward the Communist party, the Communists had shown no
inclination to compromise with the more moderate elements of the
M.L.N. On 7 October 1944 Camus had announced *Combat's*
unqualified support of the proposition, adopted in March by the
underground movement, the Congrès de Combat, that "anticommunism is the beginning of dictatorship."[1] Unfortunately, he went
on to say, in spite of his paper's position, misunderstandings on
certain issues had arisen between the Communists and other elements of the Resistance. Since no progress toward reform could be
made while such misunderstandings remained, Camus proposed to
clarify the position of the non-Communist résistants. The main
source of misunderstanding, he thought, stemmed from disagreement as to the methods to be used in initiating reforms. Social
justice and a collectivist economy were aims shared by all the
left-wing factions. But the Communists found "in a very coherent
philosophy of history the justification for political realism as a
superior means of achieving the triumph of an ideal common to
many Frenchmen." On this point *Combat* stood in firm opposition
to the Communists: those whom it represented rejected such political realism. "Our method," he added, "is different."[2] Unequivocal
as it was, this attempt at clarification did nothing to alleviate the

119

tension that existed between Communist and non-Communist—or "extra-Communist" as they were also called—elements of the Resistance movement.

Attacks against those who refused to accept conformity to Communist party discipline were soon forthcoming. On 6 December 1944 (pp. 1–2) a *Combat* editorialist confessed his perplexity at the denunciation of *extracommunisme* by Albert Bayet, the extreme left-wing Socialist editor of *Franc-Tireur*. Bayet had contended that extracommunism could only lead to anticommunism and finally to Hitlerism. The editorial writer insisted that this was not the case; *Combat* asked nothing better than to work with the Communists in settling their differences and in rebuilding France. If Bayet's premise were accepted, the writer pointed out, he and those of his persuasion would be left with a choice, pure and simple, between Doriot and Cachin.[3]

Combat refused to accept these as the only possible alternatives. The only way to realize the aims of both the non-Communist left and the Communists was to work together for the good of the nation as a whole. The editorialist repeated Camus's earlier invitation to the Communists to speak frankly about their differences, for *Combat* felt that it was only by way of a constructive dialogue that necessary unity could be achieved. This plea met with no response; the divisions within the Resistance groups continued to widen. What Camus was later to call "The War of the Left-Wing Factions" had already begun.[4]

As it became more and more evident that the Resistance had failed to bring about a successful revolution, many of the adherents of the non-Communist left shared Camus's disappointment. And many also decided that Bayet had been right. The October 1945 election, which had marked the return to political activity of many prewar political factions, also demonstrated that the Communist party was the major single political party in France and that it incontestably enjoyed the confidence of the majority of French workers. Faced with this evidence, many intellectuals decided that the only hope of ever introducing needed reforms into the French political system lay in some sort of accommodation with the Communist party, more or less on the party's own terms. Some, such as d'Astier, eventually joined the Communist party. Sartre's position was more typical: he preferred to support the party and the workers in their revolutionary aims while retaining his intellectual independence and the right to criticize specific Communist policies and actions.

Sartre and his followers were undoubtedly motivated by a sincere concern for the working class, which certainly suffered from inequities in the French social order. Camus, on the other hand, had found from his early experience both with the Communists in Algeria and as editor of *Combat* in 1944–45 that an equivocal association with the Communist party such as Sartre proposed was, if not impossible, intellectually dangerous. His warning in "Les Archives de la peste" went unheeded. As Nicola Chiaromonte observed, ever since 1945 Sartre and his followers had tended not only to act like "amateur Communists" but to adopt more and more the "arguments of the Communist catechism," while refusing to justify those arguments to those who opposed them: "They have been behaving, that is, as if, once they had declared themselves in favor of the Proletariat, the consistency of their ideas was a matter of automatic adjustment of which no account was due to 'others.' "5

Since its founding in 1945, Sartre's *Les Temps modernes* has indeed shown an almost total lack of objectivity in certain areas, especially when dealing with American social problems, with United States foreign policy, and with the political and social problems of all the Western nations. For example, as Kenneth Cornell pointed out in 1955, the biased reporting on the issue of McCarthyism, where "no effort is made by *Les Temps modernes* to indicate opposition and even corrective adjustments, reveals an almost constant inner fault in this periodical."6 More recently, the treatment of the Cuban situation in *Les Temps modernes* has been very one-sided, little attempt being made to consider any possible justification for the American position. Such reporting is to be expected from official propaganda organs, but to most impartial observers it seems out of place in a review that purports to be the voice of a distinguished group of philosophers and writers.

At the root of the shift toward communism in this particular group of French intellectuals there seems to lie that curious phenomenon of class guilt that appears to obsess many enlightened French bourgeois. It is difficult to measure the extent of the influence of this phenomenon, but its presence, particularly where Sartre is concerned, is quite discernible. Lucien Fleurier in "L'Enfance d'un chef" (*Le Mur*), Hugo in *Les Mains sales,* and Sartre's "existential psychoanalyses" of Baudelaire and Genêt all reveal his preoccupation with this social anomaly.

Camus, on the other hand, was, as Germaine Brée notes, "astonishingly free of the intellectual attitudes which most Frenchmen inherit from their long historical past and the milieu into which they were born."[7] Camus's Algerian birth and his proletarian origin were in themselves no guarantee that he was invariably right when he spoke in the name of the working class; nor was Sartre, when he did so, always wrong. But various elements in Camus's background had given him a certain objectivity about European political problems, which made him a lucid and, for the progressist intellectuals, an often dangerously accurate critic of twentieth-century political ethics.

Camus's upbringing in a proletarian environment had made him impervious to the psychological influences at work in the guilt-burdened mind of the petit bourgeois. In his experience, freedom and the natural beauty of Algeria had combined to compensate for the misery of existence in the slums of Belcourt; Camus had learned that only those means of attaining social justice that did not compromise these two precious possessions were acceptable. He understood that the worker had to protest against the injustices from which he suffered. But he also knew that the workers were not willing to live their lives in terror and oppression in return for some improvement in their material living conditions. They had other aspirations, common to all men, which Camus emphasized in his preface to Louis Guilloux's *La Maison du peuple*. There he denounced the "specialists in progress" for their lack of knowledge of the workers' real aspirations and for maintaining that the proletariat preferred bread to freedom and having no bread would have no use for freedom. To the question, "Whom do you prefer, man, him who would deprive you of bread in the name of freedom or him who would take away your freedom in order to guarantee you bread?" Camus's worker answers, "on which one should I spit first?"[8]

This may or may not truly reflect the workers' attitude. However, Jeanson presented a compelling argument when he reminded Camus that the Communist party, during the late 1940's and early 1950's, had the support of a majority of the French workers. Sartre and Jeanson used this fact as primary justification for the political positions they had taken; and, from a practical point of view, it was difficult for Camus to condemn them while claiming that justice for the working class should be the major aim of contemporary social and political reform movements.

But Camus, in contrast to Sartre and Jeanson, felt that syndicalism had not been exploited to the fullest extent. In any case, he was not willing to lead the workers, no matter how willingly they might have followed, in an effort to set up a regime patterned after that of Stalinist Russia. Camus was now gravitating slowly toward a position where he was to admit, implicitly at least, that regardless of the justice of the workers' cause other groups had certain claims and a right to recognition.

His opponents tended to look upon this position as a kind of misguided idealism or as a reluctance to recognize political realities. The opinion that Camus was not really prepared for the political role he assumed after World War II, already put forward by Jean Guitton, was stated somewhat differently by Claude Bourdet. Bourdet maintained that Camus, who had not been included in the decision-making councils of the Resistance high command, had remained unaware of the intrigues and counterintrigues among the various political factions within the Resistance. The implication was that Camus did not realize that political action inevitably involved "dirty hands," and that "one must maintain a pure heart but one must not so preciously keep one's hands chaste from every impure contact if one is to change something in this world."[9]

It is not entirely certain that Camus was wholly unaware of the existence of political intrigues beneath the surface of the Resistance movements; he certainly knew Communist tactics from first-hand experience in Algeria. His attempt to work with the Communists during 1944–45 stemmed possibly from an error in judgment or, more likely, from the acceptance of a calculated risk based on the hope that Russia's emergence from enforced isolation and the strength of the non-Communist segments of the Resistance could combine to create a favorable climate for the development of a new, more effective Popular Front.[10] When this and all other hopes failed, Camus was left little choice other than a retreat to the rather solitary and highly personal position that he set forth in *L'Homme révolté*.

L'Homme révolté appeared in October 1951. The first wave of critical reviews was favorable, although many critics expressed some reservations. It was only seven months after its publication, when the work was attacked by *Les Temps modernes,* that the controversy exploded and Camus found himself at the center of one of those scandals in which the Parisian literary world seems to specialize. A short examination of the book itself is necessary to an understanding of the subsequent disputes in the press.

For purposes of analysis the work may be divided roughly into three main sections. The first contains a study of revolt and revolution, the second a consideration of the artist as rebel and artistic creation as a form of revolt. The third section consists of an outline of what Camus called "la Pensée de Midi," intended to provide a source of ethical conduct for the rebel and the revolutionary.

The first section, which constitutes the major portion of the book, begins with the assertion that in our time methodical murder has come to be accepted as a political weapon. Modern revolutionary movements have justified terror and premeditated mass murder in the name of improvement of the human lot. Thus we find "slave camps under the banner of freedom [and] massacres justified by love for humanity or by admiration for the Superman. . . ." In order to refute this "logic of destruction," an intuitive or emotional condemnation is insufficient: "The day when crime arrays itself in the discarded attire of innocence, . . . innocence is called upon to justify itself. The intent of this essay is to accept and examine this strange challenge."[11]

Because Camus saw revolt as the basis of all desire for change in the political and social order, he began by examining in what manner revolt takes form in the human consciousness, and discussed the immediate and long-range consequences of revolt in terms of action. The moment that the slave, or any human being who becomes aware of the existence of oppression, realizes that his master has gone beyond a certain limit and has committed an intolerable transgression against certain rights which the slave feels intuitively are his, revolt is born. The slave, laboring under the master's whip, suddenly turns and faces the master. By translating his feeling of revolt into action, the slave is affirming the existence of both a value, which is represented in his very being, and a limit to the absolute freedom of the master.

As the sense of revolt becomes more firmly implanted, the slave arrives at a point where he is no longer willing to accept even qualified servitude, which he had formerly tolerated. He now insists that his inherent worth as a human being renders him equal to his master and endows him with the right to enjoy the same measure of freedom accorded the master.

Having reached this stage, the slave, now a full-fledged rebel, refuses servitude and oppression on any grounds and declares himself ready to die in defense of his newfound rights. Since death would paradoxically mean the annihilation of the slave and, at the same time, the annihilation of his ability to enjoy those rights which he has just affirmed, his willingness to defend them with his life is a further affirmation that these rights exist, not only for him but for all slaves and ultimately for all human beings.

Hence, the action born of revolt—revolution in a historical context—is an expression of the solidarity of the individual with the human race: "I rebel, therefore we are." The assertion of human equality implies complicity in the struggle against oppression, so that the rebel betrays his accomplices in equality from the moment that he in turn becomes an oppressor. Freedom thus can never be absolute, since the enjoyment of absolute freedom would inevitably imply encroachment upon those rights which the rebel had affirmed by his willingness to die. If the former slave asserts his own superiority at the expense of others, he has merely substituted one master-slave relationship for another.

Having defined revolt and the limits that are inherent in it, Camus then examines a number of literary and historical figures whose works and lives manifest the philosophy of revolt. He proceeds to study both metaphysical or individual revolt and historical revolt or revolution, concentrating on what Germaine Brée aptly calls the "monomaniacs of revolt."[12] He is primarily interested in analyzing the use which certain men, freed from the restraints imposed by Christian moral precepts, made of their freedom. Esoteric as such figures as Sade, Netchaiev, and Bakunin may seem to the average reader, their influence on modern European thinkers and on the development of twentieth-century political ideologies is unquestionable.

Camus, observing that modern man has lost sight of the relativity of all revolt, concludes that, having turned away from religion as a source of values, men have set up a new source of absolute values by deifying either man himself or history. The rigor of the absolute moral standards of the Church had been modified by the fact that final judgment and punishment were relegated to an afterlife. But with the death of God and the rejection of the belief in a hereafter, the high priests of the new religion, the dictators and their philosopher apologists, found it necessary to judge men and to punish them in this world. In their zeal to see man and the social order reflect the deified man and the perfect social order toward which they were certain the march of history was predirected, revolutionary leaders from Saint-Just to Lenin justified the destruction of those human beings who impeded the attainment of perfection within the social order.

Thus murder, conquest, and enslavement were accepted as legitimate political weapons in the attempt to establish the reign of the Superman or a utopia. Unfortunately human nature--which, Camus suggests, exists by virtue of the rebel's vague realization that his life has some intrinsic worth—since it is less than perfect, is destined to be constantly at odds with efforts to establish a perfect social order. The supreme irony lies, of course, in the fact that such efforts almost invariably derive from a desire to free humanity from oppression and injustice. Having forgotten the first generous impulse inherent in revolt, the rebel goes on to become a doctrinaire revolutionary who, like Saint-Just, tends to be impatient when he fails to discern any lessening in the discrepancy between the order prescribed by his doctrine and the existing social order: "The philosophy of revolt cannot do without the memory: it is a perpetual tension."[13] In other words, the rebel must retain the memory of the slave's former servitude. This will enable him to conceive of the consequences of his actions in terms of human suffering, the consciousness of which was the initial source of his revolt.

When he loses sight of the original cause of his revolt, the modern revolutionary, in his almost frantic effort to create new values, turns to the doctrines of Nietzsche, Marx, and Hegel, among others, rather than to the human creature himself. By corrupting Nietzsche's thought, the Nazis arrived at the concept of the Superman, which they used to justify tyranny and conquest. The followers of Marx superimposed Hegelian phenomenology on Marxian prophecy to arrive at a theory of historical determinism. They then used this theory to justify the existence of a "transitional" dictatorship, which Camus called Caesarian socialism, pointing out that in practice it seems to be not only permanent but self-perpetuating as well.

It should be noted here that Camus was not condemning Marx and Nietzsche but what he viewed as the distortion of their thought by those who came after them. He expressed strong sympathy for the motives that had inspired Marx, but attacked those of Marx's followers who have tended to hold his writings sacred despite the fact that certain of his predictions and presuppositions were proved incorrect by the actual course of historical events.

The first portion of *L'Homme révolté,* then, is a study of what lies behind the rebel's failure to attain the ends that had inspired him in the first place: the desire to free men from the restraints imposed upon them by irrelevant moral codes or by unjust political regimes. In the second section of the book, Camus deals with revolt and art. For him, the artist is the rebel par excellence. When he refuses to accept the totality of the universe on its own terms, the artist is in fact rebelling against the incoherence of the world. On the other hand, the artist cannot completely ignore reality, for it is only from the real world that he can derive his artistic vision. Thus the true artist-rebel is always obliged to take reality into consideration; through the process of artistic selection, he seeks to impose coherence on an incoherent universe.

If the artist completely ignores reality, his work is characterized by empty formalism; if he tries merely to incorporate reality as he perceives it, his work is bound to be no more than a monotonous enumeration. Camus correlates man's desire for coherence and beauty expressed in works of art and his desire for order expressed in political institutions. In both cases the artist and the statesman must constantly seek to maintain the balance between emptiness and chaos. The only way the artist and statesman can create and preserve this balance is by continually referring back to the nearest thing to absolute reality that we know, the natural world of which the human being is an integral part. In the third section of the work, Camus outlines one means whereby he thought the balance between the two extremes could be maintained. He advocated a return to the Greek ideal of moderation based on contemplation of nature and recognition of the limitations of human knowledge and capabilities.

In this third portion of the essay, Camus frequently uses the term "renaissance." This is not merely rhetoric on his part, for the "Pensée de Midi" is an appeal to turn once more to the humanistic ideals that were held in such high esteem during the Renaissance. For Camus, these ideals had been nurtured and kept alive on the shores of the Mediterranean in Spain, Italy, Greece, and North Africa.

In a sense, this part of *L'Homme révolté* is the materialization of the treatise the young Camus had planned to write, and which, as mentioned in the *Carnets,* was to deal with a political theory based on a Mediterranean culture.[14] It is quite likely that the essays in *Noces* and *L'Eté* were originally intended to be part of a development leading to the formulation of a "Pensée de Midi." However, by the 1950's any philosophical view depending for its exposition on a complex of images drawn from an Algerian or North African "culture" would inevitably be distorted by the political implications of the widespread unrest and violence in that part of the world. This undoubtedly accounts in some measure for the rather vague generalities Camus used in setting forth the "Pensée de Midi," a weakness most critics, even those otherwise sympathetic to the work as a whole, did not hesitate to point out.

Claude Bourdet, perhaps Camus's most objective left-wing critic, remarked that "in this valuable book, in which an implacable analysis leaves little to criticize, nothing or almost nothing comes forth in response to the real problem of our time."[15] His point of view, with slight variations, was to be reiterated by a number of other critics. John Cruickshank considers the work "essential to a proper understanding of present world problems. The most dangerous features of Marxism are lucidly and intelligently exposed, and yet the reasons for its success in Europe also emerge clearly." But Cruickshank feels that the final pages of the book "strike one as an unsuccessful attempt to turn a fundamentally negative argument into a positive one."[16]

These criticisms, while not without some validity, appear to me too exigent. It is true that Camus's presentation of his concept of a "Pensée de Midi" is rather lyrical and is not supported by any practical suggestions. He does not propose anything beyond a possible rejuvenation of syndicalism, and makes only a passing reference to Scandinavian experiments in social democracy. On the other hand, one cannot reasonably expect an author to provide the world singlehandedly with a definitive solution to problems that continue to perplex rulers, diplomats, political scientists, sociologists, historians, and peoples at large.

What Camus was offering in *L'Homme révolté* was not a political system or ideology, for it was clear to him that the solution to modern man's problems was not to be found in ideologies. As he had written earlier in "Ni victimes ni bourreaux": "It is quite evident that it should not be a matter of constructing a new ideology. It should be a matter of seeking a 'style of life.' "[17] This "style of life" would put revolt—and revolution when necessary— at the service of humanity rather than at the service of systematic abstractions. This was, in a sense, the underlying theme of the whole essay. But the "Pensée de Midi" is only a point of departure, a call for a return to sanity; it was not intended to supply all the answers to contemporary social and political problems. In a letter written in 1952 to Jean Gillibert, Camus further clarified his intent. The Pensée de Midi was intended only to be a beginning. Men in their struggle against history and against the misery of the human condition needed an "inexhaustible source of beauty." Never was that need greater, Camus felt, than in contemporary Europe. The Mediterranean had been a receptacle of classical culture, which still survived along its shores. In the brilliant "light" of this classical culture new works had to be brought forth to aid men in their struggle. This Camus saw as the challenge of the twentieth-century artist. As for himself, he avowed, "I only hope to have the strength and talent [to meet this challenge], but I cannot answer to that."[18]

What the artist and the intellectual must do, Camus was saying, is reexamine accepted concepts of political action in terms of their validity in relation to the realities of the human condition. Twentieth-century revolutions have, to the extent that they were based on abstract principles, derived from considerations of what humanity ought to be rather than of what it is in reality. Twentieth-century revolution, while claiming to be derived from economic theory, was fundamentally political and ideological in origin. By its very function it could not avoid doing violence to reality. Modern revolution sought "to mold reality" according to a preconceived ideological vision. True revolt, on the contrary, seeking truth, takes the path toward true realism. If revolt demands revolution it does so "in favor of life, not against it."[19]

The fundamental reality is man as he exists, not man as some ideology says he should be. Syndicalism was successful for the very reason that it dealt with the profession- and village-oriented man and did not attempt, as did authoritarian socialism, to destroy historic patterns of behavior in order to fit human beings into a preconceived political, economic, and social framework. Otherwise stated, political action and doctrines can be just only when they avoid the absolute and remain firmly based on needs that are related to man's nature and to his living conditions. Thus if man, and hence society, is perfectible—the conclusion to *La Peste* indicates that Camus thought not—perfection is not attained by forcing humanity into a perfect mold incompatible with the present form of his existence.

Since "We all carry within us our prisons, our crimes and our forces of destruction,"[20] the road to progress lies in the constant struggle against the violence inherent in human nature, and it must begin on an individual basis. The dichotomy of good versus evil exists within the individual; and since the individual is the prime element in the collectivity, the same dichotomy exists within the collectivity. The balance between the two can be maintained only by constant reference to a mean, exemplified by Nemesis, who punished those who, in the search for absolute values, go beyond the limitations of man's nature. Social order is the creation of human beings, and only so long as its point of reference is man can any social order embody that justice for which all men, faced with inevitable death, cry out. From the moment order is justified in the name of the stability of the state or in the name of a future utopia, it ceases to be relative to the living human creature for whose benefit it is presumably established.

Revolt, then, degenerates into tyranny when peoples, seeking to eliminate the causes of their sufferings, lose sight of their basic aim: a measure of individual happiness. Once they go beyond the point where they have secured their own freedom, which can never be absolute but only a measure of freedom, they have surpassed the limits imposed on the rebel by revolt itself; the rebel at this stage "is no longer Prometheus, he is Caesar."[21] Such a reversal had occurred in France when the Resistance had found itself in a position of dominance immediately after the Nazi withdrawal. While Camus had sought to maintain respect for the lives and the rights of accused collaborationists, he had soon come to feel that he himself had become infected with the nihilistic disease of ideological absolutism. The Resistance, in his view, had ultimately resorted to violent means to an end the achievement of which it could in no way guarantee. It is not surprising, then, that Camus should have insisted in *L'Homme révolté* that if the end justifies the means the means in turn must justify the end.

Camus did not deny that revolution and violence may sometimes be necessary. Essentially he was proposing for the revolutionary a source of ethical conduct posited on a profound respect for human life. If it should become necessary for the revolutionary to destroy the mean by taking a human life, he should be ready to restore the balance by giving his own life in return. There is no reason to believe that every revolutionary must, like Kaliayev, die on the gallows after having perpetrated violence in the name of justice; however, by being ready and willing to do so, the revolutionary will be inclined to resort to violence only when no other alternative is possible, and then only as an extraordinary measure, the justification for which ends the moment a *relatively* just order is established or reestablished.

Thus the rebel or the revolutionary—and these in the broadest sense include any human being who revolts against suffering inherent in the human condition—must not seek to act in the name of any absolute value. In the political sphere man's thought and action should be restricted to a mean defined by the limitations of human nature. If he violates this mean and seeks to go too far beyond his limitation, he runs into a contradiction in that he seeks to achieve that which is contrary to his very nature. Are we to infer from this that progress is impossible and that men should abandon the search for truth? No, for progress is possible within the range of man's knowledge and capabilities, and the search for truth will always be carried on by individuals. But society itself cannot define absolutes, and when a political ideal takes on the trappings of religion it quickly engenders an inquisition. Individuals will continue the search for absolutes, but "society and politics are only responsible for regulating the affairs of all so that each may have the leisure and the freedom for that common search. History . . . is only an open opportunity that remains to be rendered productive through vigilant revolt."[22]

The "Pensée de Midi" presented no new departure in Camus's thought, where it had long had a place. In its simplest form, it is an appeal for recognition of the right of the individual to achieve his own destiny within the limits of social necessity, an ideal that Camus very early saw as the greatest strength of Greek civilization. A statement he made in 1939 helps to clarify his somewhat generalized presentation of the "Pensée de Midi" in *L'Homme révolté*. In his review of a lecture given by Professor Gernet of the University of Algiers, Camus revealed how deeply he had been struck with the tendency of the Greeks to regard the human being as the touchstone of all inquiry and activity:

M. Gernet defined the essential aspect of the Greek message in what may be described as a moving manner when he said that this race of people, as much beset by misfortune as any other, nonetheless never surrendered before the problem of happiness, to the quest for which they applied their individual thought. Today, on the contrary, what one sees in neighboring countries is worship of the collectivity and negation of the individual man, derived from a desperate awareness of the adversity of the times.

Many young men, in Germany and elsewhere, thought they had found relief from their suffering by putting themselves wholly in someone else's hands. The Greeks, on the other hand, thought that man's dignity consisted in facing his destiny and in yielding to no one the concern for his own life. Such abdication is contrary to the Greek spirit, and one might add, in view of the repugnance free minds feel for that act, that they recognize the Greek ideal as a good one (*AR*, 24-1-39, p. 3).*

The emphasis here on the contrast between the Greek ideal and that of Nazi youth is significant. Camus, in 1939, had viewed the Nazi experiment as one of the cases in which justifiable revolt had gone beyond the limit. In giving form to their revolt, the German people and their leaders had reversed the master-slave relationship and thus violated the fundamental maxim of revolt: "I rebel, therefore we are." Human life had ceased to have any universal value for the Nazis.

The tendency to sacrifice individual human lives for the sake of improving the lot of the human race as a whole, Camus thought, developed largely as a consequence of the breakdown of the authority of the Church. European thinkers were the heirs of the Christian belief in a Communion of Saints in which the members of the Church Militant on earth strive against nature toward the attainment of perfection represented by the Church Triumphant in heaven. Furthermore the Church, after having dissipated its heritage of Greek thought, had emphasized historical dynamism and temporal power, the object of which was to transform nature rather than to meditate upon its mysteries and admire its beauties. Nietzsche having proclaimed the death of God, European thinkers found themselves in possession of an ascetic tradition of progressive perfection which no longer had any meaning: "It was only required that God be expelled from that historical universe in order to give birth to the German ideology wherein action is no

* French texts of starred passages may be found in Appendix A.

longer the attainment of perfection but pure conquest, that is to say tyranny."[23]

Tyranny can therefore be avoided, in a world deprived of God, by a return to a humanistic ideal: the contemplation of nature and the effort to know oneself in order better to know and understand man. On a collective level, this would entail a constant struggle to correct any social injustice that would tend to deprive the individual of the relative freedom he needs to seek happiness for himself; thus the individual is forever the yardstick of collective action. The object of political action becomes not progress toward utopian perfection but the creation of a climate of existence in which each individual can carry on his own struggle to know himself and thereby learn how to reconcile his desire for coherence with the incoherent universe in which he exists.

There is nothing in this analysis, or in the concept of a "Pensée de Midi," that implies the necessity to accept colonial exploitation, racism, and all the other ills of the modern world. Camus insisted strongly that the struggle against such injustices must not be carried on under the aegis of an ideology which seeks to "liberate" victims of injustice only to resort to prison camps, police state terrorism, and murder in order to force them into an abstract pattern of existence alien to human nature.

It is true that, as Bourdet said, Camus offered no concise system that could be substituted for historical determinism or for Communist methodology. But *L'Homme révolté* is specifically a study of the phenomenon of revolt and the process by which it loses its altruistic orientation and becomes an instrument of tyranny. Camus concluded his essay by presenting his personal philosophical reflections, suggesting that they might serve as a guide for reorienting the rebel in such a way that revolt might once more regain the constructive aspect it had lost. In a sense, the strength of Camus's "Pensée de Midi" lies precisely in the fact that it is nonsystematic and thus does not commit the rebel to any preconceived course of political action. A prescribed course of action, given the inevitable changes in the relative human condition, might eventually give rise to another conflict between means and ends like that which Camus saw in the ideals and methods of the Marxists.

L'Homme révolté was not intended to be a manual of political expediency but a warning to intellectuals as well as to every thinking individual who has a role to play in a democratic society. Camus saw history as the sum total of the actions of men in time, the end result of their attempts to give form to their dreams and aspirations. Hence he could not attribute the apocalyptic violence of the century to the fact alone that such men as Hitler and Stalin took advantage of the nihilistic currents of twentieth-century thought to maintain themselves in power. Violence was also made possible because peoples and, more important, intellectual leaders turned over to dictators their right to individual self-determination, desperately placing their lives in the hands of tyrants.

Therefore Camus's essay on revolt seems really to have been written as a sharp reminder to the intellectuals—and to all those who are impatient with the crimes and injustices rampant in the world today—that no matter how desperate the plight of oppressed peoples may be it is fatal to surrender to impatience and to commit oneself unreservedly to any despotic force. Far better to fight oppression on a day-to-day basis, always redefining values in the light of the single recognizable absolute value, inviolable human life.

This is a demanding criterion of action, but the often-repeated criticism that *L'Homme révolté* does not offer any concrete suggestions toward a solution to the present stalemate in international affairs is in itself symptomatic of the tendency of the modern intellectual to abandon the weapons of personal dissent in favor of an ideology that prescribes in advance a fixed attitude toward a given situation. By abandoning the intellectual's traditional independence of political factions in favor of militant action within a given party, French writers, Camus felt, were actually putting themselves and their art on trial.

The manner in which *Les Temps modernes* reacted to *L'Homme révolté* testifies to the accuracy of Camus's indictment of those

twentieth-century intellectuals who are committed to defense of
party ideologies rather than open discussion of all shades of political opinion. Francis Jeanson's review appeared in May 1952, seven
months after the book's publication.[24] The review was not openly
hostile; on the contrary, Jeanson took an objectively critical tone.
However, he did fail to deal with the main point of the book: the
question whether or not historical determinism has come to be a
doctrine that perpetuates tyranny and police state terrorism.

Relying on insinuation, evident in the title of the article itself—
"Albert Camus ou l'âme révoltée"—Jeanson described Camus's
entire work as being too metaphysical to have any practical application to political issues. He suggested that by Camus's own standards of "absurd" creation, as set forth in *Le Mythe de Sisyphe* and
in *L'Homme révolté* itself, Camus's essay was too balanced a work
of art to be accepted as a valid protest against social injustices.
Starting from these premises, it took only a few short steps to
consign Camus to the limbo of Hegelian "pure souls," who are
repelled by the unpleasant realities of political action.

Jeanson also implied that Camus was at least indirectly condon-
ing the murderous repression by capitalist societies of oppressed
peoples "who would undertake . . . to struggle against those
responsible for their hunger."[25] In so doing, Jeanson asserted,
Camus was helping to ease the guilty consciences of bourgeois
intellectuals and giving antiprogressist ammunition to the right.
This argument was immediately picked up by the entire left-wing
press and applied indiscriminately to nearly everything Camus
wrote and said for the remainder of his life.

Camus, acting upon an invitation from Sartre, replied to Jeanson's article in a long letter addressed not to Jeanson but to
Sartre;[26] he referred to Jeanson only as "your collaborator." This
rather haughty tone, to which Camus occasionally resorted, no
doubt proved very annoying to Sartre and to Jeanson. It probably
accounts in some measure for the atmosphere of personal insult in
which the dispute ended. This does not alter the fact that neither
Jeanson nor Sartre ever directly answered Camus's objections or

corrected the misleading slant of Jeanson's original criticism of *L'Homme révolté* and of Camus's political position.

Camus objected to a number of points in the article, contending that Jeanson had deliberately distorted not only the content of *L'Homme révolté* and his entire work but his biography as well. His major objections to the review were set forth in the form of two questions based on the essential premises of the essay: (1) Was there not a body of Marxian prophecy which the actual development of historical events had proved incorrect, and had not the Marxists adopted from Hegelian phenomenology the axiomatic conclusion that history was following a course of predetermined progress toward a utopian society? (2) Had not the prophetic aspects of Marxism and the acceptance of history as an absolute entity largely beyond human control resulted in an authoritarian form of socialism that depended on methodical terrorism and concentration camps to ensure its control of the state?

Both Sartre and Jeanson wrote lengthy replies to Camus's letter.[27] Jeanson was mainly concerned with defending his review against Camus's countercharges; the responsibility of answering Camus's questions fell to Sartre. Albert Legrand's comment that in his response "Sartre . . . chats brilliantly, like a cardsharper drawing your attention away from his tricks,"[28] while it does not take into account Sartre's sincere regret at this public disruption of a ten-year-long friendship,[29] does sum up very well Sartre's treatment of Camus's questions.

In reply to the first question, Sartre stated that *he himself* did not think that history had any predetermined end since after all history was the sum total of the actions of men, and it was up to men to determine what end or ends it should have. He then went on to say that ". . . Marx never said that history would have a final end; how could he have? . . . He only spoke of an end to prehistory, that is, of an end that would be attained within the context of history itself and ultimately surpassed like all ends."[30] This semantic somersault is typical of Sartre's whole reply.

Sartre did admit, in treating Camus's second question, that slave camps existed in the Soviet Union. He pointed out that he himself had condemned them and that while he found Soviet atrocities as repulsive as Camus did, he found even more repulsive the joy with which the right had greeted the exposure of the labor camps' existence and the use that had been made of this information to excuse the crimes the West committed against the enslaved peoples of Asia and Africa. Camus himself, Sartre charged, was exploiting the misery of Soviet slave laborers in order to justify "a quietism that refuses to distinguish those who are the masters."[31] Sartre, like Bayet in 1944, refused to recognize any middle ground between Stalin and Franco. He suggested a retreat to the Galapagos Islands as the only solution for those who recoiled at the compromises involved in effective political action. Thus he rather flippantly dismissed the possibility that there might be some justification in Camus's position or in that of all those, as Chiaromonte puts it, "who, while not pretending to have at their disposal any new systematic certainty, are aware of the sterility of the old political dogmas."[32]

Once again the lack of any political movement through which he could translate his ideas into effective action placed Camus at a disadvantage. Dissociated from any concrete political program of collectivization and social reform, the ideals of liberty and justice defended in *L'Homme révolté* could be closely identified with the professed principles of so-called bourgeois, capitalist democracy, all the more since Camus's "Pensée de Midi" derives from the same humanistic tradition as the libertarian ideals of Western democracy. But, in Camus's opinion, the fact that the bourgeois leaders of the Third Republic, in order tó perpetuate their own power, had misused Jacobin libertarian principles did not invalidate the principles themselves. He considered the confusion of the ideal of freedom with the use that had been made of it by conservative politicians one of the grave errors of the early Marxists. When they had said that freedom was merely a bourgeois fairy tale, a single word had been out of place, for "it should have been said only that bourgeois freedom, and not all freedom, was a fairy tale, . . .

that there were freedoms to be conquered and never again relinquished." Moreover, he noted, "we are still paying for that errone-
ous word order in the convulsions of our time."[33] Camus's "Pensée
de Midi," in one of its aspects, was an effort to correct this error
and to find a means of perpetuating the humanistic tradition of
liberty and justice without resorting to stultified codes of ethics and
moral values that had lost their force because they had been used to
justify a more or less rigid class structure.

The debate over *L'Homme révolté* was entirely futile so far as
bringing the two sides any nearer to a mutual understanding went.
It also succeeded in clouding the real issues, behind such side issues
as that raised by Camus's challenge to Sartre to show how he
reconciled historical determinism and existentialism. This challenge, probably motivated by Camus's long mistrust of the systematic aspects of Sartre's philosophy, might have been the basis for a
very interesting discussion, but it was beside the point. The essential point of the discussion really was whether or not Sartre had
chosen a course of political action that could eventually result in
the liberation of the working class, the avowed aim of both Camus
and Sartre.

Sartre had taken the position that the authoritarian character of
communism was the result of political rather than ideological
errors.[34] He maintained that it was therefore possible to correct
these errors and to influence the Communists to adopt more liberal
policies. But if Camus's diagnosis were correct, the Communists
could change their authoritarian policies only at the risk of bringing about the downfall of communism itself, since communism
must depend upon dictatorial methods in order to maintain a social
order that is contradictory to the natural inclinations of the people
living under its rule. If this were true, then Sartre's claim that he is
following a course of action dictated by political efficacy would
become highly questionable. Even if one assumes that such a
course of action might be instrumental in bringing the Communists
to power in France, Sartre, unless he could demonstrate that
Camus's conclusion was incorrect, would run the risk of winning a

Pyrrhic victory, since his explicitly stated goal is not Communist world domination as such but the liberation of the working class and of enslaved peoples.

There is no clear-cut criterion by which we may judge which protagonist in the quarrel was right. It is no answer to say that the course of history will decide; as Camus himself noted: "While historical dialecticism is false and criminal, the world can after all accomplish its destiny through crime by following a false idea."[35] Nevertheless, it appears to me that Camus's basic point of departure is quite sound. *L'Homme révolté* is in the final analysis an attempt to explain a posteriori the causes for a situation the existence of which had become evident in the light of Camus's own experience.

In 1944–45 Camus had attempted to compromise with the Communists in much the same way Sartre started out to compromise with them in 1946. In spite of Camus's sympathetic overtures, the Communists had refused to modify their tactics. Camus soon realized that it was he who was drifting closer and closer to an unqualified acceptance of the revolutionary myth and its consequences, while his efforts to avoid the nihilistic aspects of that myth had remained totally ineffective. He was seeking in *L'Homme révolté* to explain logically the reasons for Communist intractability, and his explanation is compelling. But whether it is entirely correct or open to question does not alter the validity of a point of departure which was empirical rather than dialectical.

Sartre on the other hand had started from the a priori assumption that present-day history makes sense only in terms of the class struggle.[36] He had recognized the proletariat as being historically on the "right" side of the class dichotomy. But the French proletariat remained stubbornly loyal to communism in spite of Sartre's efforts to woo it away. Since Soviet totalitarianism was incompatible with true revolutionary aims, Sartre was forced to rationalize its existence in terms of American aggression and to accept, against the weight of evidence, the possibility of an eventual liberalization of Communist rule.

This dialectical oversimplification put Sartre in a very vulnerable position both politically and personally. Politically, it forced him to reject any possibility of a change for the better in relatively free capitalist societies, while accepting against overwhelming odds that same possibility in Communist societies. Although the de-Stalinization program in Russia was to make it seem temporarily possible that Sartre's assumptions were well founded, Soviet suppression of the Hungarian rebellion was in turn to damage his position severely.

Personally Sartre, who is not and cannot be a member of the proletariat, is also in the difficult position of being excluded from membership in the Communist party itself. Yet he has been actively dedicated to the destruction of that portion of society which, while he finds it repugnant, guarantees his freedom to speak and constitutes his principal audience. In the eyes of some he resembles a prophet-martyr who cries out for the destruction of the old order and the rise of the new, while knowing that he will not be accepted by the new order, even, as Jeanson writes, "amid the celebrations and fireworks."[37] He knows in fact that he is doomed to be swept away with the old order.

It must be said in fairness to Sartre that he has chosen the course he follows with complete awareness of the possible pitfalls. He is certainly no Communist dupe. Furthermore, his impatience with the often complacent attitude of the West and with its sometimes hysterical approach to communism is understandable. What was disconcerting in his and Jeanson's attack on *L'Homme révolté* was not Sartre's position as such or his defense of it but the underlying implication that Camus's own position, arrived at honestly in spite of whatever flaws it may have, was absolutely untenable and constituted some sort of betrayal of oppressed humanity. Perhaps the most unfortunate aspect of the quarrel lies in the fact that two men, each sincerely dedicated to an ideal of human progress, should have been unable to find the slightest common ground on which to meet.

While Camus had admitted in *L'Homme révolté* that there was no assurance that the forces of nihilism would not finally triumph, he had also declared: ". . . that kind of resignation is rejected here: we must gamble in favor of the renaissance."[38] The wager that the forces on the side of humanitarian freedom and justice would eventually succeed in placing the world back on the road to peace and sanity was to influence his political outlook more and more deeply during the years that followed 1952.

This optimism, however, was not reflected in his personal life or in his literary work. The handful of his letters already published reveals how deeply the personal insults that had characterized the controversy raised by *L'Homme révolté* had affected him who had once written: "Even the idea of having enemies seems to me to be the most exhausting thing in the world, and only with the greatest effort could my comrades and I bear to have any."[39] The growing crisis in North Africa, the ever-increasing incursions on his time and on his personal life, along with doubts as to his capabilities, also added to this despondency.[40]

Perhaps the most eloquent testimony to Camus's state of mind at this time is the *mimodrame*, "La Vie d'artiste," first published in *Simoun* in 1953.[41] Camus later adapted part of this scenario for the short story "Jonas" (*L'Exil et le royaume*). The first part shows a talented painter who begins in poverty and gradually attains fame and fortune, which are inevitably accompanied by merchants, hangers-on, and all the trappings that money can buy. One day the throng of admirers and hangers-on holds up a mirror in which the artist beholds himself; "he looks at himself and sees what he has become" (p. 2047). He smashes the mirror and runs amok, driving out the merchants, nearly strangling an official with the ribbon of his decoration, frightening his children into a corner, divesting his wife of all her finery, and ripping apart his own canvases.

In the second part, the painter erects a floor-to-ceiling canvas and a scaffold. He mounts the scaffold and proceeds to paint madly, ignoring the merchants and hangers-on, who have returned, as well as his wife and children. Finally there are no more admirers, only creditors, who seize everything of value and leave the wife and children destitute. The children are carried off to a hospital and the wife falls sick, becomes delirious, and dies.

Descending at last from his scaffold, the painter beholds his dead wife "and with a great muffled cry, collapses all of a sudden beside the bed" (p. 2049). Neighbors rush in, and as they start toward the bed, projectors suddenly illuminate the finished canvas. The crowd stares thunderstruck, but the painter, indifferent to their awe and to his painting, weeps. Finally noticing their presence, he rises, gently ushers out the intruders, then sets up his easel beside the bed. He embraces his wife, turns to his easel, looks once more at his wife, "and begins to paint her dead face while the curtain slowly falls" (p. 2050).

What distinguishes this rather lugubrious work from "Jonas" is the ironic tone of the latter. By the time he wrote "Jonas" Camus had gained enough perspective on his own situation to satirize it. Nonetheless the problem that both these works pose was quite serious, and if Camus was smiling at his own problems in "Jonas," it was with what Quilliot calls "a kind of smile through gritted teeth."[42] Torn between the demands of his art, his private life, and political involvement, Camus seems to have experienced some temptation to abandon all political involvement. In writing to Jean Gillibert in July 1952, one month before the publication of his letter to Sartre and Sartre's reply in *Les Temps modernes,* he spoke of his work as "an ever-increasing tension." It was no longer a question for him of wondering if he would ever attain in his work the artistic level he had set for himself but rather "of knowing if I will be able to maintain that level of tension. That is why *L'Homme révolté* is such a trial for me."[43]

However strong the temptation to renounce commitment may have been, Camus did not yield to it. In "L'artiste et son temps," which first appeared in France in *Actuelles II* in 1953,[44] he restated his belief in the impossibility of the artist's remaining silent in an age such as ours where tyranny has reached a level of efficiency that it has never before attained. But he rigorously denied that there was any obligation for the artist to subordinate his art to political action or to put it at the service of an ideology. The artist, Camus felt, should speak out as a member of the human community on behalf of those of his fellow beings who suffered under tyranny and injustice. As an artist, however, he was also contributing to the defense of freedom and the condemnation of despotism by the very act of creation.

Obviously Camus's view of the dual role of the artist stood in need of further definition. What exactly were the limits of the artist's duty to participate in social and political struggles, beyond creation itself? This facet of the problem of commitment was to occupy an important place in Camus's thought during the last period of his life. He had begun to feel more and more acutely the artist's need for solitude in order to create. On the other hand, he still questioned the validity of the artist's creative vision when he becomes too detached from the turmoil of his time. The search for equilibrium was to find many forms of expression after 1952, both in Camus's political and in his creative writings.

Although in 1952–55 Camus commented far less frequently on political issues than he had previously, he made several speeches and granted a few interviews. He resigned from UNESCO in November 1952 as a protest against the admission of Spain to that body. In June 1953 he denounced the suppression of the workers' revolt in East Berlin.[45] During 1954 his only political activity was a plea on behalf of seven Tunisians condemned to death by the French government. He was asked to collaborate with *Les Temps modernes* in organizing a protest against the imprisonment of Henri Martin, a seaman in the French Navy who had been arrested for distributing Communist propaganda leaflets on a military base. In an article published in *Franc-Tireur* in December 1952, Camus asked for the release of Martin, pointing out that in a democracy the use of police state methods could not be justified on any grounds whatsoever.[46] The case was somewhat equivocal, since Martin had acted in violation of naval regulations. However, he had been tried and convicted on a charge of sabotage which carried a much heavier sentence than the nature of his infraction warranted. Under these circumstances Camus felt that Martin should be released, but he made it clear that he had arrived at this position independently and was in no way associating his appeal with that of *Les Temps modernes:* ". . . one compromises the values of freedom, among other values, in defending them in conjunction with *Les Temps modernes* and with those who approve of it."[47]

Camus's break with what he called the nihilistic forces of his times was now complete, although it was only with *La Chute* that he would eliminate the bitterness created by that association. Mid–1952 marked for him the end of an era that had begun on the morning when he read of Gabriel Péri's execution. It had been an era of crisis out of which he had hoped great things would be accomplished. The years that followed this break were to reveal a much more modest Camus, who had found that if life is to have any meaning and contain any happiness the rebel must sometimes say "yes" as well as "no." Neither an unqualified acceptance nor an unqualified refusal of men and their failings was likely to make for a better world.

7

Between Yes and No
A Balance Achieved

ALTHOUGH CAMUS'S political activities declined sharply during 1953 and 1954, these were not altogether quiescent years. He directed his own adaptations of Calderon's *Dévotion à la croix* and Larivey's *Les Esprits* at the Angers festival in the summer of 1953. *L'Eté* appeared in 1954, and Camus made a trip to Italy. In 1955 his adaptation of Dino Buzzati's *Un Cas intéressant* was staged. That May he participated in Greece in a conference on the theater. Before leaving for Greece, he had agreed to write several articles for Jacques Servan-Schreiber's left-wing weekly, *L'Express.*

Only a few articles under Camus's by-line appeared in *L'Express* from May to October 1955. In October he agreed to become a regular contributor to the paper, which had shifted temporarily from weekly to daily publication. Beginning on 8 October, he wrote a column that appeared twice weekly. He continued this association through the parliamentary crisis of November 1955 and the elections of January 1956, until 2 February 1956. No specific reasons have been given for Camus's leaving *L'Express* at that time; however, disappointment over the outcome of the January elections, which resulted in spectacular gains for the *poujadistes,*[1] and the decision of the editors of *L'Express* to make an issue of the use of torture by the French in Algeria were probably two important contributing factors.

In the articles for *L'Express,* as in those sporadically written for various other periodicals from 1956 to 1958, it became clear that

147

Camus had at last achieved in his thought that balance he had so long sought between commitment and creation, and between freedom and justice. The ideal equilibrium between freedom and justice was not reflected in the actual course of historical events, either in France or in the rest of the world, during the late 1950's. Camus nonetheless remained true to the principles he had formulated, even when his insistence upon the necessity of reaching an Algerian settlement based on justice for both sides earned him a new round of sharp attacks from the French progressists.

The themes he touched upon in his articles for *L'Express* were essentially the same ones he had treated in the past: criticism of the extremists in French politics, condemnation of the vested interests, demands for social justice in the name of the working class. Now, however, the extreme left came in for more direct criticism from him than the extreme right. Camus did not consider the right any less hostile to social reforms than it had ever been, but he believed that divisions among left-wing groups were primarily responsible for the lack of social progress. Having abandoned the orthodox left and still refusing to support the right, Camus now spoke as a sort of mediator attempting to call both sides to a reasonable acceptance of compromise in the interest of the entire nation.

Though he dealt in *L'Express* mainly with French internal affairs and the Algerian situation, he now began to show a tendency to support the West in the cold war, while still criticizing such policies as the inclusion of Spain in the Western alliance. He also carefully refrained from polemical arguments with his political opponents. He spoke as a sincerely interested citizen of some influence expressing his own point of view. When he declared that he personally supported Pierre Mendès-France and the Front Républicain in the parliamentary election campaign, he further stated that he asked no one to imitate him but hoped that his readers would at least give some consideration to the opinions of a writer who had voluntarily taken his place in the public life of his country, often to the detriment of his artistic vocation, because of a deep-felt awareness of his country's unhappy state, his love of freedom, and the hope of finding a "common dignity which would finally achieve in our country a reconciliation of the working class and the intelligentsia."[2]

Camus in fact began his series of biweekly articles with a sort of personal manifesto of the intellectual's role in society. In this article, entitled "Under the Sign of Freedom," he reiterated the stand that, as a writer, he had taken again and again, notably in *Le Mythe de Sisyphe, L'Homme révolté,* and *L'Artiste et son temps:* the artist cannot stand aside from his time and enjoy the privilege of freedom to create, without accepting the responsibility for the defense of that freedom and the freedom of all whenever and wherever freedom is threatened. The article reveals how deeply Camus had been affected by the partisan attacks and insults that had so often been the answer to his attempts to initiate a "dialogue" with those who disagreed with him.

He began the article by describing the reaction of the intellectual who repeatedly finds that his efforts meet only with derision and contempt on the part of society in general: he eventually wakes in the night to ask himself, "Que vais-je faire dans cette galère?"[3] Why, indeed, Camus asked, when the intellectual has little taste for political action, does he persist in joining in the melee? Everything seems to oppose such participation: the brevity of life, the intellectual's own insufficiency, his "already encyclopedic lack of knowledge, [which] becomes infinite in comparison with the present-day complexity of the historical scene." Finally, incapable by virtue of his nature and his profession of forgetting the ambiguities and contradictions inherent in human relations, he cannot accept the facile oversimplifications in which modern journalists and "experts in progress" have indulged (*Ex.,* 8-10-55, p. 13).

Silence, Camus admitted, becomes a temptation for the artist-intellectual, for he who remains silent deceives neither himself nor others. But silence implies acceptance of society with all its faults; and since the artist is a part of that society, when he finds certain of these faults intolerable he has no choice but to join in the struggle to correct them "on the common level, deprived of superior insight, plunged into the common ignorance." Everyone contributes in one way or another to the future of his nation and of his culture, while remaining unable to fathom the laws that govern history and the natural world. And since those who so willingly pose as intellectual leaders are not always the best informed, the writer, in spite of his limitations, must join in the common struggle (*Ex.,* 8-10-55, p. 13).

Thus Camus reaffirmed once more his conviction that the artist cannot live separated from his time. After three years during which he had seemed nearly to yield to the temptation of silence, he once more took his place in the political arena, but this time with no illusions as to the effectiveness of his opinions and with no expectation of gratitude for having spoken.

By far the greater number of the articles written for *L'Express* in 1955–56 have to do with the Algerian issue. However, Camus also mercilessly assailed the Fourth Republic and its parade of ministries for their conservatism and their failure to correct any of the ills that had become chronic in France even before World War II. As in 1938 and 1944, the working class remained central to his political thought. However, over the years he had come to view sociopolitical problems in terms not so much of the class struggle and social revolution as of a national problem, the solution for which lay in far-reaching political, social, and economic reforms from which the entire nation would benefit. He was now concerned more with what he called the reintegration of the working class into the French nation than with establishing the reign of the proletariat.

This does not mean that he was ready to ignore or to justify working-class living conditions in France at that time. He heartily endorsed Simone Weil's *La Condition ouvrière,* and pointed out that Beatrice Beck's study of the working-class position in French society, which was then printed in *L'Express,* clearly indicated that, even in 1955, the workers still lived apart as an oppressed class (*Ex.,* 13-12-55, p. 16). As long as the working class continued to be exploited by both the right and left, there could be no hope for either the workers themselves or the French nation in general. He challenged those who cried out that there was no longer any united French nation to ask themselves how there could be any unity in a France where the working class, alienated by injustice from the rest of the nation, was forced to seek the "homeland of its dreams," thereby constituting a state within the state. France, he warned, could not remain alive while the working class, her very body, was being starved and humiliated: "That is why we must neither scorn reforms in the name of some far-distant society, nor forget when reforms are proposed that our final goal is the reintegration of the working class into all its rights through the abolition of the proletariat. Sooner or later the resistance of privileges will have to give way before the general interest" (*Ex.,* 25-11-55, p. 16).

Camus felt that the first step in the direction of reintegration would be the inclusion of trade unions in official policy-making bodies assisting the direction of the national economy. This had been the aim of the establishment of the comités d'entreprise that he had championed in 1944–45; these committees had actually been instituted, but in emasculated form. To the same end, he suggested in 1955 that the trade unions themselves might well consecrate a little of the time they ordinarily devoted to political indoctrination to the formation, from within their own membership, of a technically trained elite that would be able to cooperate intelligently in such a plan. The plan could be made to work, Camus admitted, only under the direction of "a government devoted to rejuvenation" (*Ex.,* 25-11-55, p. 16), and such a government's being formed under the provisions of the Constitution of the Fourth Republic seemed highly problematical.[4]

Nonetheless it was just such a government that Camus hoped would emerge from the Front Républicain which had been formed rather hastily on the basis of little more than a "gentlemen's agreement" between Pierre Mendès-France of the Radical party and Guy Mollet of the Socialist party. Since neither had the full backing of his respective party, the success or failure of this

new attempt at a center-left coalition depended entirely on the outcome of the parliamentary elections.[5]

As the campaign for the elections gained in intensity, Camus
noted once more a state of affairs that had become characteristic of
French political life: diehard extremism on left and right that
engendered feelings of frustration among the electorate and general
apathy toward vital political questions among the French people as
a whole. In his column of 2 December 1955, Camus pointed out
that the results of a poll conducted by *Réalités,* a popular French
monthly, on the subject of happiness had revealed that whereas the
majority of Frenchmen considered good health the fundamental
asset, and 12.7 percent thought love was first in importance, only
0.4 percent considered freedom vital to the pursuit of happiness.
While cautiously admitting that such polls tended to register re-
flexes rather than reflection, Camus declared that these attitudes
were very revealing: "Slavery and good health, there is tomorrow's
slogan" (*Ex.,* 2-12-55, p. 16).

This is perhaps the harshest public statement Camus ever made
with regard to the resignation and lack of political perspective of
the French people. Criticism of such attitudes had been implicit in
the editorials of *Soir-Républicain* written on the eve of World War
II and in Camus's depiction of the Oranais in *La Peste.* The same
criticism had also been suggested in *L'Homme révolté,* where
Camus had implied that renunciation of personal liberties in
exchange for political and social irresponsibility was not a quality
peculiar to the German people alone.

But it was not on the people themselves that Camus fixed the
major blame for France's political situation. He was again address-
ing primarily the intellectuals and politicians; he repeated an indictment he had leveled against them in *L'Homme révolté* and
elsewhere: "When intellectual leadership abdicates its greatest
duty, when it deserts the endless battle for freedom, it is normal
. . . for the nation itself to withdraw and to dream of vitamins"
(*Ex.,* 2-12-55, p. 16).

There was no doubt of whom he was speaking when he mentioned "intellectual leadership." He referred specifically to the case of a German student who had recently offered as an apology for the Nazi concentration camps the excuse that individual liberties had had to be curtailed to assure the freedom of the German nation. Thus, Camus commented, ten years after the extinction of the fires in the Nazi crematoriums a German intellectual had come forward to rekindle the dead ashes.

Unfortunately, he continued, this attitude with regard to human freedom and dignity was not limited to a few German intellectuals; it was equally evident in the thinking of Western intellectuals who had become apologists for the Soviet Union, which also justified suppression of individual rights in the name of future freedom and justice for all: "Under the pretext of one day freeing everybody [the revolutionary society] has sought, to the applause of our intellectuals, to enslave each one of us without delay" (*Ex.*, 2-12-55, p. 16).

This criticism of the French intellectual had very early been implicit in Camus's works, and had become quite explicit in the exchange of polemics that followed the publication of *L'Homme révolté*. In the series of articles written for *L'Express*, it was clear that Camus had in no way changed his opinion during the three years that had elapsed since the quarrel. He accused the leftist groups of representing only "revolutionary decadence," and of blocking any truly effective action that would lead to the attainment of social justice. Only when intellectuals on both sides rejected cynicism and opportunism, renounced the compromised ideologies of both bourgeois capitalism and present-day communism, and made love and desire for freedom their supreme goal could twentieth-century revolution be placed once more on the right path. "It is on this point that a few men, of whom I am one, through a desire for true progress, stand apart from the so-called progressist movements" (*Ex.*, 4-6-55, p. 13).

In the Front Républicain Camus saw a new possibility of revitalizing the liberal left. Although he did not come forth as a party spokesman, he indicated that his sympathy very definitely lay with

Mendès-France and his movement. In an article entitled "Explication de vote" (*Ex.,* 30-12-55, p. 16) he set forth his reasons for supporting the Front Républicain. Unable to condone the "social immobility that upholds the privileges of wealth," or "the refusal to accept reforms on the pretext that they compromise the possibility of revolution," Camus preferred the middle ground of progressive reform represented by Mendès-France.

That group, as Camus saw it, not only offered hope for reforms that would benefit French workers but also suggested an enlightened policy with regard to Algeria. In addition, the general political attitude of the Front Républicain seemed to him "at once decisive and prudent, daring and well conceived," enabling its leaders to steer a middle course between the fanatic acceptance of the Franco regime by the right in the name of anticommunism and the cowardly complacence of the French Communists and their "servile followers" with regard to Russia. Camus did not think Mendès-France had all the answers to France's problems, nor did he consider that endorsement of the Front Républicain in any way compromised his own determination to criticize the movement and its leaders at any time. Once again Camus's hopes were to be disappointed.

Although the Front Républicain made a reasonable showing in the January elections—the Socialist party received the largest number of votes of any single party—it was far from achieving anything like a mandate from the people. This situation was mainly due to the large Communist vote and to the surprising strength of the poujadistes, who had openly advocated tax evasion and other irresponsible fiscal proposals. Moreover, President Coty did not call on Mendès-France to head the new government; he called instead on Mollet. Mendès-France was willing to accept this arrangement if he were given the Foreign Ministry. This was denied him, and he was offered instead the Finance Ministry. He refused, preferring to become "Ministre d'Etat," that is, a minister without portfolio, whose vaguely defined duties consisted mainly in coordinating the work of the various ministries.

For all practical purposes, then, Mendès-France, around whom a new left had seemed to be rallying and who, in Camus's opinion, had headed in 1954–55 "the only administration that has shown any intention of governing" (*Ex.,* 6-1-56, p. 16), was in little more than an advisory position in the new government. Mollet's government itself was in the very uncomfortable position of having to seek support for its legislative proposals among other minority parties, particularly Bidault's M.R.P.

Camus did not conceal his bitterness at the outcome of the elections. On 6 January 1956 he wrote: ". . . seven million Frenchmen, whether they intended to or not, have just voted for the death of their freedoms" (*Ex.,* p. 16). The meager majority won by the Front Républicain was evidence that many Frenchmen wished to see instituted a moderate but progressive government. However, their representatives did not have sufficient strength to offset the rigid opposition of the two extremes. Already, Camus pointed out, the "political realists" were trying to reach an accommodation with either the poujadistes or the Communists. There will always be, he concluded, those who think "that Berchtesgaden and Prague are excellent watering places for sick governments."

Now, Camus maintained, France's only hope was represented in the intransigence of those citizens who had voted for the Front Républicain. In political terms this intransigence meant a determined effort to see constituted a homogeneous "Republican Front" government which would have as its main objective the immediate solution of the Algerian problem, the reform of electoral laws, and the drafting of a new constitution to replace the one adopted in 1946. Although such a program proved impossible at the time, these were precisely the three primary objectives of General de Gaulle's government when it came to power in May 1958.

For Camus the Algerian question had been the paramount issue in the election campaign of December 1955. Attempts to resolve the fate of Algeria had already brought down two governments, and no progress toward any kind of settlement had been made. Organized rebellion had broken out in earnest in Algeria on 1 November

1954. The situation had quickly degenerated into a cycle of terror-istic actions by the Moslem nationalists, followed by brutal repres-sion on the part of the French. The government in an effort to win the support of the Moslems had, as we have seen, instituted certain reforms, mostly in education and medical assistance. Such efforts were not only inadequate but by now unrealistic.

As usual the left-wing and right-wing political factions in France were diametrically opposed as to the best possible solution to the Algerian problem. The right insisted that there could be no question of granting Algeria independence of any sort, much less the com-plete autonomy demanded by the nationalists. Algeria continued to be, as far as the right was concerned, a French *département,* and right-wing spokesmen generally advocated a policy of reconquest of Algeria. The Communists and the extreme left-wing contingent in general insisted that self-determination and full independence, implying complete French withdrawal, was the only solution. The left, of course, devoted much of its criticism to the repressive policies of the government and to the use of torture by French police and army units dealing with suspected nationalist sympa-thizers and insurgents. There were moderates to be sure, both in France and in Algeria, but they could scarcely be heard amid the recriminations and invective hurled at one another by the two political extremes.

Camus once more condemned the long history of French abuses in Algeria. He now equally condemned the terrorist tactics of the F.L.N. Since he insisted that the rights of both Moslems and Euro-pean Algerians had to be respected, the only solution he could see was the creation of an Algerian federation in which both groups would be given full protection under the law. Once again he made clear his belief in the impossibility of any equitable settlement other than one imposed by the government in Paris. He also called on both sides in Algeria to cease needless killing. As a preliminary step toward negotiation of a settlement, he proposed a truce which would end the killing of civilians.[6]

In late January 1956 Camus went personally to Algiers in order to launch an appeal for such a truce. His speech was accompanied by cries and insults outside the auditorium where he spoke; and although there was some organized effort in Algeria to carry through the action he had suggested, the truce was never implemented. On his return from Algiers, Camus wrote to Jean Gillibert: "I have come back from Algeria almost in despair. What is happening confirms my convictions. It is for me a personal misfortune. But we must not give up; everything cannot be compromised."[7]

What Camus meant by "What is happening confirms my convictions" is not clear. Possibly that violence in Algeria had reached a point which precluded any hope of a truce, or that, in spite of his publicly stated position, he saw little chance that the European and Moslem communities could achieve a state of peaceful coexistence. In either case, this was indeed "a personal misfortune," since both Camus's mother and his brother Lucien, to say nothing of many of his friends, were still living in Algeria.[8] Certainly, the point at which the government in Paris could still have imposed a settlement had now been passed. Two weeks after Camus's visit, Premier Mollet was greeted in Algiers by mobs and overripe fruit. Paris had lost the last shred of its authority. The Fourth Republic lumbered on toward 13 May 1958. As Camus wrote in June 1956: ". . . it is apparently not the central government that is ruling Algeria, nor M. Robert Lacoste [the Resident Minister], but just anybody at all."[9]

Because he felt that any further word from him would only be used by one extremist side or the other to justify further bloodshed, Camus refused, after the truce appeal of January 1956, to comment again on the Algerian War. The sole exception, until the publication of *Actuelles III* in May 1958, came in the form of two letters to *Le Monde* demanding the release of Jean de Maisonseul, one of Camus's close friends, who had been arrested for having supported the truce appeal launched by Camus.[10] After his return from Algiers Camus wrote but one more article in the series for *L'Express*. This article, entitled "Thanks to Mozart," is a tribute to the genius of Mozart, in whose music Camus saw a symbol of freedom, the triumph of intelligence, and the justification of all human ambition (*Ex.,* 2-2-56, p. 16).

After this date there was once more a marked decline in Camus's public participation in political affairs. When he did write, he continued to criticize the left for its conformity and its acceptance of Soviet totalitarianism. The Hungarian revolt in October 1956, followed by a pitiless repression, came as a severe shock to the left. The Communist party in France temporarily lost a number of its adherents and a good deal of its prestige. The rightist groups openly triumphed. For Camus it was only another tragic proof that communism was firmly entrenched in authoritarianism and that it had betrayed the ideals of socialism as well as the hopes of the working class and of all oppressed peoples. In March 1957 he wrote in *Franc-Tireur:* "What Spain was for us twenty years ago, Hungary will be today."[11] What had happened in Budapest should be a bitter lesson to those who persisted in the hope that Russia might gradually abandon her totalitarian ways. Absolute power was inevitably used absolutely, he maintained, and could only engender terror and police state oppression. Terror in turn spawned new terror in a never-ending cycle, and there was no hope for liberaliza- tion in a police state. He warned both intellectuals and workers that "no privilege, no supreme reason can justify torture or terror."[12]

These statements were undoubtedly intended as an indirect reply to Sartre's long article, "Le Fantôme de Staline," which appeared in *Les Temps modernes* in January 1957.[13] Once again Camus and Sartre took opposing positions. In his article Sartre had maintained that the suppression of the Hungarian rebellion was unjustifiable not only because of its brutality but also because it represented a political blunder on the part of the Soviet Union, committed in order to cover a series of earlier blunders made by the Hungarian Communist regime. From Sartre's point of view, repression of the rebellion had been nothing more than political backsliding marked by a return to Stalinist tactics. As such it had tended to negate whatever progress had been made toward liberalization of Soviet authoritarianism through the de-Stalinization program. Nevertheless, Sartre in no way showed that his loyalty to the Communist cause had lessened.

On the other hand, it was after the Hungarian affair that Camus, for the first time, explicitly defended the West. "The defects of the West are innumerable," he wrote in the *Franc-Tireur* article, "its crimes and errors very real. But in the end let's not forget that we are the only ones who have the possibility of improvement and emancipation that lies in free genius."[14] In a later article, in which he stated his belief in an eventual "renaissance" in the West, he further outlined his reasons for advocating the superiority of the Western position in the cold war. Asked if he thought it right to ignore the failings of the West in order to combat the worse evil of communism, he answered that it was sometimes necessary, as Richard Hillary had said before his death in World War II, to combat a lie in the name of a half-truth. Even if one fought in the name of a quarter truth, if that quarter truth were on the side of freedom one was still justified in fighting, for "Without freedom heavy industry can be perfected, but not justice or truth."[15] In short, as Camus himself said in another article summing up his position: "None of the evils which totalitarianism . . . claims to remedy is worse than totalitarianism itself."[16]

It seemed to Camus that the Hungarian rebellion and its aftermath should have finally cleared up the mystifications surrounding communism and the Soviet Union. In his view, the failure of the neutral nations gathered at the Bandung Conference to condemn Soviet intervention in Hungary only proved that no nation had a monopoly on peace and that, in the twentieth century, new nations matured very rapidly, all too quickly attaining the status of power-seekers. Therefore, he believed, one could no longer assume that there were nonbelligerent nations in the world, only more or less belligerent ones. The left, which Camus described as "schizophrenic," would have to recognize this fact and shake off its fatal fascination with communism before any real progress toward social justice could be made. "Socialism, as well as capitalism, can engender wars," he noted. "We did not know this before for the simple reason that there was no Socialist state. Now we know."[17]

Camus's criticism of the progressist intellectuals and their attitudes was not limited to articles. It carried over into his creative works as well. Both *La Chute* and "Le Renégat" (*L'Exil et le royaume*) are probably more telling indictments of the "moral abdication" and passion for absolutes of modern intellectuals than any of the straight accusations that Camus made in various articles. As Victor Brombert pointed out, the priest in "Le Renégat," on one symbolic level at least, "is the modern intellectual, heir to a Humanist culture, but now impatient with the 'seminary' coziness of this tradition and with its sham, and who, in search of systems and ideologies, espouses totalitarian values that have long ago declared war (and he knows it) on the thinker and his thought. Thus amorous hate and amorous surrender are the logical consequence of a denial of life in favor of abstraction."[18]

La Chute too is on one level an analytical portrait of those modern intellectuals who, Camus wrote in *Discours de Suède,* "by seeking to outdo each other in despairing, have claimed the right to dishonor, and have plunged headlong into the nihilism of the age."[19] Jean-Baptiste Clamence, rather than being a modern John the Baptist *clamens in deserto* as many critics have thought, comes nearer to being a satirical portrait of left-wing intellectuals as Camus saw them, lost in the nihilistic desert of twentieth-century ideologies, led astray by their own systematic abstractions. In its setting and in the character of Clamence, *La Chute* further suggests the immobility into which Camus felt the progressist intellectuals had drifted as a consequence of their exaggerated sense of guilt and responsibility. Clamence tells his tale against a cold, empty background where the horizon disappears into the uniform gray of sea and sky. There is no action at all in the novel, even in the background, and Clamence himself is not a man of action but a man of "words, words, words."

In much the same way Sartre and other progressist intellectuals are caught in an intellectual and political no-man's land. Sartre, for example, rejects bourgeois society and its values but is forever excluded from *being* a member of the proletariat. Jeanson sees this situation as one of ultimate freedom, where Sartre "escapes from dizziness, that is, from the temptations of Good and Evil, from all the provocations, from all the pathetic and ignoble evasions that we know so well." What other contemporary writer, Jeanson asks, has been better able to set forth an understanding of the problems of all oppressed peoples and at the same time retain for himself "such supreme freedom?"[20]

Camus took a somewhat different view of Sartrian freedom. He had early noted that it led the Sartrian character into an impasse from which he seemed unable to escape. In 1939, reviewing Sartre's volume of short stories, *Le Mur,* he had said:

In M. Sartre's works there is a certain taste for impotence, in the broad sense of the word as well as in the physiological sense, which compels him to take characters who have reached their farthest limits and who stumble against an absurdity that they cannot go beyond. It is with their own lives that they collide, and, if I dare say so, through an excess of freedom. These beings remain without attachments, without principles, without any guide line, free to the point of being torn apart by their very freedom, deaf to the appeal of either action or creation (*AR*, 12-3-39, p. 5).*

Camus had already suspected, despite his admiration for Sartre, that Sartrian "freedom" might be no more than a trap which would doom one to a state of perpetual suspension between conflicting forces that would lead to inaction. He therefore came to question Sartre's implied claim that he had at last solved Hamlet's dilemma by shaking off the "pale cast of thought" and had transformed thought into action. If anything, as far as Camus was concerned, Sartre and other progressist intellectuals had only succeeded in adding fuel to the fires of reaction so that progress toward political reform was blocked by the intransigence of the two extremes of right and left. A political movement bereft of all liberalism and sunk into a welter of meaningless words: this was Camus's view of the entire phalanx of extreme left-wing groups in France and all

* French texts of starred passages may be found in Appendix A.

over Europe. In an interview with Jean Bloch-Michel, he again charged the left with being in a state of "full decadence, a prisoner of words, bogged down in its own vocabulary." He reiterated his belief in the necessity for a thorough reappraisal of left-wing aims and methods, adding that "until considerable progress has been made on this work of reform, any group action will be useless and even harmful."[21]

In criticizing the progressists' position, Camus was in no way questioning the validity of commitment itself. He still felt that commitment was not only useful but necessary. The duty of the intellectual was clear, he thought, but it existed within certain fairly narrow limits that Camus felt he was at last able to define. The duty of the intellectual was above all to tell the truth, to point out that "the king is naked when he is naked," and not to describe ecstatically the magnificence of his nonexistent robes.[22] Beyond that it was a question of giving form to a relevant doctrine of liberty and justice badly needed in the world as well as in France.

In pointing out the need for such a doctrine as a prerequisite for social reforms, Camus had written in *L'Express:* "The responsibility of intellectuals, more limited than they like to think, but of capital importance within the limits of that responsibility, is involved herein for a long time to come" (*Ex.*, 3-1-56, p. 20). In a later article he indicated precisely what he thought those limits should be. The intellectual should not wear himself out with talking too much. He should channel his energies into creative works in which he confronts the problems of his age. However, when flagrant injustice erupts, as in the Hungarian rebellion, then he should make it known in no uncertain terms where he stands. Above all he should avoid ambiguous pronouncements and sophistry, but should always stand resolutely in defense of freedom.[23]

In a speech he delivered at the University of Uppsala, after having received the Nobel Prize for literature in 1957, Camus further expounded his views on the artist's role in society. This speech, which draws together many facets of Camus's thought concerning commitment, once more emphasized the limitations of direct political involvement and reaffirmed the value and necessity of the creative artist in a free society.[24]

With *La Chute* Camus seems to have rid himself of some of the bitterness engendered by the quarrel over *L'Homme révolté*. At about the same time, he seems at last to have come to terms with the problem of solitude versus solidarity and to have achieved the balance sought between creation and commitment. He turned once more to his writing and began work on a projected novel, *Le Premier Homme*. In 1958 he purchased a house in Lourmarin in the Var so that he could escape from the suffocating intellectual atmosphere of Paris. But he found it impossible to escape entirely from political entanglements and quarrels. Like a tragic leitmotiv, the crisis in Algeria continued to intrude into the pattern of both his private and his public life.

Camus's "silence" with regard to the Algerian War, about which he had written nothing in France since January 1956, became a live issue in 1957. The announcement that he had won the Nobel Prize for literature that year was the signal for a new round of insults and attacks on Camus's reputation both as an artist and as an intellectual. Although the *presse d'information,* led by such dailies as *Le Monde* and *Le Figaro,* wrote congratulatory announcements, the *presse d'opinion,* particularly a large number of left-wing weeklies, was extremely caustic. At their worst, the insults came from minor critics and writers who were obviously venting their jealousy of Camus and of his recognized position as an international literary figure.

Even the more respectable left-wing reviews made no attempt to hide the political basis for their criticism. Roger Stéphane in *France-Observateur* echoed the general opinion, expressed by Camus himself, that the prize should have gone to Malraux. Stéphane went on to condemn Camus for not speaking out against the well-known use of torture in Algeria and sarcastically asked for what higher purpose Camus might be keeping himself so pure.[25] Pierre Daix, writing in Aragon's Communist *Lettres françaises,* called Camus's works a source of "intellectual comfort and evasion," and Camus himself "a pacifier . . . a preacher against revolution, honored the same year that the Nobel Prize for peace is awarded to the founder of N.A.T.O."[26] He also reproached Camus for his silence with respect to French crimes in Algeria.

Camus did not immediately reply to this charge, although in a letter to *Encounter* in June 1957 he had already answered a similar criticism made by Peter L. Caracciola. There he had pointed out that he had been criticizing French policies in Algeria for twenty years, and proceeded to give a summary of his most recent proposals for a solution of the Algerian problem. But he refused, "as an Algerian Frenchman," to approve of F.L.N. terrorism, which, he said, claimed more Moslem civilians as victims than French. He added: "One cannot ask me to protest against a particular repression, which I have done, and to justify a particular terrorism, which I shall never do."[27]

Early in 1958, however, *Actuelles III* was published, which contains selections from the report on the Kabylian famine, the survey of conditions in Algeria after the rebellion at Sétif in 1945, and a number of the articles printed in *L'Express* in 1955–56. Camus also added a preface and an essay, "L'Algérie 1958," in which he once more clearly stated his personal feelings and outlined the only solution to the Algerian problem that he found acceptable. He called for an Algerian federation with close ties to France. Such a federation appeared to him to be eminently preferable to an "Islamic empire" which, he felt, would do twofold harm by merely adding to the suffering of the Moslems while uprooting the European Algerians from "their natural homeland."[28]

In "L'Algérie 1958," he amplified this statement by presenting a detailed plan for setting up a quasi-independent Algeria linked to metropolitan France by federal ties.[29] He also emphatically stated that, while recognizing the justice of Moslem claims against French abuses, he considered Algerian nationalism without historical basis and politically unsound. There had never been an Algerian nation, he maintained, pointing out that the Moslem population was by no means homogeneous. Furthermore the European community, by virtue of the length of its implantation there, had the full right to consider itself indigenous to Algeria.

He denounced Pan-Islamism and Nasser's United Arab Republic as historically unrealistic, asserting that if there was a basis for a Moslem empire there was just as much basis for a Christian empire, but that one was obviously as ridiculous as the other. Furthermore, because of her demographic explosion and lack of industrial resources, full independence for Algeria could only mean economic and ultimately political dependence on some other nation. Under the existing circumstances, he declared, this would certainly mean that Algeria would be drawn into the Cairo-Moscow orbit. Thus France, by granting Algeria total independence, would not only be sealing the fate of one million European Algerians but be playing up to the Soviet strategic aim of encircling Western Europe. At the same time the French would be delivering up the Algerian Moslems to be used as pawns of Soviet imperialism and cold war strategy. Algeria would be irrevocably lost, with terrible consequences for the Moslems as well as for the French, Camus stated flatly, if some proposal such as he advocated did not prevail. With understandable weariness he added: "This is the final comment, before returning to silence, of a writer devoted to the service of Algeria for twenty years."[30]

Actuelles III met with almost unanimous silence in the French press. In order to draw attention to the book, on the second printing "Chroniques algériennes" was added in bold red type to the cover and to the title page—but to little avail. The book was already at the printers' when the revolt of 13 May 1958, which ultimately brought General de Gaulle to power, took place. A short note at the beginning of the collection pointed out that although the volume had been prepared before 13 May the rebellion and its consequences had changed nothing with regard to the basic problem as outlined in it.

Camus never again publicly commented on the Algerian situation. He did, however, tell Jean Bloch-Michel in October 1959 that when a referendum on independence took place he would ask for space in an Algiers newspaper and campaign for self-determination, but against complete independence. He had had an interview with General de Gaulle in 1957 and had received the impression that the General did not understand the Algerian character or the full implications of the situation there. Camus still thought it possible that the Moslems, given the choice in a truly free election, might accept a federal association with France.

Shortly before his death, however, Camus confided to Bloch-Michel that he had changed his mind. He remarked that his last efforts publicly to seek a solution to the Algerian crisis—the truce appeal in 1956—had ultimately resulted only in the replacement of the moderate General Catroux by Robert Lacoste as Resident Minister of Algeria. Lacoste, as it happened, was unexpectedly conservative in his approach to the Algerian conflict.[31] Furthermore, Camus did not believe the F.L.N. would be any more inclined than the French had been to allow free elections to take place. As far as I have been able to determine, this was Camus's last word on the Algerian problem.

It is impossible here to discuss and evaluate all the aspects of Camus's position with regard to Algeria. How accurate his assessment of the political implications, international as well as internal, of Algerian independence will prove to be is a question that historians will be able to decide only in the course of time.[32] However, apart from the political issues, Camus, in his defense of the Algerian Europeans, raised a vital question the import of which goes far beyond the specific problem itself.

Whether one agrees or not with Camus's defense of the European community in Algeria, in defending it he posed one of the most disturbing moral problems in an age in which the "displaced person" has too often been summarily dismissed as merely the unfortunate victim of historical circumstances. Whatever the wrongs of which the Algerian Europeans may have been guilty, they were after all frightened human beings who felt they were being abandoned by France and who stood in mortal fear of losing the homes they knew and loved. When Camus wrote, "There are other ways of establishing necessary justice than to replace one form of injustice by another,"[33] he issued a challenge to all those who claim to be working to free oppressed peoples, for suffering and death are not confined to any one group of human beings but afflict all men. Jules Roy, also an Algerian and a friend of Camus, attempted to answer this challenge when he made the following statement in a book dedicated to Camus's memory: "I agree that one should render justice to one group without depriving others of justice at the same time. But I respect an order based on urgency: I yield to the injustice that cries out, since the other, for the moment, only constitutes a hypothetical injustice."[34] This may well be the only answer; but when the hypothetical injustice becomes a real one, as it did in Algeria during the summer of 1962, what then? If human progress is to be interpreted to mean progress from one form of injustice to another, then the future of the human race takes on a rather derisive aspect.

Writing of Dostoevski, Camus once declared that the Russian author "knew that henceforth our civilization would demand salvation for everyone or for no one. But he knew that salvation cannot be offered to everyone if we forget the suffering of one lone human being."[35] The same might be said of Camus himself, for this is the basic problem with which not only his political writings but all his works and his own life confront a century that has often seemed only too willing to damn whole peoples to assure the salvation of one "elect" or another.

Camus, of course, like all men, made mistakes, and it is easy enough in retrospect to find fault with certain of his judgments. Thody reproached Camus for the lack of "practical value" in his political pronouncements.[36] But how are we to measure their practical value? If it can be measured only in terms of immediate efficacy, perhaps Thody's criticism is justified. On the other hand, as Léon Roudiez points out in his review of Thody's book, while it is well to have intellectuals who are willing to give themselves fully to the day-to-day political struggle, "It is even more important that there be a few others, who, even if ignored and scorned, will rise to remind us that the concept of man transcends that of an efficient political animal."[37] It is here that one finds the very practical value of Camus's political writings. Underneath every word lies a sincere concern for the human creature in all his grandeur and weakness, a concern for his aims, his hopes, and his aspirations. Camus's words are a constant reminder that political institutions are conceived by men to serve man, to enhance his grandeur and to offset his weaknesses, to help him achieve, as an individual and as a member of society, his just ambitions. Above all he reminds us that life is too precious a gift to be taken away without the gravest justification. When he criticized institutions, governments, political ideologies, or other men, Camus was defending a concept of humanity that is incompatible with any form of tyranny no matter how just may seem the cause that gives rise to it.

Sartre may well be the "bad conscience" of the French Communist party; Camus was and, through his works, remains a bad conscience for all who are tempted to use tyrannical means to any end whatsoever. His example for a long time to come will be useful to those who, while unsure of the best means to human progress, must constantly revaluate and choose anew the way to that progress.

Camus himself belonged to that minority who are able constantly to review and correct their opinions in the light of new experience and changing conditions. Above all, he had the rare courage to admit, as he does in the preface to *Actuelles I* (p. 14), that he had sometimes been wrong and that he had changed his way of thinking. Essentially, Camus was a true nonconformist in a time when even nonconformity has become organized; he refused to conform not for the sake of nonconformity itself but because what he held to be true was out of line with contemporary shibboleths and fashionable fetishes.

Perhaps because of its suddenness, Camus's death on 3 January 1960 seemed like a tragic interruption of a life and a talent that had not yet borne its best fruits. Despite his two-year silence after the publication of *Actuelles III,* many were sure that he would speak again, and they waited tensely to hear what he would say. Not only was his novel, *Le Premier Homme,* left unfinished, but his *témoignages* as he called them seem fragmentary, as though an epoch of which he had been so much a part had closed at a climactic moment of turmoil and crisis. One year after Camus's death the sense of loss felt by many, even those who had been his enemies, was expressed by Guy Dumur: "He would have been a force in reserve, a bridge between the past and the future: he would have been one from whom we awaited a response that, when it came, would have been heard by all."[38]

Reference
Matter

APPENDIX A

French Texts of Selected Citations from Uncollected Articles by Camus in *Alger-Républicain, Soir-Républicain, Combat,* and *Rivages.*

These passages are starred in the text.*

Page 7 . . . mais je sais qu'aucune n'est possible si elle n'a commencé dans le coeur et l'esprit de ceux qui comptent la faire. L'échec de tant de révolutions tient peut-être à cette idée.

8 . . . Albert Ollivier pense que cette préparation doit se faire loin du tumulte et des mensonges, et qu'elle demande du temps, ce qui n'est rien, mais aussi des hommes et de la lucidité, ce qui est tout. . . . le livre se termine par quelques lignes qui devraient être méditées . . . : "Le véritable révolutionnaire doit . . . s'éloigner de la place publique. . . . Il doit résister à cette tentation de l'action immédiate, si forte soit-elle, et pour cela on accordera qu'il lui faut beaucoup d'humilité et beaucoup d'orgeuil."

8 . . . on aura intérêt (et même les communistes), à lire un livre à la fois ému et documenté qui reste lucide jusque dans son hostilité au régime soviétique. Ce qui peut nuire le plus à l'U.R.S.S., en effet, ce ne sont pas les critiques de bonne foi, mais . . . les admirateurs maladroits qui la présentent comme le paradis de l'homme.

10 On ne comprend pas justement que ce qui attache tant de nous à l'Espagne républicaine, ce ne sont pas de vaines affinités politiques, mais le sentiment irrépressible que, de son côté se trouve le peuple espagnol, si pareil à sa terre, avec sa noblesse profonde et son ardeur à vivre. . . . Mais à quoi bon insister. Rien ne changera aujourd'hui le jeu stupide des haines. L'assassinat méthodique de ce peuple se poursuit. Nous pouvons être fiers: nous avons fait tout ce qu'il fallait pour ça. . . .

12 C'est la question sociale qui aborde Guibert et le pousse dans ses retranchements. L'artiste aujourd'hui doit, d'une façon

173

Page   ou d'une autre, lui trouver une solution. C'est à la fois sa servitude et sa grandeur.

12 . . . il n'est point d'oeuvre révolutionnaire sans qualité artistique. Ceci peut paraître paradoxal. Mais je crois que si l'époque nous enseigne quelque chose à cet égard, c'est que l'art révolutionnaire ne peut se passer de grandeur artistique, sans retomber aux formes les plus humiliées de la pensée.

13 Depuis quelques années, on a beaucoup écrit et discuté autour de l'adhésion. Mais, tout compte fait, c'est un problème aussi futile que celui de l'immortalité, une affaire qu'un homme règle avec lui-même et sur quoi il ne faut pas juger. On adhère comme on se marie. Et quand il s'agit d'un écrivain, c'est sur son oeuvre que l'on peut juger des effets de l'adhésion.

Malraux, qui adhère, est un grand écrivain. On aimerait pouvoir en dire autant d'Aragon. . . . Montherlant, qui se refuse à tout enrégimentement, demeure un des plus étonnants prosateurs du siècle.

13 . . . c'est par une erreur d'optique qu'on a fait tant de bruit autour du Gide partisan. Car sur le plan social, son opinion n'a PAS PLUS d'importance que celle de n'importe quel Français cultivé, généreux et raisonnablement idéaliste.

14 . . . qu'on ne croie pas que nous relevons toutes ces illégalités pour le plaisir de marquer des points. . . . Mais une injustice profonde se trahit toujours dans les détails. . . . Et l'on pourra encore juger de l'état d'esprit d'un homme innocent, accusé injustement, soumis à l'arbitraire, souillé dans tous ses sentiments humains et sans défense contre l'autorité démesurée dont sont investis des hommes inférieurs à leurs fonctions. C'est cet homme qui marque ici des points.

15 Il ne s'agit pas ici de pitié, mais de toute autre chose. Il n'y a pas de spectacle plus abject que de voir des hommes ramenés au-dessous de la condition de l'homme. C'est de ce sentiment qu'il s'agit ici. . . . Ces hommes, nous n'avons pas à les juger, d'autres l'ont fait. Ni à les plaindre, ce serait puéril. Mais il s'agissait seulement ici de décrire ce destin singulier et définitif par lequel des hommes sont rayés de l'humanité. Et peut-être est-ce le fait que ce destin soit sans appel qui crée toute son horreur.

Page 18 . . . les hommes politiques n'imaginent pas à quel point il est difficile d'être un homme tout court. De vivre, sans être injuste, une vie pétrie d'iniquités, avec 1,200 francs par mois, une femme, un enfant, et la certitude de mourir sans être inscrit au manuel d'Histoire.

19 . . . la générosité est une vertu de grande allure. Personne n'aurait eu l'idée de la lui demander. . . . nous n'essaierons pas de "faire plier" M. Rozis. Il s'agit maintenant de défendre le pain de nos camarades. Le ressentiment n'a pas de fondement légal et une décision à ce point arbitraire est inacceptable. Les employés révoqués se pourvoiront en Conseil de préfecture.

20 La presse constitue à notre époque une arme terrible dans les mains qui la contrôlent. Elle fait ou elle défait l'opinion, elle la dirige, la freine, ou l'exaspère. . . .

20 . . . les pouvoirs meurtriers de la presse s'expliquent autant par la corruption de ceux qui la dirigent que par le manque de sens critique de ceux qui la lisent.

22 Nous disons qu'il ne s'agit pas de sauver les apparences, qu'il ne s'agit pas d'une condamnation de principe. Si la justice s'est trompée, elle doit le reconnaître. . . . Et si paradoxal que cela puisse paraître, il peut être bon pour la justice que les juges parfois soient confondus.

23 Il faut mettre autant de force à exalter l'impartialité qu'à dénoncer le parti pris. . . . remercions les juges de Tiaret d'avoir su rendre une justice entière dans une affaire à la fois si évidente et si délicate.

23 Souhaitons seulement que la sentence du tribunal y aide. Et aux termes de cette longue campagne, devant une justice que nous reconnaissons enfin pour telle, ce ne sont pas de félicitations que nous adressons à Michel Hodent. Il n'en a que faire.

23 Cette lettre, j'ignore si vous la lirez. Il le faudrait pourtant. . . . nous savons que derrière les grands de ce monde, il arrive que l'homme surgisse. . . . C'est cet homme que nous voudrions toucher. . . . à cette dernière minute, nous ne voulons songer qu'à l'inexplicable espoir que nous plaçons en vous—à cet espoir singulier et tenace qu'un langage humain suffit à provoquer des décisions humaines.

29 300 kilos de couscous, 10 moutons, 300 kilos de figues et 40 kilos de beurre auront servi à calmer la faim de centaines

Page   de miséreux, pour un jour seulement. . . . beaucoup trop d'enfants s'y voyaient. J'ai vu de petites mauresques cacher sous leur voiles les morceaux de viande qui leur revenaient. Cela en dit long sur la prospérité de leur foyer.

29 Je sais bien que ce n'est pas facile et je ne pense pas qu'on supprime la pauvreté en un jour. Mais je dois dire aussi que je n'ai jamais vu une population européenne aussi misérable que cette population arabe—et cela doit bien tenir à quelque chose. C'est à supprimer cette disproportion et cet excès de pauvreté qu'il faut s'attacher. On ne peut croire du moins que cela soit utopique.

32 . . . la Grèce évoque irrésistiblement une certaine gloire du corps et de ses prestiges. Et dans aucun pays que je connais, le corps ne m'a paru plus humilié que dans la Kabylie. Il faut l'écrire sans tarder: la misère de ce pays est effroyable. . . . Je sentais bien . . . qu'il n'y avait rien pour ces hommes, ni univers, ni guerre mondiale, ni aucun des soucis de l'heure, en face de l'affreuse misère qui met des plaques sur tant de visages kabyles.

36 A l'heure où tant de voix importantes ou supposées telles s'époumonnent pour nous vanter on ne sait quels idéaux de basse qualité, il est plus urgent de mettre tout en oeuvre pour freiner l'injustice chaque fois que c'est possible.

Si la démocratie doit avoir un sens, c'est ici qu'elle le prendra et non dans les discours officiels du dimanche. Et il est permis de supposer que l'innocence reconnue des condamnés d'Auribeau lui fera rattraper le temps et le prestige que la mobilisation morale à sens unique lui a déjà fait perdre en ce pays.

Aucun homme libre n'est assuré de sa dignité devant de semblables procédés. Et lorsque les méthodes abjectes parviennent à conduire au bagne des malheureux dont la vie n'était déjà qu'une suite de misères, alors elles constituent pour chacun de nous une sorte d'injure personnelle qu'il est impossible de souffrir.

37 Cette accusation serait . . . ridicule si elle n'était pas malfaisante. Car c'est là qu'il faut en venir. On a voulu punir. On veut frapper, décapiter le P.P.A. La défense nationale l'ordonne comme elle a permis les reniements de M. Daladier. Mais la réponse dans les deux cas est la même.

Page   Car défendre la démocratie, c'est d'abord la fortifier. Si les propositions du P.P.A. gênent tant l'administration, l'administration ne doit pas y donner prétexte. C'est la seule solution conforme à la justice et à la liberté. . . . chaque fois que le P.P.A. a été frappé, son prestige a grandi un peu plus. La montée du nationalisme algérien s'accomplit sur les persécutions dont on le poursuit. Et je puis dire sans paradoxe que l'immense et profond crédit que ce parti rencontre aujourd'hui auprès des masses est tout entier l'oeuvre des hauts fonctionnaires de ce pays.

37   . . . la seule façon d'enrayer le nationalisme algérien, c'est de supprimer l'injustice dont il est né.

38   Nous jugeons ici et avec nous la population musulmane et ouvrière toute entière. . . . Le spectacle gracieux qu'offrait le Conseil Municipal n'est qu'une faible compensation aux charges fiscales qui vont nous accabler.

40   A ce peuple neuf dont personne encore n'a tenté la psychologie (sinon peut-être Montherlant dans ses "Images d'Alger"), il faut une langue neuve et une littérature neuve. Il a forgé la première pour son usage personnel. Il attend qu'on lui donne la seconde.

40   A l'heure où le goût des doctrines voudrait nous séparer du monde, il n'est pas mauvais que des hommes jeunes sur une terre jeune, proclament leur attachement à ces quelques biens périssables et essentiels qui donnent un sens à notre vie: mer, soleil et femmes dans la lumière. Ils sont le bien de la culture vivante, le reste étant la civilisation morte que nous répudions. S'il est vrai que la vraie culture ne se sépare pas d'une certaine barbarie, rien de ce qui est barbare ne peut nous être étranger.

46   Dans cette guerre où sa vie même est engagée, où chaque heure qui s'écoule peut décider de son sort, le public a soif de nouvelles et d'informations vraies.

    Ce journal les lui apporte. Il le fera sans outrance ni vaine forfanterie.

    Une cause juste peut se passer de l'indigne et futile "bourrage de crâne."

    Seuls prévaudront ici les droits de la froide raison.

    Aucune autre considération ne nous fera dévier de notre route. Fidèles à notre idéal, nous serons fidèles à la vérité.

47   On me dira que les gouvernements représentent les peuples.

Page   Mais nous lisons tous les jours dans les journaux que ce n'est pas vrai pour certains pays. Et pour les autres, on me permettra de sourire d'une façon discrète.

47   . . . une certaine tradition de notre littérature actuelle qui s'est spécialisée dans le genre "produit supérieur de la civilisation."

47   M. Giraudoux sera le premier à s'en réjouir. Son passé supprimé, il sera plus à l'aise dans ses nouvelles fonctions.

48   Je crois qu'il faut aujourd'hui un certain courage pour oser dire qu'il y a *aussi* un impérialisme des démocraties. Beaucoup parmi nous le savaient. Presque tous l'ont oublié. Et pourtant, les destins des peuples sont inséparables et on peut tenir pour certain que l'appétit de pouvoir entraîne l'appétit de pouvoir, que la haine suscite la haine, que l'impérialisme fait naître l'impérialisme et que le traité de Versailles est le père spirituel des accords de Munich.

48   Nous avons été les premiers à répudier un régime où la dignité humaine était comptée pour rien et où la liberté devenait une dérision. Mais en même temps, nous ne cessions de dire que cet excès de la bestialité trouvait sa source dans le désespoir d'un peuple. Les nations sont ici comme des individus. C'est dans leur plus grande misère qu'elles forgent leur volonté de puissance.

49   Nous croyons . . . qu'il n'y a qu'une fatalité dans l'histoire, celle que nous y mettons. Nous croyons que ce conflit pouvait être évité et peut encore être arrêté à la satisfaction de tous. Nous croyons que s'il n'existait à cela qu'une seule chance, il serait encore défendu de désespérer avant de l'avoir tenté.

49   Jamais peut-être les militants de gauche n'ont connu tant de raisons de désespérer. Bien des croyances se sont effondrées en même temps que cette guerre. Et parmi toutes les contradictions où le monde s'agite, contraints à la lucidité, nous sommes alors conduits à tout nier.

Nous comprenons. Nous comprenons tout. Et nous comprenons même très bien. Beaucoup d'entre nous n'avaient pas bien compris les hommes de 1914. Nous sommes plus près d'eux maintenant, car nous savons qu'on peut faire la guerre sans y consentir. Nous savons qu'à une certaine extrémité du désespoir, l'indifférence surgit et avec elle le sens et le goût de la fatalité.

Page 50 . . . toutes les expériences ont été faites, sauf celle-là. Et toutes ces expériences nous ont amené la guerre. On aurait pu dire que l'honnêteté intellectuelle exigeait du moins que, l'ultime tentàtive fût entreprise, avant de juger du caractère fatal des guerres.

50 Nous avons des voeux à formuler, précis, généreux, ardents. Nous désirons et nous appelons de toutes nos forces un monde nouveau, une vie où l'homme garde ses chances de dignité. Nos lecteurs savent bien ce que nous voulons et attendons. Alors, qu'ils pensent avec nous qu'il est vain de souhaiter cette année bienheureuse, mais qu'il est essentiel de travailler pour la construire. Ne souhaitez rien, mais accomplissez. N'attendez pas d'un destin que d'autres fabriquent de toutes pièces, ce qui est encore entre vos mains. *Le Soir-Républicain* ne vous souhaite pas d'être heureux, puisqu'il sait que vous êtes meurtris dans vos chairs et vos espoirs. Mais du fond du coeur, il vous souhaite de garder la force et la lucidité nécessaires pour forger vous-même votre bonheur et votre dignité.

51 Montherlant ne se pose pas la question de prévenir ou de guérir, mais cherche seulement comment subir la guerre. Et quel autre problème se pose à cette heure aux esprits sincères de ce pays?

51 On nous partage aujourd'hui en deux clans selon que nous choisissons entre la servitude et la mort. Mais nous sommes beaucoup à refuser ce dilemme, à ne pas vouloir choisir, à admirer ceux qui, délibérément, ont arrêté leur action. Montherlant n'est pas de ceux-là.

52 . . . la prendra comme une maladie et tentera d'y trouver encore des raisons de vivre. Il n'y a peut-être pas dans notre littérature de passage plus viril et plus amer que celui où Montherlant affirme qu'il combattra sans croire, sans autre idéal que celui d'être à la hauteur d'un destin venu sans qu'on l'appelle.

62 Beaucoup d'hommes jeunes, en Allemagne et ailleurs, ont cru trouver un soulagement à leurs misères en se remettant tout entiers entre les mains d'un autre.

64 C'est bien un nouvel ordre qui se trouve fondé. . . . La politique n'est plus dissociée des individus. Elle est l'adresse directe de l'homme à d'autres hommes.

66 Aucun de nous n'aimait la guerre. . . . Nous n'avions pas

Page de goût pour la haine et nous avions l'idée de la justice. C'est pourquoi nous nous demandions alors si la justice était avec nous. Et pendant que nous nous le demandions, la foudre nous frappait et nous jetait dans la poussière.

67 . . . ce serment que nous n'avons jamais fait qu'au fond de nous-mêmes, nous avons fait à nos camarades morts, nous le tiendrons jusqu'au bout.

67 [Le pays] n'a pas besoin de Talleyrand. . . . Il a besoin de Saint-Just.

72 Un peuple qui veut vivre n'attend pas qu'on lui apporte sa liberté. Il la prend.

74 Nous voulons réaliser sans délai une vraie démocratie populaire et ouvrière . . . une Constitution où la liberté et la justice recouvrent toutes leurs garanties, les réformes de structure profondes sans lesquelles une politique de liberté est une duperie, la destruction impitoyable des trusts et des puissances d'argent, la définition d'une politique étrangère basée sur l'honneur et la fidélité à tous nos alliés sans exception. Dans l'état actuel des choses, cela s'appelle une Révolution. Il est probable qu'elle pourra se faire dans l'ordre et dans le calme. Mais de toutes façons, c'est à ce prix seulement que la France reprendra ce pur visage 'que nous avons aimé et défendu par-dessus tout.

74 La révolution n'est pas forcément la guillotine et les mitrailleuses, ou plutôt ce sont les mitrailleuses quand il le faut.

75 Si demain, le peuple de France, appelé à s'exprimer librement, désavouait la politique de la Résistance, la Résistance s'inclinerait. . . .

76 . . . ils parlaient au nom d'une force intérieure qui les dépasse, qui les a portés pendant quatre ans et qui, dans certaines conditions, pourrait prendre demain sa vraie forme. . . . Ce qui a porté la Résistance pendant quatre ans, c'est la révolte. C'est-à-dire le refus entier, obstiné, presque aveugle au début, d'un ordre qui voulait mettre les hommes à genoux. La révolte, c'est d'abord le cœur.

76 . . . passe dans l'esprit où le sentiment devient idée, où l'élan spontané se termine en action concertée.

76 Nous ne croyons pas ici aux révolutions définitives. Tout effort humain est relatif. L'injuste loi de l'histoire est qu'il faut à l'homme d'immenses sacrifices pour des résultats sou-

Page

vent dérisoires. Mais si mince que soit le progrès de l'homme vers sa propre vérité, nous pensons qu'il justifie toujours ces sacrifices. Nous croyons justement aux révolutions relatives.

77 . . . qui n'inspirent plus que l'indifférence ou le mépris, pourront toujours s'employer à la rédaction de leurs Mémoires destinés à n'être jamais lus.

78 . . . nous nous sommes décidés à supprimer la politique pour la remplacer par la morale.

78 . . . cela contrarierait la justice que les hommes que le peuple français avait déjà condamnés reparussent sur la scène politique avec le sourire de l'innocence.

78 . . . ces milieux bourgeois que Jouvenel hait pour tant de raisons, les lecteurs moyens dont nous sommes peuvent les mépriser seulement. Ainsi ne rejoindrons-nous pas l'auteur du fait que celui-ci, à tort ou à raison, estime que ces milieux sont à juger quand nous pouvons les considérer déjà comme jugés. . . . Appeler M. Renault "un grand exploiteur des ouvriers français," c'est un peu enfoncer une porte ouverte.

80 Nous savons maintenant que les vies françaises sont irremplaçables. Mais il faut que cette classe comprenne, qu'elle nous laisse enfin après nous avoir tant lassés. Et qu'après avoir tant manqué de courage et de générosité, elle ne se prive pas de cette intelligence élémentaire qui lui permettrait encore d'être le témoin d'une grandeur dont elle n'a pas su être l'ouvrière.

81 Nous avons eu l'imagination qu'il fallait devant les mille nouvelles de nos frères arrêtés, déportés, massacrés ou torturés. Ces enfants morts qu'on faisait entrer à coups de pied dans les cerceuils, nous les avons portés en nous pendant quatre ans. Maintenant nous aurons de la mémoire. Nous ne sommes pas dans la haine. Mais il faut que nous soyons des hommes de justice.

81 . . . notre difficile entreprise est de juger au nom d'une vérité qui n'a pas encore pris forme de loi.

82 Qu'avons-nous à opposer à cette argumentation? La simple intuition que l'un des devoirs les plus sacrés d'un homme et d'un citoyen a été violé. . . . Il faut . . . si nous voulons condamner que nous donnions un sens à notre accusation. . . . Il ne faut pas avoir honte de dire que cette accusation

Page   est morale, et qu'elle est sans recours. Pour tout dire d'un mot, le problème est dans la responsabilité. . . . Les hommes doivent porter la responsabilité de leurs privilèges.

82   . . . il n'est pas question d'épurer beaucoup, mais d'épurer bien.

83   . . . à l'extrémité du doute, il nous faut une résolution. Nous savons bien que le jour où la première sentence de mort sera exécutée dans Paris il nous viendra des répugnances. Mais il nous faudra penser alors à tant d'autres sentences de mort qui ont frappé des hommes purs, à de chers visages retournés à la terre et à des mains que nous aimions serrer. Quand nous serons tentés de préférer aux noires besognes de la justice les généreux sacrifices de la guerre, nous aurons besoin de la mémoire des morts et du souvenir insupportable de ceux d'entre nous dont la torture a fait des traîtres. Si dur que cela soit, nous saurons alors qu'il est des pardons impossibles et de nécessaires révolutions.

85   Ce n'est pas la voie que nous avons choisie et nous maintenons la liberté au profit même de ceux qui l'ont toujours combattue.

88   . . . non pas le bonheur humain, qui est une autre affaire, mais les conditions nécessaires et suffisantes pour que chaque homme puisse être le seul responsable de son bonheur et de son destin. Il s'agit simplement de ne pas ajouter aux misères profondes de notre condition une injustice qui soit profondément humaine.

90   Nous appellerons . . . justice un état social où chaque individu reçoit toutes ses chances au départ, et où la majorité d'un pays n'est pas maintenue dans une condition indigne par une minorité de privilégiés. Et nous appellerons liberté un climat politique où la personne humaine est respectée dans ce qu'elle est comme dans ce qu'elle exprime.

94   Un pays qui manque son épuration se prépare à manquer sa rénovation. . . . Faute de cela, nous allons avoir besoin de dérisoires consolations. On voit bien que M. Mauriac a raison, nous allons avoir besoin de la charité.

99   Nulle politique ne serait plus aveugle. Nous ne trouverons d'appui réel dans nos colonies qu'à partir du moment où nous les aurons convaincues que leurs intérêts sont les nôtres et que nous n'avons pas deux politiques: l'une qui

Page   donnerait la justice au peuple de France et l'autre qui consacrerait l'injustice à l'égard de l'Empire.

99 On avait ainsi le spectacle d'un peuple occupé (ne faisons pas d'idéalisme) dépossédé de sa terre, acceptant pour finir la civilisation du vainqueur et demandant à y être intégré complètement. La tradition, une psychologie aveugle, les intérêts d'une seule classe, ont empêché nos représentants d'apercevoir la grandeur de la tâche qui leur était proposée. Ils ont gardé dans leur vocabulaire le mot d'assimilation, et ils ont continué à faire pratiquement l'occupation quelquefois bienveillante.

107 . . . cette vie personnelle et ces bonheurs plus faciles dont les a tirés un moment, au milieu de la défaite, le sentiment, alors justifié, que quelque chose était à faire et ne pouvait se faire sans eux.

110 . . . l'erreur d'une certaine littérature, c'est de croire que la vie est tragique parce qu'elle est misérable. Elle peut être bouleversante et magnifique, voilà toute sa tragédie. Sans la beauté, l'amour et le danger, il serait presque facile de vivre. Et le héros de M. Sartre n'a peut-être pas fourni le vrai sens de son angoisse lorsqu'il insiste sur ce qui le répugne dans l'homme, au lieu de fonder sur certaines de ses grandeurs des raisons de désespérer. Constater l'absurdité de la vie ne peut être une fin, mais seulement un commencement. . . . Ce n'est pas cette découverte qui intéresse, mais les conséquences et les règles d'action qu'on en tire.

116 Je sais que certains d'entre vous donnent volontiers à choisir entre la pendaison ou la fusillade. C'est l'idée qu'ils se font de la liberté humaine. Nous, nous faisons ce que nous pouvons pour que ce choix ne devienne pas inévitable. Vous, vous faites ce qu'il faut pour que ce choix devienne inévitable.

116 Je sais que Paulhan trouve sot de dire que les guerres sont funestes parce qu'elles détruisent des êtres humains. Je m'obstine personnellement dans cette sottise. . . .

117 Ils savent bien que leur voie est ailleurs, et leur vrai métier. Ils ont seulement poussé un cri d'alerte, selon leur état, et il est bien possible que ce cri soit poussé dans le désert.

133 L'essentiel du message grec, M. Gernet le définit d'une

Page   façon qu'on peut estimer pathétique lorsqu'il dit que ce peuple, qui fut aussi malheureux que d'autres, n'abdiqua cependant jamais devant le problème du bonheur, à la recherche duquel il appliquait sa réflexion individuelle. Ce que l'on voit aujourd'hui au contraire dans des pays voisins, c'est la religion du groupe et la négation de l'homme, issues d'une conscience désespérée du malheur des temps.

      Beaucoup d'hommes jeunes, en Allemagne et ailleurs, ont cru trouver un soulagement à leurs misères en se remettant tout entiers entre les mains d'un autre. Les Grecs pensaient au contraire que la dignité de l'homme était de regarder en face et de ne remettre à personne le soin de sa propre vie. Cette abdication est contre l'esprit grec, et nous pouvons ajouter qu'à cette répugnance que les esprits libres éprouvent devant elle, ils reconnaissent que l'idéal grec était bon.

161   Il y a chez M. Sartre un certain goût de l'impuissance, au sens plein et au sens physiologique, qui le pousse à prendre des personnages arrivés aux confins d'eux-mêmes et trébuchant contre une absurdité qu'ils ne peuvent dépasser. C'est contre leur propre vie qu'ils butent, et, si j'ose dire, par excès de liberté. Ces êtres restent sans attaches, sans principes, sans fil d'Ariane, libres au point d'en être désagrégés, sourds aux appels de l'action ou de la création.

227*n*2 Nous savons ce qu'est une occupation. . . . Nous le savons si bien que nous n'en voulons plus et que ce seul mot suffit à réveiller nos plus profondes colères.

APPENDIX B

Articles and Editorials by Camus

Listed here are those articles that I was able to identify as having been written by Camus for the following periodicals: *Alger-Républicain*, *Soir-Républicain*, clandestine *Combat*, postliberation *Combat*, and *L'Express*. A number of articles for *Soir-Républicain* and *Combat* that he may have written are grouped separately; they are discussed in more detail below. In addition I have listed, from miscellaneous periodicals, uncollected articles written by Camus.

AI, AII, and *AIII* indicate those articles from the five periodicals mentioned above that have been included in one of the three volumes of *Actuelles*. I have not listed articles contained in Justin O'Brien's translation of Camus's articles, *Resistance, Rebellion and Death*, or in the Pléiade edition of Camus's works, *Théatre, récits, nouvelles* (see "Works by Camus" in List of Works Consulted). Most of the *Combat* editorials were without titles. I have supplied brief descriptions in English of the general content of these.

All of the articles from *Alger-Républicain* were signed either with Camus's full name or with his initials. The articles from *Soir-Républicain*, clandestine *Combat*, and postliberation *Combat* presented certain problems of identification. Partly to evade the censors and partly because Camus preferred to work anonymously with a "team," he did not sign his articles and editorials in *Soir-Républicain* and postliberation *Combat*. The articles in clandestine *Combat* of course could not be signed for reasons of secrecy.

In the case of *Soir-Républicain*, Madame Camus was able to acquire photocopies of various articles identified as Camus's by one of his Algerian associates of the period 1939–1940. Thody accepts most of these articles as Camus's; however, I think a certain amount of caution is necessary. At least two of the articles in this group attributed to Camus must be classed as doubtful: those written on 12 and 16 November 1939. Both are extremely long and somewhat verbose, very unlike Camus's other articles and editorials. Until more conclusive evidence can be found, I shall consider these two articles along with a number of others as being of uncertain authorship.

In questioning these and other articles, I may be overly cautious.

It is quite possible that under the pressure of the times and in an attempt to deal with difficult questions of international law, etc., Camus's style tended to become somewhat prolix. In any case, Camus's preference for editorial teamwork resulted in his working so closely with his newspaper staffs that any of the opinions expressed in the editorial columns of *Soir-Républicain* would almost certainly reflect his own. In fact, views set forth in the articles I have listed as uncertain are quite similar to those expressed in some of the articles that I have accepted as by Camus himself.

All those articles for which I could find further evidence to corroborate previous identifications I have listed as being Camus's. These include: (1) Those front page editorials signed *"Le Soir-Républicain"*: Since these usually included some statement of policy, and Camus was editor-in-chief, they seem certain to be his. Moreover, the editorial of 17 September 1939, "La Guerre," is very close to passages in *Lettres à un ami allemand* and in the essay "Les Amandiers" (*Noces*), and to certain editorials in postliberation *Combat*. (2) Articles signed "Jean de Meursault," and one entitled "Le Temps du mépris." Meursault is, of course, the main character in *L'Etranger*, on which Camus was working in 1939–40. Camus wrote and staged his own adaptation of Malraux's *Le Temps du mépris* in 1938. Also *Combat* for 30 August 1944 has an editorial by Camus bearing this title (*Actuelles I*, p. 25). (3) The article of 19 December 1939 entitled "La Folie continue" is included because a reference in it to that of 13 December 1939 (signed Jean de Meursault) would indicate that the same author wrote both articles: "Nous avons défini ici même, il y a quelque jours, la position qui nous paraissait souhaitable vis-à-vis du conflit finno-russe . . ." (*SR*, 19-12-39, p. 2). All the articles listed from page two of *Soir-Républicain* appeared under the rubric "Sous les éclairages de guerre."

The articles from the clandestine issues of *Combat* remain unidentified except for two that Camus himself identified for Germaine Brée and which she cites in her study (*Camus* [New Brunswick, 1961], p. 41). Further information on Camus's clandestine activities is given in the course of the present book (see Chapter 3, pp. 59–61).

The editorials written in 1944–45 for postliberation *Combat*, the majority of which were unsigned, presented the greatest difficulty. Although these were theoretically the result of a "team" effort, most were in fact written by Camus himself or by Albert Ollivier. Ollivier published a great many of his own editorials in a collection entitled *Fausses Sorties* (Paris, 1946). In the preface to this he wrote:

J'ai eu le privilège et le périlleux honneur de parler au nom de l'équipe de ce journal [*Combat*], plus souvent qu'un autre, par suite du hasard des circonstances, et notamment de l'éloignement d'Albert Camus, appelé par d'autres préoccupations et d'autres travaux. Au demeurant, l'équipe de *Combat* n'a jamais été "monolithique," ses membres ont toujours joui les uns envers les autres d'une grande indépendance. Elle a trouvé son unité sans discussions, sans qu'il soit besoin de la préciser quotidiennement (pp. 14–15).

This statement corroborated information that I had received during interviews with several of Camus's fellow journalists, all of whom assured me that, in spite of the team spirit Camus had sought to foster in editing *Combat,* the editorials were invariably written by individual authors, mostly Camus himself and Ollivier during the first few months after the liberation. I was therefore able to eliminate all the editorials contained in *Fausses Sorties* from those that might possibly have been written by Camus.

A dossier containing carbon copies of Camus's editorials written between 21 August 1944 and 1 January 1945 was placed at my disposal by Madame Camus. Although this file was incomplete, most of the articles missing from it had been reprinted in *Actuelles I.* This raised the question whether Camus might not have taken from the file a number of carbon copies that he had not subsequently included in *Actuelles I.* Unfortunately, neither Madame Camus nor Mme. Suzanne Agnely, Camus's secretary at Gallimard, was able to find any other file containing either the missing copies or copies of later editorials.

One group of editorials—those that appeared in *Combat* between 11 December 1944 and 10 February 1945—was signed with the writers' initials. With the combined material from *Actuelles I,* the dossier mentioned above, and the initialed editorials, I was able to identify most of the editorials written by Camus from 21 August 1944 to 9 February 1945. These are among the more important ones, and it was during this period that Camus was most active in running the paper.

In order to identify the editorials written after 9 February 1945, it was necessary to ascertain, if possible, when and how often Camus's absences, to which Ollivier refers in the above citation, occurred. Camus wrote no editorials between 11 January and 9 February 1945. On 18 January a note at the foot of the editorial column referred to Camus's absence and quoted a letter from him in which he stated that "Les sérieuses raisons de santé . . . me tiennent éloigné de 'Combat' . . ." (p. 1). On 9 February an editorial restating *Combat's* position on a number of questions was signed "Albert Camus." Whether this was an isolated piece written in order to answer criticism of *Combat*'s editorial policies or whether it signaled Camus's return to active participation on the paper is uncertain, all subsequent editorials being unsigned. However, since *Actuelles I* contains no editorials dating from the period between 9 February and 13 May 1945, when Camus wrote a series of signed articles on Algeria, it seems probable that he was absent during much of that period, or at least that his activities were curtailed.

A number of editorials written between 13 May and 20 September 1945 do appear in *Actuelles I.* Therefore, once again during the late spring and the summer of 1945 Camus was probably actively engaged in running the paper and in writing editorials. Thody states that Camus left the paper again in late 1945 in order to work on *La Peste* (*Camus: 1913–1960,* p. 92). Although he gives no precise date, I assume that he received this information from Camus himself, since at the time that he was writing the first version of his study Thody was in personal contact with Camus.

Marcel Gimont, one of Camus's associates on both clandestine and postliberation *Combat,* recalled that after Camus's departure in 1945 another editorialist, Phillipe Diole, had tried to carry on the editorial dialogue that had been established earlier between Camus and François Mauriac. Mauriac immediately realized that Camus had not written the editorial in question and demanded to know why *Combat* had replaced his usual interlocutor with "le dernier de la classe." The article written by Diole appeared on 23 November 1945. Gimont and Roger Grenier, another of Camus's associates at the time, were kind enough to look over for me the editorials for the period between 9 February and 23 November 1945. Neither was able to identify any of these as being definitely by Camus, but both agreed—and I saw them separately —that none of those written after 1 October 1945 seemed to have been Camus's.

I was unable to see either Pascal Pia, the directeur of *Combat* from 1944 to 1947, or Albert Ollivier during my sojourn in Paris. However, after returning to the United States, I had photographed from among the unidentified editorials a selection of those that I thought most important and sent them to Ollivier with the request that he tell me whether or not they were his own. In his reply he wrote: "Je puis vous dire qu'aucun des éditoriaux en question n'est de moi. Je ne peux pas vous garantir que les autres articles que vous m'avez soumis sont de la plume d'Albert Camus. Je suis même persuadé qu'il faut en distraire tous les articles consacrés à la politique étrangère qui sont l'oeuvre de Marcel GIMONT. . . ." Gimont had, of course, already identified these same editorials as probably having been written by Camus. Therefore, although this attribution cannot be considered unimpeachable, it seems fairly certain that these editorials, the dates of which I have included in the Appendix, were written by Camus. Nevertheless, I preferred not to rely on them in the body of the study itself, where I have cited, unless otherwise indicated, only those editorials of whose authorship I am certain.

I have included in the inventory the four following articles from *Combat* that were not in Madame Camus's file: (1) 12 September 1944: This article contains the passage cited above on p. 66, a passage very similar in tone, wording, and sentiment expressed to parts of the first letter to a German friend (See *Lettres à un ami allemand*, pp. 23–27). It was also one of the articles I had photocopied for Ollivier. Since he was not the author, it is almost certain that Camus was. (2) 1 October 1944: This article is in part a statement of policy and in part a definition of the term "conciliation de la liberté et de la justice," a term Camus used a number of times in other editorials. (3) 30 November 1944: This article is an attack on Pierre-Henri Teitgen, minister of information and a personal friend of Camus. Both Grenier and Gimont were certain that only Camus would have taken the responsibility for writing this editorial. (4) 24 December 1944: This is not an editorial, but a satirical vignette signed "Suétone." Grenier distinctly recalled the circumstances under which Camus wrote it, and was able to make a positive identification.

After a year's absence Camus returned to *Combat* in November 1946, when "Ni victimes ni bourreaux" appeared. He again took over as full-time editor after a month-long printers' strike, in March 1947, had crippled the paper financially. He wrote a few editorials in the spring of 1947, all of which seem to have been signed and most of which were reprinted in *Actuelles I*. After that period, as far as I know, Camus signed all the articles that he wrote for periodicals. All articles listed below, unless otherwise indicated, have been identified as Camus's.

Alger-Republicain
1938

Oct. 9 p. 5 *Marina di Vezza,* le nouveau roman d'Aldous Huxley.

  10 p. 5 *Les Camarades,* par Erich-Maria Remarque.

11	p. 3	L'Affaire Zittel: Réunis hier soir à la Bourse du Travail, les "municipaux" ont vigoureusement répliqué à la décision arbitraire de M. Rozis.
11	p. 5	*La Sève des justes,* par Blanche Balain.
20	p. 5	*La Nausée,* par J.-P. Sartre.
23	p. 5	*André Gide,* par Jean Hytier.
Nov. 2	p. 4	*Les Salopards,* par René Janon.
11	p. 5	*La Conspiration,* par Paul Nizan.
19	p. 1	Au Pays du mufle.
22	p. 3	*Les Fables bônoises,* d'Edmond Brua.
26	p. 2	Quand la France abandonne la Méditerranée aux pirates.
27	p. 3	Les Travailleurs contre les décrets-loi.
28	p. 4	Les Revues. "Poésie," numéro spécial de la revue Aguedal (Rabat); la revue algérienne, *Vendredi,* disparaît.
Dec. 1	pp. 1–2	Ces Hommes qu'on raie de l'humanité.
3	pp. 1, 3	Dialogue entre un président du Conseil et un employé à 1,200 francs par mois.
7	pp. 1, 3	Poursuivant de sa haine les employés syndiqués, M. Rozis suspend et veut révoquer cinq "municipaux."
18	p. 2	Gazette de Renaudot: Petit Portrait dans le goût du temps.
21	pp. 1, 3	156 "municipaux" seront mis à pied pendant 8 jours.
24	pp. 1, 3	Un Conseil municipal pittoresque. Le Budget d'Alger est voté dans la confusion par 24 voix contre 13.
29	pp. 1–2	L'Enquête sur la catastrophe de la rue Blanchard amène l'arrestation d'Ait Sidoun pour . . . trafic des armes.
30	p. 1	Une cassure dans une conduite de gaz est mise au jour rue Blanchard. Est-elle la conséquence d'une explosion?
31	pp. 1–2	L'Enquête sur l'explosion de la rue Blanchard continue dans le secret.

1939

Jan. 3	p. 3	*Commune Mesure,* par Renaud de Jouvenel; *Lettre aux paysans sur la pauvreté et la paix,* par Jean Giono.

9	p. 1	L'Affaire Hodent; comment on circonvient et on éloigne un témoin gênant.
12	p. 5	*Le Mur,* par Jean-Paul Sartre.
13	p. 1	L'Affaire Hodent; un homme juste plaide pour un innocent.
16	p. 1	Les "Complices" de Michel Hodent et les fantaisies de l'instruction.
18	pp. 1–2	L'Affaire Hodent; pour s'effondrer dans le ridicule l'instruction n'en est que plus odieuse.
19	pp. 1–2	L'Affaire Hodent; c'est demain matin au tribunal correctionnel de Tiaret que l'innocence des inculpés sera reconnue.
21	pp. 1–2	L'Affaire Hodent devant le tribunal correctionnel de Tiaret.
22	pp. 1–2	Le Jugement de l'affaire Hodent sera rendu ce matin; les défenseurs ont souligné hier l'inanité des accusations que le ministère public a eu le tort de ne pas abandonner.
23	pp. 1–2	L'Innocence de Hodent et du magasinier Mas a fini par triompher; le tribunal correctionnel a acquitté tous les prévenus et mis à la charge des parties civiles les dépens du procès.
28	p. 4	*Forêt vierge,* par Ferreiro de Castro; *L'Exploration du Sahara,* par Henri-Paul Sydoux.
Apr. 4	p. 2	Comment les assurances sociales défavorisent les ouvriers nord-africains de Paris.
9	p. 5	*Bahia de tous les saints,* par Jorge Amado.
13	p. 2	Peut-on réparer l'injustice faite aux assurés sociaux nord-africains qui résident en France?
16	p. 6	Le Roman d'aventures. *Aranga,* par Gabriel Saint-Georges; *Baudouin des mines,* par O. P. Gilbert; *Chez Krull,* par Simenon.
20	pp. 1–2	Notre Enquête sur les assurances sociales; la situation des Nord-Africains travaillant en France.
21	pp. 1–2	Notre Enquête sur les assurances sociales; la C.G.T. est favorable à la réforme proposée.
23	pp. 1–2	Notre Enquête sur les assurances sociales; l'opinion de M. le Professeur Amédée Laffont.
24	pp. 1, 3	Notre Enquête sur les assurances sociales; l'opinion des médecins de colonisation—la réforme est possible dans les villes, impossible dans les campagnes.

25	p. 3	Les Ecrivains et leur critiques. *Constantin Léontieff,* par Nicolas Berdiaeff; *Henri Heine,* par E. Vermeil; *Introduction à Swift,* par A. M. Petitjean.
26	p. 1	L'Assassinat du Muphti devant la cour criminelle; aujourd'hui plaidoirie de la partie civile et réquisitoire de l'avocat général.
27	pp. 1–2	L'Avocat général renonce à soutenir l'invraisemblable accusation portée contre Cheikh El Okbi et Abbas Turqui.
28	pp. 1–2	Les Défenseurs d'Akacha, Mohara et Boukheir ont réclamé l'acquittement de ces trois accusés.
29	pp. 1–2	La Cour criminelle reconnaissant l'innocence de Cheikh El Okbi et Abbas Turqui les a acquittés.
July 4	p. 3	La Pensée engagé. *Scandale de la vérité,* par Georges Bernanos; *La Commune,* par Albert Ollivier; *Les Nouveaux Cahiers.*
15	p. 2	*Oiseau privé,* par Armand Guibert.
24	p. 3	L'Edition algérienne. *Keboul,* par A. E. Breugnot; *Quinta Pugneta,* par Jean Lavergne; *Coplas populaires andalouses.*
25	pp. 1–2	L'Affaire des "incendiaires" d'Auribeau en cassation; l'histoire d'un crime, ou comment on imagine un crime pour les besoins d'une accusation.
26	pp. 1–2	L'Affaire des "incendiaires" d'Auribeau; comme au moyen âge, la torture au service des accusateurs.
28	pp. 1–2	L'Affaire des "incendiaires" d'Auribeau; un odieux déni de justice.
31	pp. 1–2	L'Affaire des "incendiaires" d'Auribeau; des innocents condamnés aux travaux forcés et les leurs condamnés à la misère "au nom du peuple français."
Aug. 18	p. 1	De malencontreuses poursuites.

Soir-Républicain

The following articles and editorials may be reliably accepted as having been written by Camus:

1939

| Sept. 15 | p. 1 | A nos lecteurs. |
| 17 | p. 1 | La Guerre. |

Oct.	4	p. 1	A nos lecteurs.
	30	p. 1	Notre Position.
Nov.	6	p. 1	Notre Position.
Dec.	6	p. 1	A nos lecteurs.
	13	p. 2	Pas de croisade. (Signed Jean de Meursault.)
	14	p. 2	Le Temps du mépris.
	15	p. 2	La Société des peuples. (Signed Jean de Meursault.)
	19	p. 2	La Folie continue.
	23	p. 2	Lettre à un jeune Anglais sur l'état d'esprit de la nation française. (Signed Jean de Meursault.)

1940

Jan.	1	p. 1	1940.

The following articles and editorials are of somewhat uncertain attribution:

1939

Nov.	6	p. 2	Notre Revue de presse indépendante.
	7	p. 2	Un Effort généreux.
	10	p. 2	La France est libre.
	12	p. 2	Les Conditions d'une collaboration.
	15	p. 2	Ils sont sincères.
	16	p. 2	Comment aller vers un ordre nouveau.
	25	p. 2	Une interview avec Dieu le Père.
	27	p. 2	La Censure avec nous.
Dec.	17	p. 2	Défense de notre liberté nationale.
	18	p. 2	Pétrone et les ciseaux.
	29	p. 2	Le Socialisme devant les événements actuels. (Signed Alius.)
	30	p. 2	Recherche du possible.

Combat Clandestin

1944

Mar.	pp. 1–2	A guerre totale, résistance totale.
May	pp. 1–2	Pendant trois heures ils ont fusillé des Français.

Combat

1944

Aug.	21	p. 1	Le Combat continue.
	21	p. 1	De la Résistance à la révolution.

22	pp. 1–2	Le Temps de la justice.
23	p. 1	Ils ne passeront pas.
24	pp. 1–2	Le Sang de la liberté. (*AI.*)
25	pp. 1–2	La Nuit de la vérité. (*AI.*)
29	pp. 1–2	Le Réalisme politique.
30	pp. 1–2	Le Temps du mépris. (*AI.*)
31	pp. 1–2	Critique de la nouvelle presse.
Sept. 1	pp. 1–2	Réforme de la presse.
2	pp. 1–2	La Démocratie à faire.
4	p. 1	La Morale et la politique
6	pp. 1–2	La Fin d'un monde.
7	pp. 1–2	Nos Frères d'Espagne.
8	pp. 1–2	Le Journalisme critique. (*AI.*)
12	pp. 1–2	[*Combat* shall not forget those who died in the war or those who are still prisoners.]
15	pp. 1–2	[On the rise of Hitler and the disastrous effects of his policies.]
16	pp. 1–2	[Pays tribute to Christian members of the Resistance, but condemns Church's failure to speak out clearly against injustice.]
17	pp. 1–2	[German people have done nothing to erase the dishonor of the crimes committed in their name.]
19	pp. 1–2	[On meeting of the M.L.N. at the Salle Pleyel.]
20	pp. 1–2	[The German people have chosen to accept defeat in silence with Hitler.]
23	pp. 1–2	[Pays tribute to England for having stood alone in the early days of the war.]
26	pp. 1–2	[On trial of Louis Renault.]
27	pp. 1–2	[France must punish her traitors.]
28	pp. 1–2	[Sees government decision to requisition Renault factories as first positive step toward economic reform.]
29	pp. 1–2	[Battle with Germany will be a fight to the bitter end. No easy victory.]
30	pp. 1–2	[Americans seem to mistrust de Gaulle, but the Resistance and the French people support him.]
Oct. 1	pp. 1–2	[What the Resistance and *Combat* seek is "la conciliation de la justice avec la liberté."]
3	pp. 1–2	[Denounces criticism of French press by Allan Forbes of the *Daily Mail*.]
4	pp. 1–2	[Objects to government's regulation of the press.]

17 pp. 1–2 [Quotes a speech made in 1868 by Edgar Quinet on the progressive steps in undermining a revolutionary movement. Points out that history seems to be repeating itself.]

18 pp. 1–2 [Approves Franco-Soviet treaty.]

20 pp. 1–2 [Von Rundstedt's new offensive shows that Germany is still far from defeated.]

22 pp. 1–2 [On the agony of being separated from loved ones.] (*AI.*)

24 p. 1 Le Poète et le général de Gaulle. (Signed Suétone.)

29 pp. 1–2 [Strongly criticizes government for not following sufficiently energetic policies.]

30 p. 1 Ne jugez pas.

1945

Jan. 3 pp. 1–2 [On Polish question. The government should state its position clearly; there must be no equivocation as under the Third Republic.]

5 pp. 1–2 [The purge has gone completely awry.]

7 pp. 1–2 [Criticizes government for receiving the Falangist ambassador to France.]

11 pp. 1–2 Justice et charité. (*AI.*)

Feb. 9 pp. 1–2 [Reviews and restates *Combat*'s policies.]

May 13 pp. 1–2 Crise en Algérie. (*AIII.*)

15 pp. 1–2 La Famine en Algérie. (*AIII.*)

16 pp. 1–2 L'Algérie demande des bateaux et de la justice. (*AIII.*)

17 pp. 1–2 [Condemns American treatment of PW's.] (*AI.*)

18 pp. 1–2 Les Indigènes nord-africains se sont éloignés d'une démocratie dont ils se voyaient écartés. (*AIII.*)

19 pp. 1–2 [Continues editorial of 17-5-45; reply to *France-Soir*.] (*AI.*)

20 pp. 1–2 Les Arabes demandent pour l'Algérie une constitution et un parlement. (*AIII.*)

23 p. 1 C'est la justice qui sauvera l'Algérie de la haine. (*AIII.*)

June 27 pp. 1–2 [Attacks speech by Edouard Herriot.] (*AI.*)

Aug. 8 pp. 1–2 [On atomic explosion at Hiroshima.] (*AI.*)

30 pp. 1–2 [On purge]: "Le mot d'épuration était déjà assez pénible. La chose est devenue odieuse." (*AI.*)

1946

The following eight articles were printed under the collective title "Ni victimes ni bourreaux." (*AI,* pp. 140–97.)

Nov. 19	p. 1	Le Siècle de la peur.
20	p. 1	Sauver les corps.
21	p. 1	Le Socialisme mystifié.
23	p. 1	La Révolution travestie.
26	p. 1	Démocratie et dictature internationale.
27	p. 1	Le Monde va vite.
29	p. 1	Un Nouveau Contrat social.
30	p. 1	Vers le dialogue.

1947

Mar. 17	p. 1	La République sourde et muette.
21	p. 1	Radio 47.
22	p. 1	Le Choix.
Apr. 30	p. 1	Démocratie et modestie. (*AI.*) [Incorrectly dated February 1947 in *Actuelles I.*]
May 7	p. 1	Anniversaire. (*AI.*)
10	p. 1	La Contagion. (*AI.*)
June 3	p. 1	A nos lecteurs. [Camus announces his resignation as editor of *Combat.*]

1948

| Dec. 9 | pp. 1, 3 | A quoi sert l'O.N.U. |
| 25 | pp. 5, 6 | Réponse à l'incrédule: Albert Camus à François Mauriac. |

The following editorials, which appeared in *Combat* in 1945, each on pp. 1–2, were probably written by Camus:

Feb. 15, 16.
Mar. 14, 28, 29.
Apr. 10.
June 15, 22.
Aug. 4, 5, 7, 9, 14, 15, 16, 17, 21, 22, 25, 29.

L'Express

1955

| May 14 | p. 15 | Le Métier d'homme. |
| June 4 | p. 13 | Le Vrai Débat. |

Articles Written by Camus for Miscellaneous Periodicals

"Un Nouveau Verlaine," *Sud,* No. 4 (March 1932), p. 59.
"Jean Rictus," *Sud,* No. 6 (May 1932), pp. 90–91.
"Essai sur la musique," *Sud,* No. 7 (June 1932), pp. 125–30.
"La Philosophie du siècle," *Sud,* No. 7 (June 1932), p. 144.

"Présentation de la revue *Rivages*," *Rivages*, No. 1 (1939), pp. 1–2.

"Barrès ou la querelle des héritiers," *La Lumière*, No. 674 (5 April 1940), p. 5.

"Giraudoux ou Byzance au théâtre," *La Lumière*, No. 679 (10 May 1940), p. 5.

"L'Intelligence et l'échafaud," *Confluences*, Nos. 21–24 (July–August 1943), pp. 218–23.

"Portrait d'un élu," *Les Cahiers du sud*, No. 225 (April 1943), pp. 306–11.

"Sur une philosophie de l'expression," *Poésie 44*, No. 17 (1944), pp. 15–23.

"Tout ne s'arrange pas," *Les Lettres françaises*, No. 16 (May 1944), p. 4.

"Remarque sur la politique internationale," *Renaissances*, No. 10 (May 1945), pp. 16–20.

"*La Vallée heureuse*, par Jules Roy," *L'Arche*, No. 24 (February 1947), pp. 117–21.

"Les Archives de la peste," *Les Cahiers de la Pléiade* (April 1947), pp. 149–54.

"Pluies de New York," *Formes et couleurs*, No. 6 (1947).

"Les Meurtriers délicats," *La Table ronde*, No. 1 (January 1948), pp. 42–50.

"La Démocratie exercice de la modestie," *Caliban*, No. 20 (September 1948), pp. 17–19.

"L'Artiste est le témoin de la liberté," *Empédocle*, No. 1 (April 1949), pp. 71–76.

"Le Meurtre et l'absurde," *Empédocle*, No. 1 (April 1949), pp. 19–27.

"Nietzsche et le nihilisme," *Les Temps modernes*, No. 70 (August 1951), pp. 193–208.

"Lettre au journal Arts," *Arts*, No. 334 (23 November 1951), pp. 1, 3.

"Chroniques," *Esprit*, No. 182 (April 1952), pp. 725–26.

"Une Lettre de M. Albert Camus," *Le Monde*, No. 2638 (19–20 July 1953), p. 4.

"Calendrier de la liberté," *Témoins,* No. 5 (Spring 1954), pp. 1–10. This article is a reprint of two speeches by Camus dated 19 July 1936 (pp. 1–6) and 17 June 1953 (pp. 6–10). The two speeches were again reprinted in a fascicule entitled "Presence de Camus," which appeared as *Témoins,* No. 26 (March 1961), pp. 5–13.

"Lettre à Roland Barthes, sur *La Peste,*" *Club* (February 1955), p. 7.

"Lettre au sujet du 'Parti Pris,' " *NRF,* No. 45 (September 1956), pp. 386–92.

"Réponse à l'appel des écrivains hongrois," *Franc-Tireur,* No. 3823 (10–11 November 1956), pp. 1, 3.

"Le Socialisme des potences," *Demain,* No. 63 (21–27 February 1957), pp. 10–11. Translated as "Parties and Truth," *Encounter,* 8 (April 1957), 3–5.

"Le Parti de la liberté," *Monde nouveau–Paru,* Nos. 110–11 (April–May 1957), pp. 1–9.

"Letter of Reply to Peter L. Caracciola," *Encounter,* 8 (June 1957), 68.

"Le Pari de notre génération," *Demain,* No. 98 (24–30 October 1957), pp. 11–13.

"Hommage à un journaliste exilé," *La Revue prolétarienne,* No. 442 (November 1957), pp. 2–4.

"Albert Camus nous parle de son adaptation des Possédés," *Spectacles,* No. 1 (March 1958), p. 6.

"Dostoïevski, prophète du vingtième siècle," *Spectacles,* No. 1 (March 1958), p. 5.

"Ce que je dois à l'Espagne," *Preuves,* No. 85 (March 1958), pp. 41–43.

"Il aidait à vivre: à propos de Roger Martin du Gard," *Le Figaro littéraire,* No. 645 (30 August 1958), p. 1.

"Camus nous parle," *Le Figaro littéraire,* No. 682 (16 May 1959), pp. 1, 4.

"Réponses à Jean-Claude Brisville (1959)," in Jean-Claude Brisville, *Camus* (Paris: Gallimard, 1959), pp. 256–61.

"Les Vraies Tâches," *Cahiers des saisons,* No. 20 (1960), pp. 615–16.

"Lettres d'Albert Camus à Jean Gillibert," *Revue d'histoire du théâtre,* No. 4 (October–December 1960), pp. 355–59.

LIST OF WORKS CONSULTED

The dates in this list indicate the printing I consulted, not necessarily the first editions of the works listed. In most cases, the text and pagination of later printings of Camus's works are the same as those of earlier printings. Exceptions are *"Le Malentendu" suivi de "Caligula,"* where I consulted the "nouvelles versions," and *"Noces" suivi de "L'Eté,"* where the two collections of essays, originally published separately, are combined.

Since current practice among most French publishers is to print the copyright date on the back of the title page instead of a date of publication on the title page itself, I have dispensed with the use of brackets to indicate citation of the copyright date.

For bibliographical data on articles by Camus other than those cited from *Actuelles I, II,* and *III; Resistance, Rebellion and Death;* or *Théâtre, récits, nouvelles,* see Appendix B.

Works by Camus

Actuelles I: Chroniques 1944–1948. Paris: Gallimard, 1950.

Actuelles II: Chroniques 1948–1953. Paris: Gallimard, 1953.

Actuelles III: Chroniques algériennes (1939–1958). Paris: Gallimard, 1958.

Carnets: Mai 1935–février 1942. Paris: Gallimard, 1962.

La Chute. Paris: Gallimard, 1956.

Discours de Suède. Paris: Gallimard, 1958.

L'Envers et l'endroit. Paris: Gallimard, 1958.

L'Etat de siège. Paris: Gallimard, 1948.

L'Etranger. Paris: Gallimard, 1957.

L'Exil et le royaume. Paris: Gallimard, 1957.

L'Homme révolté. Paris: Gallimard, 1951.

Les Justes. Paris: Gallimard, 1950.

Lettres à un ami allemand. Paris: Gallimard, 1948.

"Le Malentendu" suivi de "Caligula." Nouvelles versions. Paris: Gallimard, 1958.

Le Mythe de Sisyphe. Paris: Gallimard, 1942.

"Noces" suivi de "L'Eté." Paris: Gallimard, 1959.

Notebooks: 1935–1942, trans. Philip Thody. New York: Knopf, 1963.

La Peste. Paris: Gallimard, 1947.

Resistance, Rebellion and Death, trans. Justin O'Brien. New York: Knopf, 1961.

Théâtre, récits, nouvelles, ed. Roger Quilliot. Bibliothèque de la Pléiade. Paris: Gallimard, 1962.

Works Written by Camus in Collaboration or for Collections

Désert vivant: Images en couleurs de Walt Disney. Textes de Marcel Aymé, Louis Bromfield, Albert Camus. . . . Paris: Société Française du Livre, 1954.

"Herman Melville," in Raymond Queneau, ed., *Les Ecrivains célèbres,* 3 (Paris: Mazenod, 1953), 128–29.

Koestler, Arthur, and Albert Camus. *Réflexions sur la peine capitale.* Paris: Calmann-Lévy, 1954.

"Remarque sur la révolte," in Jean Grenier, ed., *L'Existence* (Paris: Gallimard, 1945), pp. 9–23.

Works with Prefaces by Camus

Bieber, Konrad. *L'Allemagne vue par les écrivains de la Résistance française.* Genève: Droz, 1954.

Camus, Albert. *L'Etranger,* eds. Germaine Brée and Carlos Lynes, Jr. New York: Appleton-Century-Crofts, 1955.

Chamfort, Nicolas Sébastien Roch de. *Maximes et anecdotes.* Monaco: Dac, 1944.

Char, René. *Feuillets d'Hypnos.* Paris: Gallimard, 1946.

Clairin, Pierre-Eugène. *Dix Estampes originales, présentées par Albert Camus.* Paris: Rombaldi, 1946.

Faulkner, William. *Requiem pour une nonne,* trans. Maurice E. Coindreau. Paris: Gallimard, 1957.

Grenier, Jean. *Les Iles.* Paris: Gallimard, 1959.

Guilloux, Louis. *La Maison du peuple.* Paris: Grasset, 1953.

Héon-Canonne, Jeanne. *Devant la mort.* Paris: Siraudeau, 1951.

Leynaud, René. *Poésies posthumes.* Paris: Gallimard, 1947.

Martin du Gard, Roger. *Oeuvres complètes.* 2 vols. Bibliothèque de la Pléiade. Paris: Gallimard, 1955.

Mauroc, Daniel. *Contre-Amour.* Paris: Editions de Minuit, 1952.

Méry, Jacques. *Laissez passer mon peuple.* Paris: Editions du Seuil, 1947.

Rosmer, Alfred. *Moscou sous Lénine: Les Origines du communisme.* Paris: Editions de Flore, 1953.

Salvet, André. *Le Combat silencieux.* Paris: Editions France-Empire, 1945.

Targuebayre, Claire. *Cordes-en-Albigeois*. Toulouse: E. Privet, 1954.

La Vérité sur l'affaire Nagy. Paris: Plon, 1958.

Wilde, Oscar. *La Ballade de la geôle de Reading*. Paris: Falaize, 1952.

Other Works Consulted

A Albert Camus, ses amis du livre. Paris: Gallimard, 1962.

Albérès, R.-M. "Albert Camus dans son siècle," *La Table ronde*, No. 146 (February 1960), pp. 9–15.

————. *L'Aventure intellectuelle au vingtième siècle*. Paris: Albin-Michel, 1959.

————. *La Révolte des écrivains d'aujourd'hui*. Paris: Corréa, 1949.

Amoureux, Henri. *La Vie des Français sous l'occupation*. Paris: Fayard, 1961.

Anthologie des écrivains morts à la guerre. Paris: Albin-Michel, 1960.

Aron, Raymond. *De l'armistice à l'insurrection nationale*. Paris: Gallimard, 1945.

————. *France, Steadfast and Changing*. Cambridge: Harvard University Press, 1960.

————. *L'Opium des intellectuels*. Paris: Calmann-Lévy, 1955.

————. "Un Seul Homme, un homme seul," *Preuves*, No. 109 (March 1960), pp. 3–12.

————. *La Tragédie algérienne*. Paris: Plon, 1957.

Aron, Robert. *Histoire de la libération de la France: Juin 1944–mai 1945*. Paris: Fayard, 1959.

————. *Histoire de Vichy: 1940–1944*. Paris: Fayard, 1954.

Astier, Emmanuel d'. "Arrachez la victime aux bourreaux: Résponse à Albert Camus," *Caliban*, No. 15 (April 1948), pp. 12–17.

Astorg, Bertrand d'. "L'Homme engagé: De *La Peste* ou d'un nouvel humanitarisme," *Esprit*, No. 10 (October 1947), pp. 615–21.

Aubarède, Gabriel d'. "Rencontre avec Albert Camus," *Les Nouvelles littéraires*, No. 1236 (10 May 1951), pp. 1, 6.

Audry, Colette. *Léon Blum ou la politique du juste*. Paris: Julliard, 1955.

Ayer, A. J. "Albert Camus," *Horizon*, 13 (March 1946), 155–68.

Aymé, Marcel. *Le Confort intellectuel*. Paris: Flammarion, 1949.

Barrier, M.-G. *L'Art du récit dans "L'Etranger" d'Albert Camus*. Paris: Nizet, 1962.

Barthes, Roland. "*La Peste*, annales d'une épidémie ou roman de la solitude," *Club* (February 1955), p. 6.

Barzun, Jacques. *The House of Intellect.* New York: Harper, 1959.

Bataille, Georges. "L'Affaire de *l'Homme révolté,*" *Critique,* No. 67 (December 1952), pp. 1077–81.

————. "Le Temps de la révolte: Albert Camus, l'Homme révolté," *Critique,* No. 55 (December 1951), pp. 1019–27; No. 56 (January 1952), pp. 29–41.

Beau de Loménie, E. *La Mort de la Troisième République.* Paris: Editions du Conquistador, 1951.

Beauvoir, Simone de. *Les Mandarins.* Paris: Gallimard, 1954.

Behr, Edward. *The Algerian Problem.* New York: Norton, 1962.

Bellanger, Claude. *La Presse clandestine: 1940–1944.* Paris: Armand Colin, 1961.

Benda, Julien. *La Trahison des clercs.* Paris: Grasset, 1927.

Berger, Pierre. "Camus a-t-il cessé d'être romancier?" *Arts,* No. 415 (18 June 1953), p. 12.

Berl, Emmanuel. "Lettre à Albert Camus," *La Table ronde,* Nos. 103–4 (July–August 1956), pp. 301–6.

Bespaloff, R[achel]. "Le Monde du condamné à mort," *Esprit,* No. 169 (January 1950), pp. 1–26.

Bieber, Konrad. *L'Allemagne vue par les écrivains de la Résistance française.* Genève: Droz, 1954.

————. "*Engagement* as a Professional Risk," *Yale French Studies,* No. 16 (Winter 1955–56), pp. 29–39.

————. "The Rebellion of a Humanist," *The Yale Review,* 43 (March 1954), 473–75.

Blanchet, André. "*L'Homme révolté* d'Albert Camus," *Etudes,* 272 (January 1952), 48–60.

————. "La Querelle Sartre-Camus," *Etudes,* 275 (November 1952), 239–46.

Blanchot, Maurice. "La Confession dédaigneuse," *La Nouvelle Revue française,* No. 48 (December 1956), pp. 1050–56.

————. "Réflexions sur l'enfer," *NRF,* No. 16 (April 1954), pp. 677–86.

————. "Réflexions sur le nihilisme," *NRF,* No. 17 (May 1954), pp. 850–59.

————. "Tu peux tuer cet homme," *NRF,* No. 18 (June 1954), pp. 1059–69.

Blin, Georges. "Albert Camus et l'idée de la révolte," *Fontaine,* 10 (June 1946), 109–17.

————. "Albert Camus, ou le sens de l'absurde," *Fontaine,* 5 (1943), 553–61.

Bloch-Michel, Jean. "Albert Camus et la nostalgie de l'innocence," *Preuves,* No. 110 (April 1960), pp. 3–9.

———. "Solitaire ou solidaire," *Demain,* No. 68 (28 March–3 April 1957), p. 16.

Blocq-Mascart, Maxine. *Chroniques de la Résistance.* Paris: Corréa, 1945.

Bodin, Paul. "Une Grande Bataille se poursuit," *Arts,* No. 378 (26 September–2 October 1952), pp. 1, 5.

Boisdeffre, Pierre de. *Métamorphoses de la littérature.* 2 vols. Paris: Editions Alsatia, 1951.

Bollinger, Renate. *Albert Camus: Eine Bibliographie der Literatur über ihn und sein Werk.* Cologne: Greyen Verlag, 1957.

Bonnier, Henri. *Albert Camus ou la force d'être.* Lyon: E. Vitte, 1959.

Bourdet, Claude. "Camus et la révolte de Sisyphe," *L'Observateur,* No. 83 (13 December 1951), pp. 17–18.

———. "Camus et la révolte de Sisyphe," *L'Observateur,* No. 84 (20 December 1951), pp. 17–18.

———. "Camus ou les mains propres," *France-Observateur,* No. 505 (7 January 1960), p. 18.

Brace, Richard, and Joan Brace. *Ordeal in Algeria.* Princeton: Van Nostrand, 1960.

Brée, Germaine. "Albert Camus and *The Plague,*" *Yale French Studies,* No. 8 (1951), pp. 93–100.

———. *Camus,* rev. ed. New Brunswick: Rutgers University Press, 1961.

———. "Introduction to Albert Camus," *French Studies,* 4 (January 1950), 27–37.

———, ed. *Camus: A Collection of Critical Essays.* Englewood Cliffs, N.J.: Prentice-Hall, 1962.

Breton, André. "Sucre jaune: A propos de Lautréamont," *Arts,* No. 328 (12 October 1951), pp. 1, 3.

Breton, André, and Aimé Patri. "Dialogue entre A. Breton et A. Patri à propos de *l'Homme révolté* d'Albert Camus," *Arts,* No. 333 (16 November 1951), pp. 1, 3.

Brisville, Jean-Claude. *Camus.* Paris: Gallimard, 1959.

———. "Hommage à Albert Camus," *Le Figaro littéraire,* No. 601 (26 October 1957), p. 5.

Brogan, D. W. *The French Nation from Napoleon to Pétain.* London: Hamish Hamilton, 1957.

Brombert, Victor. *The Intellectual Hero: Studies in the French Novel (1880–1955).* New York: J. B. Lippincott, 1960.

Bruckberger, Raymond-Leopold. "The Spiritual Agony of Europe," *Renascence,* 7 (Winter 1954), 70–80.

Caillet, Gérard. "Sartre contre Camus," *France Illustration,* No. 362 (20 September 1952), p. 280.

Caracciola, Peter L. "M. Camus and Algeria," *Encounter,* 8 (June 1957), 68.

Casanova, Laurent. *Le Parti Communiste, les intellectuels et la nation.* Paris: Editions Sociales, 1949.

Catalogue des périodiques clandestines (1939–1945). Paris: Bibliothèque Nationale, 1954.

Cate, Curtis. "Turmoil in Algeria," *The Atlantic,* 210 (December 1962), 49–55.

Catroux, Georges. *Dans la bataille de la Méditerranée.* Paris: Julliard, 1949.

Champigny, Robert. *Stages on Sartre's Way.* Bloomington: Indiana University Press, 1959.

———. *Sur un héros païen.* Paris: Gallimard, 1959.

Char, René. "Hommage à Albert Camus: Je veux parler d'un ami," *Le Figaro littéraire,* No. 601 (26 October 1957), p. 5.

Charney, Hanna. "Le Héros anonyme: De Monsieur Teste aux Mandarins," *Romanic Review,* 50 (December 1959), 268–75.

Cherki, M. "Polémique ou haine," *La Nef,* No. 12 (December 1957), p. 96.

Chiaromonte, Nicola. "Albert Camus and Moderation," *Partisan Review,* 25 (October 1948), 1142–45.

———. "La Résistance à l'histoire," *Preuves,* No. 110 (April 1960), pp. 17–20.

———. "Sartre versus Camus: A Political Quarrel," in Germaine Brée, ed., *Camus: A Collection of Critical Essays* (Englewood Cliffs, N.J.: Prentice-Hall, 1962), pp. 31–37.

Chonez, Claudine. "Portrait d'Albert Camus," *Paru,* No. 47 (October 1948), pp. 7–13.

Clark, Michael K. *Algeria in Turmoil.* New York: Praeger, 1959.

Clavel, Maurice. "Une Rencontre dans la Résistance," *Le Figaro littéraire,* No. 716 (9 January 1960), p. 7.

Colin, P. "Athéisme et révolte chez Camus," *La Vie intellectuelle,* No. 7 (July 1952), pp. 30–51.

Cornell, Kenneth. "*Les Temps modernes:* Peep Sights across the Atlantic," *Yale French Studies,* No. 16 (Winter 1955–56), pp. 24–28.

Crépin, Simone. *Albert Camus: Essai de bibliographie.* Bruxelles: Commission Belge de Bibliographie, 1960.

Crossman, R. H. S. "A Frustrated Intellectual," *The New Statesman and Nation,* 47 (16 January 1954), 72, 74.

Cruickshank, John. *Albert Camus and the Literature of Revolt.* New York: Oxford University Press, 1960.

Daix, Pierre. "Albert Camus: Prix Nobel," *Les Lettres françaises,* No. 693 (24–30 October 1957), pp. 1, 5.

Defosse, Jean, "Albert Camus: *Actuelles III,*" *La Revue nouvelle,* 28 (October 1958), 358–59.

Delpech, Janine. " 'Non, je ne suis pas existentialiste,' nous dit Albert Camus," *Les Nouvelles littéraires,* No. 954 (15 November 1945), p. 1.

Doubrovsky, Serge. "Camus en Amérique," *La Nouvelle Revue française,* 98 (1 February 1961), 292–96.

———. "The Ethics of Albert Camus," in Germaine Brée, ed., *Camus: A Collection of Critical Essays* (Englewood Cliffs, N.J.: Prentice-Hall, 1962), pp. 71–84.

———. "A Study in Incarceration," *Yale French Studies,* No. 25 (Spring 1960), pp. 85–92.

Druon, Maurice. "Le Prix Nobel d'Albert Camus: Le Respect qu'on doit à l'esprit," *La Nef,* No. 12 (December 1957), p. 94.

Duhrssen, Alfred. "Some French Hegelians," *Review of Metaphysics,* 7 (December 1953), 323–37.

Dumur, Guy. "Albert Camus et la solitude," *Demain,* No. 14 (15–21 March 1956), p. 15.

———. "Une Bouteille à la mer: A propos de *l'Homme Révolté,*" *Les Cahiers du sud,* No. 311 (1952), pp. 154–60.

———. "Il y a un an, Albert Camus . . . ," *France-Observateur,* No. 557 (5 January 1961), p. 16.

Durand, Anne. *Le Cas Albert Camus.* Paris: Editions Fischbacher, 1961.

Etiemble. "Peste ou péché," *Les Temps modernes,* No. 26 (November 1947), pp. 911–20.

Fauvet, Jacques. *La Quatrième République.* Paris: Club du Meilleur Livre, 1959.

Favrod, Charles-Henri. *La Révolution algérienne.* Paris: Plon, 1959.

Feraoun, Mouloud. "Le Dernier Message," *Preuves,* No. 110 (April 1960), pp. 21–24.

Fitch, Brian T. *Narrateur et narration dans "L'Etranger" d'Albert Camus.* Paris: Archives des Lettres Modernes, 1960.

Fraisse, Simone. "De Lucrèce à Camus, ou les contradictions de la révolte," *Esprit,* No. 3 (March 1959), pp. 437–53.

Frank, Bernard. "Une Bonne Oeuvre," *La Nef*, No. 11 (November 1957), pp. 61–63.

Frank, Waldo. "Life in the Face of Absurdity," *New Republic*, 133 (19 September 1955), 18–20.

Gaidenko, Pyama P. "Existentialism and the Individual," *The Soviet Review*, 3 (July 1962), 8–25.

Gavin, Catherine. *Liberated France*. New York: St. Martin's Press, 1955.

Gillespie, Joan. *Algeria: Rebellion and Revolution*. London: Ernest Bean Ltd., 1960.

Goguel, François. *Le Régime politique français*. Paris: Editions du Seuil, 1955.

Granet, Marie. *"Défense de la France": Histoire d'un mouvement de résistance (1940–1944)*. Paris: Presses Universitaires de France, 1960.

Granet, Marie, and Henri Michel. *Combat*. Paris: Presses Universitaires de France, 1957.

Grenier, Jean. "Un Oui, un non, une ligne droite," *Le Figaro littéraire*, No. 601 (26 October 1957), pp. 1, 5.

Guehenno, Jean. "Mais non, la vie n'est pas absurde," *Le Figaro littéraire*, No. 292 (24 November 1951), pp. 1, 6.

Guérard, Albert L. *France: A Modern History*. Ann Arbor: University of Michigan Press, 1959.

Guitton, Jean. "Extraits d'un journal," *La Table ronde*, No. 146 (February 1960), pp. 169–73.

Hanna, Thomas. *The Thought and Art of Albert Camus*. Chicago: Henry Regnery Co., 1958.

Harrington, Michael. "Ethics of Rebellion," *The Commonweal*, No. 59 (29 January 1954), pp. 428–31.

Hartman, Geoffrey. "Camus and Malraux: The Common Ground," *Yale French Studies*, No. 25 (Spring 1960), pp. 104–10.

Herbette, François. *L'Expérience marxiste en France*. Paris: Génin, 1959.

Hervé, Pierre. *La Révolution et les fétiches*. Paris: La Table Ronde, 1956.

Hourdin, Georges. *Camus le juste*. Paris: Les Editions du Cerf, 1960.

Jeanson, Francis. "Albert Camus ou l'âme révoltée," *Les Temps modernes*, No. 79 (May 1952), pp. 2070–90.

———. *Notre Guerre*. Paris: Editions de Minuit [1960].

———. "Pour tout vous dire," *Les Temps modernes*, No. 82 (August 1952), pp. 354–83.

————. *Sartre par lui-même.* Paris: Editions du Seuil, 1960.

Johnson, Gerald W. "Government as a Creative Act," *New Republic,* 138 (2 June 1958), 16–17.

Julien, Charles-André. *L'Afrique du Nord en marche.* Paris: Julliard, 1952.

Kanapa, Jean. *Situation de l'intellectuel.* Paris: Editions Sociales, 1957.

Kanters, Robert. "L'Homme malade de la peste," *La Gazette des lettres,* No. 39 (28 June 1947), pp. 4–5.

————. "Les Possédés, contre-expertise," *L'Express,* No. 399 (5 February 1959), pp. 30–31.

Kemp, Robert. "Actuelles III," *Les Nouvelles littéraires,* No. 1610 (10 July 1958), p. 2.

————. "L'Homme révolté," *Les Nouvelles littéraires,* No. 1263 (15 November 1951), p. 2.

Kréa, Henri. "Le Malentendu algérien," *France-Observateur,* No. 557 (5 January 1961), p. 16.

Kristol, Irving. "The Shadow of the Marquis," *Encounter,* 8 (February 1957), 3–5.

Lalou, René. "De la révolte: *L'Homme révolté,*" *Hommes et mondes,* No. 67 (February 1952), pp. 287–93.

Laurent, Jacques. "Albert Camus contre-guillotin," *Arts,* No. 631 (13 August 1957), pp. 1, 3.

————. "Le Nobel couronne une oeuvre terminée," *Arts,* No. 642 (23 October 1957), pp. 1, 3.

Lebesque, Morvan. "Albert Camus, l'Algérien," *Le Canard enchaîné,* No. 1931 (23 October 1957), p. 2.

Legrand, Albert. "The Anguish of the Left," *Culture,* 15 (1954), 164–74.

Lehrman, Hal. "Book in the News: *The Algerian Problem* by Edward Behr," *Saturday Review,* 45, No. 5 (3 February 1962), 18–19.

Lewis, Wyndham. *The Writer and the Absolute.* London: Methuen, 1953.

Luppé, Robert de. *Albert Camus.* Paris: Editions Universitaires, 1958.

————. "Albert Camus ou le retour aux sources," *La Revue française,* No. 101 (May 1958), pp. 58–59.

Lüthy, Herbert. *A l'heure de son clocher: Essai sur la France.* Paris: Calmann-Lévy, 1955.

Maquet, Albert. *Albert Camus ou l'invincible été.* Paris: Editions Debresses, 1955.

Marcus, John T. *French Socialism in the Crisis Years: 1933–1936.* New York: Praeger, 1958.

Matthews, J. H., ed. *Configuration critique No. 5: Albert Camus I.* Paris: *Lettres Modernes,* 1961.

Maulnier, Thierry. "Faut-il détruire des vivants?" *Le Figaro littéraire,* No. 192 (24 December 1949), p. 8.

Mauriac, Claude. *"L'Homme révolté,* d'Albert Camus," *La Table ronde,* No. 48 (December 1951), pp. 98–109.

———. *Hommes et idées d'aujourd'hui.* Paris: Albin-Michel, 1953.

Mauriac, François. *Le Bâillon dénoué.* Paris: Grasset, 1945.

———. "Une Jeune Voix à laquelle une génération fait écho," *Le Figaro littéraire,* No. 601 (26 October 1957), p. 1.

———. "Lettre III: Réponse à Albert Camus," *La Table ronde,* No. 14 (February 1949), pp. 199–206.

———. "Le Mépris de la charité," *Le Figaro,* No. 122 (7–8 January 1945), p. 1.

———. "Réponse à *Combat,*" *Le Figaro,* No. 55 (22–23 October 1944), p. 1.

———. "La Vocation de la Résistance," *Le Figaro,* No. 91 (3–4 December 1944), p. 1.

Memmi, Albert. "Camus ou le colonisateur de bonne volonté," *La Nef,* No. 12 (December 1957), pp. 95–96.

Mesnil-Amar, Jacqueline. *Ceux qui ne dormaient pas.* Paris: Editions de Minuit, 1957.

Michel, Henri. *Histoire de la Résistance.* Paris: Presses Universitaires de France, 1950.

Michel, Henri, and Boris Guetzévitch. *Les Idées politiques et sociales de la Résistance.* Paris: Presses Universitaires de France, 1954.

Milosz, Czeslaw. "L'Interlocuteur fraternel," *Preuves,* No. 110 (April 1960), pp. 14–16.

Montherlant, Henri de. *Textes sous une occupation.* Paris: Gallimard, 1953.

Mounier, Emmanuel. "Camus parle," *Esprit,* No. 1 (January 1947), pp. 156–57.

Nadeau, Maurice. "Albert Camus et la révolte," *Mercure de France,* No. 1061 (January 1952), pp. 106–11.

Nora, Pierre. *Les Français d'Algérie.* Paris: Gallimard, 1961.

———. "Pour une autre explication de *L'Etranger,*" *France-Observateur,* No. 557 (5 January 1961), p. 17.

Ollivier, Albert. *Fausses Sorties.* Paris: La Jeune Parque, 1946.

Pauthe, Jacqueline. "Lettre à Camus," *Esprit,* No. 5 (May 1954), pp. 644–51.

Peyre, Henri. "The Resistance and Literary Revival in France," *The Yale Review*, 25 (September 1945), 84–92.

Picon, Gaëtan. "*La Chute* d'Albert Camus," *Mercure de France*, No. 1116 (August 1956), pp. 688–93.

———. "Entretien avec Albert Camus," *Le Figaro littéraire*, No. 21 (18 August 1946), pp. 2–3.

———. *Panorama de la nouvelle littérature française.* Paris: Gallimard, 1949.

———. "Remarques sur *La Peste* d'Albert Camus," *Fontaine*, No. 61 (September 1947), pp. 453–60.

Pouillon Jean. "L'Optimisme de Camus," *Les Temps modernes*, No. 26 (November 1947), pp. 921–29.

Quilliot, Roger. "L'Algérie d'Albert Camus," *La Revue socialiste*, No. 120 (October 1958), pp. 121–31.

———. "Autour d'Albert Camus et du problème socialiste," *La Revue socialiste*, No. 20 (April 1948), pp. 342–52.

———. *La Mer et les prisons: Essai sur Albert Camus.* Paris: Gallimard, 1956.

———. "La Querelle est politique," *La Nef*, No. 12 (December 1957), p. 96.

———. *La Société de 1960 et l'avenir politique de la France.* Paris: Gallimard, 1960.

Rossi, Louis. "Albert Camus: The Plague of Absurdity," *The Kenyon Review*, 20, No. 3 (Summer 1958), 399–422.

Roudiez, Léon S. "The Literary Climate of *L'Etranger:* Samples of a Twentieth-Century Atmosphere," *Symposium*, 12 (Spring–Fall 1958), 19–35.

———. "To Him Sisyphus Symbolized Man," *Saturday Review*, 45 (10 March 1962), 20.

Rousseaux, André. "Albert Camus et notre espoir," *Le Figaro littéraire*, No. 601 (26 October 1957), p. 2.

———. "*L'Homme révolté* d'Albert Camus," *Le Figaro littéraire*, No. 291 (17 November 1951), p. 2.

Roussel, Jean. "Le Siècle de la trahison est aussi le temps du nihilisme," *L'Age nouveau*, 1 (February 1952), 78–81.

Roy, Claude. "Camus solidaire et solitaire," *France-Observateur*, No. 505 (7 January 1960), p. 19.

———. "Sur l'espèce humaine. Albert Camus: *La Peste* et 'Remarque sur la révolte' dans *Existence*," *Europe*, No. 22 (October 1947), pp. 99–101.

Roy, Jules. *Autour du drame*. Paris: Julliard, 1961.

―――. *La Guerre d'Algérie*. Paris: Julliard, 1960.

Roynet, L. "Albert Camus chez les chrétiens," *La Vie intellectuelle*, No. 4 (April 1949), pp. 336–51.

Sartre, Jean-Paul. "Albert Camus," *France-Observateur*, No. 505 (7 January 1960), p. 17.

―――. "Les Communistes et la paix: I," *Les Temps modernes*, No. 81 (July 1952), pp. 1–50.

―――. "Les Communistes et la paix: II," *Les Temps modernes*, Nos. 84–85 (October–November 1952), pp. 695–763.

―――. "Les Communistes et la paix: III," *Les Temps modernes*, No. 101 (April 1954), pp. 1731–1819.

―――. *Explication de "L'Etranger."* Paris: Gallimard, 1947.

―――. "Le Fantôme de Staline," *Les Temps modernes*, Nos. 129–31 (November–December 1956; January 1957), pp. 577–696.

―――. "Matérialisme et révolution: I," *Les Temps modernes*, No. 9 (June 1946), pp. 1537–63.

―――. "Matérialisme et révolution: II," *Les Temps modernes*, No. 10 (July 1946), pp. 1–32.

―――. "Réponse à Albert Camus," *Les Temps modernes*, No. 82 (August 1952), pp. 334–53.

Saulnier, Adam. "Albert Camus, Prix Nobel . . . un Homme!" *Force ouvrière*, No. 608 (24 October 1957), p. 11.

Sénard, Jean. "Un Certain Journaliste," *Le Figaro littéraire*, No. 601 (26 October 1957), p. 5.

Siegfried, André. *De la Troisième à la Quatrième République*. Paris: Grasset, 1956.

Simon, Pierre-Henri. *Présence de Camus*. Paris: Nizet, 1962.

"La Source de nos malheurs communs: Lettre d'un Algérien musulman." *Preuves*, No. 91 (September 1958), pp. 72–75.

Spiegelberg, Herbert. "French Existentialism: Its Social Philosophies," *The Kenyon Review*, 16 (Summer 1954), 446–62.

Stéphane, Roger. "A défaut de Malraux . . . ," *France-Observateur* (24 October 1957), p. 16.

Thody, Philip. *Albert Camus: A Study of His Work*. New York: Grove Press, 1959.

―――. *Albert Camus: 1913–1960*. London: Hamish Hamilton, 1961.

―――. "Albert Camus and 'Remarque sur la révolte,' " *French Studies*, 10 (October 1956), 335–38.

―――. *Jean-Paul Sartre*. London: Hamish Hamilton, 1960.

———. "Meursault et la critique," in J. H. Matthews, ed., *Configuration critique no. 5: Albert Camus I* (Paris: Lettres Modernes, 1961), pp. 12–22.

Thoorens, Léon. *A la rencontre de Albert Camus.* Paris: La Sixaine [1946?].

Tillion, Germaine. "Albert Camus et l'Algérie," *Preuves,* No. 91 (September 1958), pp. 69–72.

———. *L'Algérie 1957.* Paris: Editions de Minuit, 1957.

Tournoux, J.-R. *Secrets d'état.* Paris: Plon, 1960.

Troyat, Henri. "Réponse à Albert Camus," *La Nef,* No. 14 (January 1946), pp. 145–48.

Truc, Gonzague. "La Querelle Sartre-Camus," *Hommes et mondes,* No. 76 (November 1952), pp. 370–75.

Ubersfeld, Annie. "Albert Camus ou la métaphysique de la contre-révolution," *Nouvelle Critique,* No. 92 (January 1958), pp. 110–30.

V[iggiani], C[arl] A. "Camus and *Alger-Républicain:* 1938–1939," *Yale French Studies,* No. 25 (Spring 1960), pp. 138–43.

———. "Camus in 1936: The Beginnings of a Career," *Symposium,* 12 (Spring–Fall 1958), 7–18.

———. "Camus's First Publication," *Modern Language Notes,* 75 (November 1960), 589–96.

Wahl, Nicholas. *The Fifth Republic.* New York: Random House, 1959.

Werth, Alexander. *France: 1940–1955.* London: R. Hale, 1956.

———. *The Twilight of France: 1933–1940.* New York: Harper, 1942.

Williams, Phillip. *Politics in Post-War France.* London: Longmans, 1954.

Wollheim, Richard. "The Political Philosophy of Existentialism," *The Cambridge Journal,* 7 (October 1953), 3–19.

Wright, Gordon. *France in Modern Times.* Chicago: Rand McNally, 1960.

Wurmser, André. "Le Diagnostic du confesseur: *La Chute,* récit d'Albert Camus," *Les Lettres françaises,* No. 624 (20 June 1956), p. 2.

NOTES

Introduction

1 The journalistic writings have of course been discussed to a greater or lesser extent in all the full-length critical studies of Camus and his work. Philip Thody's *Albert Camus: 1913–1960* (London, 1961) contains the most thorough treatment of the articles and editorials up to the present time. Carl Viggiani has published an inventory of Camus's articles from *Alger-Républicain* in the special issue of *Yale French Studies* (Spring, 1960) devoted to Camus. Philip Thody, in an appendix to his translation of Camus's notebooks, includes a complete listing of the articles from both *Alger-Républicain* and *Soir-Républicain*. Justin O'Brien has published a translation of selected articles by Camus entitled *Resistance, Rebellion and Death* (New York, 1961).

2 Appendix B contains a list of Camus's uncollected articles and editorials, including those from *Combat* that I was able to identify. Since many of these articles are hard to obtain, I have quoted some of them at length in the text—particularly the articles from *Alger-Républicain, Soir-Républicain,* and *Combat.* Quotations in the book are in English. All translations, unless otherwise indicated, are my own. French texts for selected quotations from uncollected articles will be found in Appendix A.

Chapter 1

1 Historical background material for this chapter is taken mainly from the following sources: D. W. Brogan, *The French Nation from Napoleon to Pétain;* François Herbette, *L'Expérience marxiste en France;* John T. Marcus, *French Socialism in the Crisis Years: 1933–1936;* Alexander Werth, *The Twilight of France: 1933–1940.*

2 Albert Camus, *"La Galère,* par André Chamson," *Alger-Républicain,* No. 229 (23 May 1939), p. 2. All subsequent references to Camus's articles in *Alger-Républicain* and *Soir-Républicain* will be given in the text *(AR* and *SR).*

3 Camus gave this as the date of his break with the Communist party in an interview with Germaine Brée in 1956. He gave the same date in a letter to Roger Quilliot, which Quilliot refers to in the biographical outline in the Pléiade edition of Camus's works: *Théâtre, récits, nouvelles,* p. xxix.

219

4 "Biographie" in *Théâtre, récits, nouvelles,* p. xxix.
5 Messali Hadj organized the Etoile Nord-Africaine party in 1927. It was outlawed in 1929 and reorganized in 1933. Hadj was arrested at this time, then amnestied under the Popular Front in 1937. Originally affiliated with the Communists, the party became associated with the Ulema, a Pan-Arab movement, when the Communists withdrew their support. In 1937 the Etoile Nord-Africaine was again reorganized as the Parti du Peuple Algérien.
6 "Biographie" in *Théâtre, récits, nouvelles,* p. xxix.
7 Roger Quilliot, "Albert Camus's Algeria," in Germaine Brée, ed., *Camus: A Collection of Critical Essays,* p. 40.
8 Camus continued to feel, until at least 1945, that Russia was forced into isolation by the hostility of the rest of the European nations. Concerning the Russian invasion of Finland in 1939 he wrote: "At the present time everything seems to indicate that the Soviet Union has taken her place among the imperialist nations. The causes for that change are perhaps more psychological than economic . . ." (*SR,* 13-12-39, p. 2). In 1944 he again stated that Russia had resorted to a narrowly nationalistic foreign policy only because she had been forced to do so by other nations. He noted that it was Russia that had offered, "with no hope of any gain," a plan for international disarmament before World War II (*Combat,* 18-12-44, p. 2). This attitude toward Russia was typical of a great number of left-wing intellectuals in the 1930's. Russia's belated joining of the British-American-French alliance in 1942 strengthened their hopes that, once she had emerged from her isolation, Russia would liberalize her internal policies and join the rest of the world in an effort to establish a sound world peace.
9 Alius, "Le Socialisme devant les événements actuels," *Soir-Républicain,* No. 106 (29 December 1939), p. 2.
10 Camus, "Révolte dans les Asturies," in *Théâtre, récits, nouvelles,* pp. 401–38.
11 Marcus, p. 185.
12 Camus, *Carnets,* p. 29. Jean Grenier, philosopher, writer, and teacher, was Camus's professor at both the lycée and the University of Algiers. Grenier's admiration for Greek culture did much to form Camus's thought. He and Grenier remained close friends throughout Camus's lifetime.
13 Jean-Claude Brisville, *Camus,* p. 256.
14 *Carnets,* p. 89.
15 *Ibid.,* p. 41.

16 *Ibid.,* p. 57.
17 Camus, *Actuelles III,* p. 88.
18 Germaine Brée, *Camus,* p. 8.
19 "Biographie" in *Théâtre, récits, nouvelles,* p. xxxiii.
20 Albert Camus, "De la Résistance à la révolution," *Combat,* No. 59 (21 August 1944), p. 1.
21 Charles Maurras, French writer and journalist, was the leader of the ultra conservative Action Française.
22 Camus, *Actuelles I,* pp. 31–39.
23 Philip Thody, *Albert Camus: 1913–1960,* p. 10.

Chapter 2

1 Historical background material on Algeria for this and for subsequent chapters is taken mainly from the following sources: Edward Behr, *The Algerian Problem;* Richard and Joan Brace, *Ordeal in Algeria;* Michael K. Clark, *Algeria in Turmoil;* Charles Henri Favrod, *La Révolution algérienne.*
2 There is some confusion as to the accepted terminology to be used when referring to the various racial groups that make up the Algerian population. Some writers object to the use of the term "Arab" in reference to the indigenous inhabitants since a large number of these inhabitants—especially the Kabylians, who are Berbers—are not of the same racial strain as the Arabs. As for the "white" population, the terms "settler" and *colon* have recently come to take on a somewhat unpleasant connotation. Since "Algerian" alone, probably the preferred designation of all the racial groups, is confusing, the "white" inhabitants are most often referred to in French as Français d'Algérie or Français de souche. Some foreign writers, however, feel that these are inaccurate and misleading terms; though most of the Français d'Algérie are French citizens, many are of Italian, Spanish, Maltese, or Greek origin. For purposes of simplification I will use "Moslem" to refer collectively to the indigenous population, except where speaking specifically of a particular group such as the Kabylians. For the white population I will use "European Algerian."
3 Brace, p. 20.
4 *Actuelles III,* p. 49.
5 This series of eleven articles appeared in *Alger-Républicain* from 5 through 15 June 1939. (See Appendix B.) All but four of the articles were reprinted in *Actuelles III* in 1958.
6 *Actuelles III,* pp. 47–48.

7 Roger Quilliot, "Albert Camus's Algeria," in Germaine Brée, ed., *Camus: A Collection of Critical Essays*, p. 41.

8 These proposals are mentioned in various places throughout the series. Most of them, however, are contained in one article: "L'Avenir économique et social," *Actuelles III*, pp. 74–85.

9 *Ibid.*, p. 85.

10 *Ibid.*, p. 87.

11 *Ibid.*, p. 88.

12 Thody, *Albert Camus: 1913–1960*, p. 13.

13 *Actuelles III*, pp. 89–90.

14 Thody, p. 12.

15 *Actuelles III*, p. 88.

16 Albert Camus, "Présentation de la revue *Rivages*," *Rivages*, No. 1 (1939), p. 1.

17 *Carnets*, p. 50.

18 Camus, *"Noces" suivi de "L'Eté,"* p. 73.

19 *"Noces,"* p. 73.

20 Camus, "Présentation," *Rivages*, p. 2.

21 Jean Bloch-Michel, "Albert Camus et la nostalgie de l'innocence," *Preuves*, No. 110 (April 1960), p. 5.

22 *"Noces,"* p. 78.

23 Brée, *Camus*, p. 117.

24 Philip Thody, "Meursault et la critique," in J. H. Matthews, ed., *Configuration critique No. 5: Albert Camus I*, pp. 15–16.

25 *"Noces,"* p. 68.

26 Gaëton Picon, "Entretien avec Albert Camus," *Le Figaro littéraire*, No. 21 (18 August 1946), p. 2.

27 Bloch-Michel, p. 5.

28 Louis Rossi, "Albert Camus: The Plague of Absurdity," *The Kenyon Review*, 20, No. 3 (Summer 1958), 399–422.

29 *Actuelles III*, p. 41.

30 Henri Kréa, "Le Malentendu algérien," *France-Observateur*, No. 557 (5 January 1961), p. 16.

31 Pierre Nora, "Pour une autre explication de *l'Etranger*," *France-Observateur*, No. 557 (5 January 1961), p. 17.

Chapter 3

1 These steps are given briefly in the editorial cited, but were set forth in detail a short time later. On 12 and 16 November 1939 two lengthy articles in *Soir-Républicain* outlined a plan for a

truce that would stipulate Germany's withdrawal from Czechoslovakia and Poland. Reparations were to be paid to these two countries by Germany and "other states," presumably Russia and Austria. These reparations would be based on a realistic evaluation of ability to pay. Meanwhile international control of armaments with provisions for sanctions against any state that had recourse to arms during the truce period would assure the possibility of peaceful talks among the belligerent nations. This truce would be concluded "with respect for the dignity, the economic needs, freedom and unity of the German people and of all other peoples; there would be no conquerors, no '*Diktat*,' no conquered . . ." (*SR*, 16-11-39). The truce would last as long as might be necessary to facilitate discussions and negotiations that would found a new order in Europe based on mutual cooperation among nations, the right to self-determination for all peoples, and total disarmament.

    These articles are signed "Irénée." Their authorship is not certain. For further details, see Appendix B, pp. 185 ff.

2 Albert Camus, *"Le Malentendu" suivi de "Caligula,"* p. 125.

3 Brée, *Camus,* p. 37.

4 *Carnets,* p. 170.

5 *Ibid.,* pp. 167–68.

6 *Ibid.,* pp. 166–67.

7 *Ibid.,* pp. 178–82.

8 *Ibid.,* pp. 181–82.

9 This date, which conflicts with that given by other biographical sources, was furnished by Madame Camus in a letter to Germaine Brée.

10 Historical background material concerning the Resistance period is taken mainly from the following sources: Raymond Aron, *De l'armistice à l'insurrection nationale;* Claude Bellanger, *La Presse clandestine: 1940–1944;* Marie Granet and Henri Michel, *Combat;* Henri Michel, *Histoire de la Résistance;* Henri Michel and Boris Guetzévitch, *Les Idées politiques et sociales de la Résistance;* Alexander Werth, *France: 1940–1955.*

11 Granet, *Combat,* p. 134.

12 *Ibid.,* p. 138.

13 Werth, *France: 1940–1955,* p. 197.

14 "Manifeste des M.U.R.," *Combat clandestin,* No. 34 (September 1942), p. 1. Hereafter all references to *Combat clandestin* (*Com. cl.*) will be included in the text.

15 Robert Aron, *Historie de la libération de la France,* p. 121.
16 Werth, *France: 1940–1955,* p. 197.
17 Albert Camus, "Avant-propos," in Konrad Bieber, *L'Allemagne vue par les écrivains de la Résistance française,* p. 3.
18 Thody, *Albert Camus: 1913–1960,* pp. 11–12.
19 *Actuelles I,* p. 185. Camus wrote that he read the news of Péri's death in a morning newspaper in Lyon. Yet Péri was shot in December 1941 and there is no indication that Camus was in Lyon at that time: Madame Camus states that he did not return to France, after having left in January 1941, until August 1942. It is possible that what Camus read was an account of Péri's death written at a later date, or that by 1948 the place he had read the article was no longer clear in his mind.
20 Granet, *Combat,* pp. 145–46.
21 Claude Bourdet, "Camus ou les mains propres," *France-Observateur,* No. 505 (7 January 1960), p. 18.
22 Granet, p. 146. Mlle Bernard states that the entire editorial staff in Paris assisted in the preparation and dissemination of the mimeographed issue.
23 For a more detailed study of this aspect of the French Resistance movement, see Bieber, *L'Allemagne vue par les écrivains de la Résistance française.*
24 *Carnets,* pp. 247–48.
25 Camus, *Lettres à un ami allemand,* p. 23.
26 *Carnets,* p. 64.
27 Camus, *La Peste,* p. 14.
28 *"Noces" suivi de "L'Eté,"* p. 132.
29 *Lettres à un ami allemand,* p. 74.
30 "Rien sans la résistance," *Combat,* No. 62 (1 September 1944), p. 1. All subsequent references to *Combat* (*Com.*) will be included in the text.
31 The survey appeared in *L'Observateur* in late August 1952. Information concerning it was taken from Werth, *France: 1940–1955,* pp. 173–78. Werth discusses and analyzes the survey in some detail.
32 Albert Camus, "Tout ne s'arrange pas," *Les Lettres françaises,* No. 16 (May 1944), p. 4.
33 *Ibid.*
34 Albert Camus, "Les Vraies Tâches," *Cahiers des saisons,* No. 20 (1960), p. 616. This article is actually a letter written by Camus in 1950 but published only after his death in 1960.

Chapter 4

1 Historical background material for this and the following chapter is taken mainly from Robert Aron, *Histoire de la libération de la France;* Catherine Gavin, *Liberated France;* Alexander Werth, *France: 1940–1955;* Gordon Wright, *France in Modern Times.*

2 Werth, *France: 1940–1955,* p. 217.

3 *Actuelles I,* p. 20.

4 Raymond Aron, "Un Seul Homme, un homme seul," *Preuves,* No. 109 (March 1960), p. 3.

5 The Mouvement de Libération Nationale was the rank-and-file organization of the united Resistance movements. It had pretensions to becoming a political party but actually remained a loosely organized, strife-torn movement.

6 *Carnets,* p. 106.

7 Philip Thody, *Albert Camus: 1913–1960,* p. 233n. A copy of this editorial, written on 6 November 1944, was not in the file I used to identify Camus's editorials. (See Appendix B, p. 187.)

8 Claude Bourdet, "Camus et la révolte de Sisyphe," *L'Observateur,* No. 84 (20 December 1951), pp. 17–18.

9 *Actuelles I,* p. 21.

10 Camus, "Tout ne s'arrange pas," *Les Lettres françaises,* No. 16 (May 1944), p. 4.

11 René Gérin was a pacifist journalist in the 1930's, literary critic for *L'Oeuvre* from 1940 to 1944. Arrested in September 1944, he was tried and condemned to eight years at hard labor. His sentence was commuted and he was released in October 1946, recovering his civil rights, and became a journalist for *Le Figaro.*

   Gaston Bergery, French lawyer and statesman, was vice-president of the Radical party in 1928 and ambassador to Moscow in 1940. One of the leading thinkers connected with the Popular Front, he switched loyalties and joined the Vichy government in 1941, becoming Vichy's ambassador to Turkey. After the liberation he in turn offered his services to de Gaulle, who refused them. Finally brought to trial in 1947, he was acquitted and subsequently entered private law practice.

12 Robert Brasillach, a novelist, was also a journalist for the ultra-rightist *Je suis partout.* Coadministrator of the Germanophile publishing house, La Rive Gauche, during the occupation, he was tried in January 1945, found guilty, and executed in February.

   Stéphane Lauzanne, writer and journalist for *Le Matin,* one of the more openly collaborationist Parisian dailies, was tried in late 1944, found guilty, and sentenced to twenty years at hard labor.

Georges Suarez was a journalist and editor of the pro-German *Aujourd'hui.* He was tried, found guilty, and executed in December 1944.

13 François Mauriac, "Réponse à Combat," *Le Figaro,* No. 55 (22–23 October 1944), p. 1.

14 Henri Béraud was a writer and critic associated with *Gringoire,* an ultrarightist but anti-German weekly. He was tried and sentenced to death in January 1945; de Gaulle commuted his sentence to life imprisonment. He was released and given conditional freedom in 1950.

15 The Assemblée Consultative Provisoire was first constituted by de Gaulle in Algiers in 1943. It consisted of members of the Resistance movements and of the major prewar political parties. Its function was to serve as an interim legislative body. In September 1944 de Gaulle enlarged it to 248 seats, 148 of them going to representatives of the metropolitan Resistance groups. This enlarged body started to function in November 1944 and was superseded by the Constituent Assembly in November 1945.

16 *Actuelles I,* p. 40.

17 *Ibid.,* p. 63.

18 *Ibid.,* p. 64.

19 Serge Doubrovsky, "The Ethics of Albert Camus," in Brée, ed., *Camus: A Collection of Critical Essays,* p. 72.

20 François Mauriac, "La Vocation de la Résistance," *Le Figaro,* No. 91 (3–4 December 1944), p. 1.

21 Werth, *France: 1940–1955,* pp. 243–44.

22 The *comités d'entreprise* were labor-management committees organized to increase production and to give the workers a greater voice in the direction of the national economy. Although they were made compulsory after 22 February 1945 in all businesses employing over one hundred persons, they never actually became much more than grievance committees for the workers.

23 In the trials held in 1940 at Riom, Blum, Daladier, and other ministers associated with the Popular Front were brought before the Cour Suprême de la Justice, instituted by the Vichy government that July. The trials ended in a stalemate and no decision was ever handed down. Nevertheless, the trials and the charges of having "betrayed their duties and their responsibilities," made

against these ministers became an odious symbol of Vichy reaction and hatred of the Popular Front.

24 Albertini was an associate of Marcel Déat, a former Deputy and air minister who advocated a Franco-German entente in 1938–39. Déat became political director of *L'Oeuvre* during the occupation. In 1944 he fled to Germany. Tried and condemned to death in absentia in 1945, he was never found.

25 François Mauriac, "Le Mépris de la charité," *Le Figaro*, No. 122 (7–8 January 1945), p. 1.

26 *Actuelles I*, pp. 72–73.

27 *Ibid.*, p. 74.

28 *Ibid.*, pp. 212–13.

29 *Ibid.*, p. 146.

30 *Ibid.*, pp. 78–81.

Chapter 5

1 René Pleven, at that time colonial minister, had made a speech in which he noted the part played by the colonies in the liberation movement. He then added: "That fidelity of the indigenous populations implies for us great responsibilities. . . . A new phase of our colonial life must therefore be opened. It will be a question of pursuing the conquest of hearts" (*Com.*, 13-10-44, p. 1).

2 The reference to the "occupation" of Algeria was particularly strong for the time at which this editorial was written—only two months after the liberation. In a reply to a British journalist who had suggested that the British and Americans set up an occupation government in France, Camus had written: "We know what an occupation is. . . . We know it so well that we want no more of them, and the very word serves to reawaken in us our deepest-felt anger" (*Com.*, 22-10-44, p. 2).*

3 Entitled "Crise en Algérie," this series appeared in *Combat* from 13 to 23 May 1945. It is reprinted in *Actuelles III*, pp. 93–122.

4 *Actuelles III*, p. 106.

5 *Ibid.*, p. 109.

6 *Ibid.*, p. 119.

7 The F.L.N. was a Moslem rebel political organization that grew out of the Comité Révolutionnaire pour l'Unité et l'Action (C.U.R.A.) in 1954. Its leaders were Ferhat Abbas, Belkacem

* French texts of starred passages may be found in Appendix A.

Krim, and Ahmed Ben Bella. It claimed to be the legal Algerian government and functioned with headquarters in Tunis and Cairo. It was with the F.L.N. that Louis Joxe and Charles de Gaulle negotiated the settlement of the Algerian War, which led to independence for that country.

8 *Actuelles III*, p. 122.

9 Nicola Chiaromonte, "La Résistance à l'histoire," *Preuves*, No. 110 (April 1960), p. 20. A reconstruction of Camus's speech from notes Chiaromonte made at the time.

10 For further remarks made by Camus while he was in the United States, see Justin O'Brien, "Albert Camus: Militant," in Brée, ed., *Camus: A Collection of Critical Essays*, pp. 20–25.

11 Albert Camus, "Remarques sur la politique internationale," *Renaissances*, No. 10 (May 1945), pp. 16–20.

12 "Ni victimes ni bourreaux" appeared in *Combat* from 19 to 30 November 1946. The date is incorrectly given as 1948 in *Actuelles I*, where the articles were reprinted (pp. 141–79).

13 *Actuelles I*, p. 146.

14 *Ibid.*, p. 167.

15 *Ibid.*, p. 169.

16 Albert Camus, "Ni victimes ni bourreaux," *Caliban*, No. 11 (November 1947), pp. 10–22.

17 Emmaneul d'Astier [de la Vigerie], "Arrachez les victimes aux bourreaux," *Caliban*, No. 15 (April 1948), pp. 12–17.

18 The letter from Camus to Albert Ollivier is in the possession of Madame Camus.

19 Claude Bourdet, "Albert Camus ou les mains propres," *France-Observateur*, No. 505 (7 January 1960), p. 18.

20 Sartre's association with the Communists developed gradually from 1946 to 1952. From 1944 to 1946 Sartre, along with most other French left-wing intellectuals, championed the Resistance revolution. By late 1946, however, the last hope of accomplishing even a "renovation" was lost. Sartre decided about this time that the only chance for the revolutionary movement lay in some kind of accommodation with the Communist party. However, like Camus, he had grave misgivings concerning Communist ideology. In 1947 he attempted to organize a workers' movement, Le Rassemblement Démocratique et Révolutionnaire (R.D.R.), as a "bad conscience" of the Communist party. Camus steadfastly refused to join this movement or to give it anything but qualified support. The indifference of the workers caused the failure of the R.D.R. From

this point on (1947), Sartre and *Les Temps modernes,* which was founded in 1945, have drifted closer and closer to Communist orthodoxy, although Sartre claims to have retained his intellectual and political independence. Sartre's ideological evolution can be traced in a number of articles on communism and revolution that he wrote for *Les Temps modernes.* The more important ones are: "Le Matérialisme et la révolution" (June and July 1946); "Sommes-nous en démocratie?" (August 1952); "Les Communistes et la paix" (July, October 1952; April 1954).

21 Jean Guitton, "Extraits d'un journal," *La Table ronde,* No. 146 (February 1960), p. 172.

22 Jean-Paul Sartre, "Réponse à Albert Camus," *Les Temps modernes,* No. 82 (August 1952), p. 345.

23 Bourdet, "Albert Camus ou les mains propres," p. 18.

24 Camus, "Lettre à Monsieur le Directeur de *La Nef,*" in *Théâtre, récits, nouvelles,* p. 1743. The letter originally appeared in *La Nef,* No. 14 (January 1946), pp. 144–45.

25 "In the Italian museums, the little painted screens that the priest held before the faces of the condemned so that they could not see the scaffold. The existential leap is the little screen" (*Carnets,* pp. 177–78).

26 Roland Barthes, "*La Peste,* annales d'une épidémie ou roman de la solitude," *Club* (February 1955), p. 6.

27 Albert Camus, "Lettre à Roland Barthes sur *La Peste,*" *Club* (February 1955), p. 7.

28 Albert Camus, "Les Archives de la peste," *Les Cahiers de la Pléiade* (April 1947), pp. 149–54.

29 Camus, "Lettre à Roland Barthes," p. 7.

30 Etiemble, "Peste ou péché?" *Les Temps modernes,* No. 26 (November 1947), pp. 911–20. Jean Pouillon, "L'Optimisme de Camus," *Les Temps modernes,* No. 26 (November 1947), pp. 921–29.

31 Etiemble, p. 920.

32 Sartre, "Réponse à Albert Camus," p. 345.

33 *Actuelles I,* pp. 183–207.

34 Garry Davis was an American who, in 1948, renounced his nationality to become a "citizen of the world." He began a one-man picket campaign in front of the Palais de Chaillot in Paris where the United Nations was in session. He was joined by a few followers and received the support of some French intellectuals, Camus and Gide among them. His movement, however, never got be-

yond the incipient stage, and Davis himself became the object of ridicule.

35 Albert Camus, "A quoi sert l'O.N.U.?" *Combat,* No. 1377 (9 December 1948), pp. 1, 3.

36 Albert Camus, "Réponse à l'incrédule," *Combat,* No. 1391 (25–26 December 1948), pp. 5–6.

37 Jean Paulhan, a critic and editor of the *Nouvelle Revue française,* was secretary of the *NRF* in 1920, its editor from 1925 to 1940. During the occupation he founded, with Jacques Decour, *Les Lettres françaises,* the Resistance organ of the Comité Nationale des Ecrivains (C.N.E.). After 1945 he broke with the C.N.E., which had become Communist-dominated. He thereafter followed a pro-Western, anti-Communist political line. He founded the *Cahiers de la Pléiade* in 1945, and in 1952 again became editor of the *NRF.*

38 Camus, "Réponse à l'incrédule," p. 6.

39 *Actuelles I,* p. 206.

40 Albert Camus, "Les Vraies Tâches," *Cahiers des saisons,* No. 20 (1960), p. 615. (See Chap. 3, n. 34.)

41 See "La Création absurde," in *Le Mythe de Sisyphe,* pp. 127–57.

Chapter 6

1 *Actuelles I,* p. 48.

2 *Ibid.,* pp. 49–50.

3 Marcel Cachin was a Communist deputy and parliamentary leader. Editor of *Humanité,* he was acting chairman of the Communist party in 1944 until Maurice Thorez' return from Moscow that November.

Jacques Doriot, founder of the Fascist Parti Populaire Français (1936), was leader of the French Nazis during the occupation. He fled to Germany in 1944. From there he broadcast pro-Nazi propaganda to France. He was killed by gunfire from an Allied fighter plane while riding in an automobile in Germany in late 1944.

4 Albert Camus, "Le Vrai Débat," *L'Express,* No. 106 (4 June 1955), p. 13.

5 Nicola Chiaromonte, "Sartre versus Camus: A Political Quarrel," in Brée, ed., *Camus: A Collection of Critical Essays,* p. 36.

6 Kenneth Cornell, "*Les Temps modernes:* Peep Sights across the Atlantic," *YFS,* No. 16 (Winter 1955–56), p. 28.

7 Brée, *Camus,* p. 7.

8 Albert Camus, "Préface" in Louis Guilloux, *La Maison du peuple*, p. 12.

9 Claude Bourdet, "Camus ou les mains propres," *France-Observateur*, No. 505 (7 January 1960), p. 18.

10 See Chap. 1, n. 8.

11 Camus, *L'Homme révolté*, p. 14.

12 Brée, *Camus*, p. 224.

13 *L'Homme révolté*, p. 35.

14 *Carnets*, p. 50.

15 Claude Bourdet, "Camus et la révolte de Sisyphe," *L'Observateur*, No. 84 (20 December 1951), p. 18.

16 John Cruickshank, *Albert Camus and the Literature of Revolt*, pp. 116–17.

17 *Actuelles I*, p. 173.

18 Albert Camus, "Lettres à Jean Gillibert," *Revue d'histoire du théâtre*, No. 4 (October–December 1960), p. 356.

19 *L'Homme révolté*, p. 368.

20 *Ibid.*, p. 372.

21 *Ibid.*, p. 301.

22 *Ibid.*, p. 373.

23 *Ibid.*, p. 370.

24 Francis Jeanson, "Albert Camus ou l'âme révoltée," *Les Temps modernes*, No. 79 (May 1952), pp. 2070–90.

25 *Ibid.*, p. 2077.

26 Albert Camus, "Lettre au directeur des *Temps modernes*," No. 82 (August 1952), pp. 316–33; reprinted in *Actuelles II*, pp. 85–123.

27 Francis Jeanson, "Pour tout vous dire," *Les Temps modernes*, No. 82 (August 1952), pp. 354–83. Jean-Paul Sartre, "Réponse à Albert Camus," *Les Temps modernes*, No. 82 (August 1952), pp. 334–53.

28 Albert Legrand, "The Anguish of the Left," *Culture*, 15 (1954), 167.

29 Sartre expressed this regret and paid touching tribute to Camus at at the time of the latter's death (see "Albert Camus," *France-Observateur*, No. 505 [7 January 1960], p. 17; translated into English in *The Reporter Magazine* [4 February 1960], p. 34, and reprinted in Brée, ed., *Camus: A Collection of Critical Essays*, pp. 173–75).

30 Sartre, "Réponse à Albert Camus," p. 353.

31 *Ibid.*, p. 343.

32 Chiaromonte, "Sartre versus Camus," p. 33.

33 *Actuelles II*, p. 162.
34 Francis Jeanson, *Sartre par lui-même*, pp. 153–54.
35 *L'Homme révolté*, p. 305.
36 Jeanson, *Sartre par lui-même*, p. 153.
37 *Ibid.*, p. 160.
38 *L'Homme révolté*, p. 305.
39 *Actuelles I*, p. 73.
40 Albert Camus, "Lettre à P. B.," in *Théâtre, récits, nouvelles*, p. 2051.
41 Albert Camus, "La Vie d'artiste," *Simoun*, No. 8 (April 1953), pp. 14–20. Reprinted in *Théâtre, récits, nouvelles*, pp. 2043–50. The page references in the text are taken from the latter volume.
42 Roger Quilliot, "Présentation" to "Jonas" in *Théâtre, récits, nouvelles*, p. 2043.
43 Camus, "Lettres à Jean Gillibert," p. 355.
44 *Actuelles II*, pp. 173–82.
45 Albert Camus, "Calendrier de la liberté," *Témoins*, No. 5 (Spring, 1954), pp. 6–10.
46 *Actuelles II*, pp. 127–33.
47 *Ibid.*, p. 127.

Chapter 7

1 The *poujadistes* were followers of Pierre Poujade, founder of a political party known as the Union pour la Défense des Commerçants et des Artisans. Poujade and his party advocated abolition of the income tax, and other fiscal measures presumably designed to benefit the small shopkeepers. The party also had racist tendencies and has generally been considered neo-Fascist. After winning a large number of votes in the 1956 parliamentary election, the poujadistes went into a decline, and the movement seems to have all but disappeared.
2 Albert Camus, "Sous le signe de la liberté," *L'Express*, No. 124 (8 October 1955), p. 13. All subsequent references to Camus's articles from *L'Express* (*Ex.*) will be given in the text.
3 "What am I doing here?" A play on Géronte's often-quoted line in Molière's *Les Fourberies de Scapin:* "Que diable allait-il faire dans cette galère?"
4 Historical background material concerning the Fourth Republic is taken mainly from Jacques Fauvet, *La Quatrième République* (Paris, 1959).
5 The Front Républicain was formed as a result of the parliamentary

crisis that had caused the fall, on 29 November 1955, of Edgar Faure's government. The no-confidence vote in the Assembly passed by 318 to 218 votes, six votes more than was needed by the Faure government to dissolve Parliament and call new elections. Earlier in November, Pierre Mendès-France had won control of the Radical party leadership. According to Jacques Fauvet (p. 207), one of Faure's aims in calling for new elections was to force Mendès-France into a political campaign before the latter had had time to solidify the "nouvelle gauche" that was forming around him. Faced with elections on 2 January 1956, Mendès-France quickly concluded a loose agreement with Guy Mollet of the Socialist party, François Mitterand of the Democrat and Socialist Union of the Resistance, and Chaban-Delmas of the Social Republican party. This grouping became known as the Front Républicain; its platform was based on two burning issues of the time: economic reform and the Algerian problem.

6 Most of the articles written for *L'Express* on Algeria can be found in *Actuelles III* (pp. 133–66). The truce appeal is also included (pp. 169–84).

7 Albert Camus, "Lettres à Jean Gillibert," *Revue d'histoire du théâtre,* No. 4 (October–December 1960), p. 359.

8 Camus's mother died in Algiers in 1960. Lucien Camus was forced to flee Algeria during the disturbances following the declaration of Algerian independence on 4 July 1962.

9 *Actuelles III,* p. 192.

10 *Ibid.,* pp. 185–96.

11 Albert Camus, "Kadar Had His Day of Fear," in *Résistance, Rebellion and Death,* trans. Justin O'Brien, p. 160. This article originally appeared in *Franc-Tireur* on 18 March 1957.

12 *Ibid.,* pp. 161–62.

13 Jean-Paul Sartre, "Le Fantôme de Staline," *Les Temps modernes,* Nos. 129–31 (November–December 1956; January 1957), pp. 577–696.

14 Camus, "Kadar Had His Day of Fear," p. 163.

15 Albert Camus, "Le Pari de notre génération," *Demain,* No. 98 (24–30 October 1957), p. 13. Richard Hope Hillary, a British writer and officer in the R.A.F., was killed in the Battle of Britain in 1943. Some of his writings have been recently published under the title *The Last Enemy* (London: Macmillan, 1961).

16 Albert Camus, "Parties and Truth," *Encounter,* 8 (April 1957), 5. This is the translation of an interview between Camus and Jean

Bloch-Michel; it originally appeared under the title "Le Socialisme des potences," *Demain*, No. 63 (21–27 February 1957), pp. 10–11.

17 *Ibid.*, p. 4.
18 Victor Brombert, *The Intellectual Hero*, p. 230.
19 *Discours de Suède*, p. 17.
20 Jeanson, *Sartre par lui-même*, p. 162.
21 Camus, "Parties and Truth," p. 5.
22 *Ibid.*
23 *Ibid.*, pp. 4–5.
24 *Discours de Suède*, pp. 25–70.
25 Roger Stéphane, "A défaut de Malraux . . . ," *France-Observateur* (24 October 1957), p. 16.
26 Pierre Daix, "Albert Camus: Prix Nobel," *Les Lettres françaises*, No. 693 (24–30 October 1957), p. 5.
27 Albert Camus, "Letter of Reply to Peter L. Caracciola," *Encounter*, 8 (June 1957), 68.
28 *Actuelles III*, p. 28.
29 *Ibid.*, pp. 200–12.
30 *Ibid.*, p. 212.
31 It was General Catroux who had proposed a revival of the Blum-Violette Project in 1945. In 1956 Mollet appointed Catroux Resident Minister in Algeria. Algerian officials refused to receive this "bradeur d'Empire" (liquidator of empires), and Mollet went personally to Algiers to have him installed in office. Riots followed, as a result of which Catroux resigned and Mollet, giving in to mob pressure, appointed Robert Lacoste Resident Minister in his place. Lacoste, although considered a liberal at the time, soon became a defender of the extremely conservative European Algerians. It was under his administration that the scandals concerning the use of torture in Algeria by the French police became a major political issue.
32 It should be pointed out that Camus's view of the Algerian problem is not without support outside the usual right-wing elements in France, which, in any case, would not have accepted his criticisms of French misrule in the colonies. Hal Lehrman, in a review of Edward Behr's *The Algerian Problem* (New York, 1962), pointed out that many "liberal" commentators outside France have leapt to the defense of the Algerian rebels in order categorically to condemn the French position. Whereas American writers sometimes seem instinctively to sympathize with the "underdog," Lehrman rightly marks that the Algerian situation was a far more com-

plex matter than simply the attempt of an oppressed people to throw off the bonds of servitude. "The wonder is that there are so many Behrs, though he is the best and fairest among them. To this writer's knowledge, only one book in English worth noting and published here since the 1954 outbreak of the Algerian insurrection has taken a contrary line: 'Algeria in Turmoil,' done in 1959 by Michael Clark. . . ." All the other studies, Lehrman goes on to say, "more or less preach identical articles of faith. Their chief and common fallacy is not that they espouse the rebellion—which would be their right and even pride if they reached this preference by intellectual sweat and open-minded inquiry— but that they make it axiomatic, and filter every inconvenient fact through a set of unexamined dogmas." ("Book in the News," *Saturday Review,* 45, No. 5 [3 February 1962], 18.)

Concerning the abilities and intentions of the F.L.N. to rule equitably, Curtis Cate, writing in the *Atlantic,* points out that "By midsummer 1962 . . . Camus's forebodings had been largely confirmed." ("Turmoil in Algeria," the *Atlantic,* 210, No. 6 [December 1962], 49.)

33 *Actuelles III,* p. 28.
34 Jules Roy, *La Guerre d'Algérie,* p. 207.
35 Albert Camus, "Dostoïevski, prophète du vingtième siècle," *Spectacles,* No. 1 (March 1958), p. 5.
36 Thody, *Albert Camus: 1913–1960,* p. 205.
37 Léon Roudiez, "To Him Sisyphus Symbolized Man," *Saturday Review,* 45 (10 March 1962), 20.
38 Guy Dumur, "Il y a un an, Albert Camus . . . ," *France-Observateur,* No. 557 (5 January 1961), p. 16.

INDEX

Abbas, Ferhat, 100, 227n7
Absurd, The, 42, 110–11
Actuelles, xii
Actuelles III: publication of, 157, 165; contents of, 164
Adhésion: of French intellectuals in 1934, 5. *See also* Commitment
Albertini (assistant to Marcel Déat), 94, 227n24
Algeria: famine in Kabylia, 25, 32–34; resistance of European Algerians to reform in, 26, 27, 34, 35, 98–99; French rule in, 26, 27, 102; nationalist movements in, 26, 99, 100–101, 102, 164, 166, 227n7; rebellion at Sétif, 97, 100; at end of World War II, 98–102; 1954 rebellion in, 155–56; French reaction to rebellion in, 156. *See also* Camus, Albert, and Algeria; European Algerians; Front de Libération Nationale (F.L.N.); Moslems (Algerian); Parti du Peuple Algérien; Progressist Party (Algerian)
Algerian nationalists. *See* Algeria
"L'Algérie 1958," 164
Alger-Républicain, xi, 3. *See also* Camus, Albert
Algiers: Camus and, 39, 40; truce appeal made in, 156–57; Mollet's visit to, 157
Allied Armies: entry of, into Paris, 64, 72; effect of presence in France, 72, 75
Allied Military Government for Occupied Territories, 75
Amado, Jorge, 7
"Les Amandiers," 55
Aragon, Louis, 13
"Les Archives de la peste," 113
Aron, Raymond, 107

Artist and artistic creation. *See L'Homme révolté*
Astier [de la Vigerie], Emmanuel d': and controversy over "Ni victimes ni bourreaux," 106; mentioned, 56, 65, 95
Audisio, Gavriel, 40
Austria, 223n1

Bahia de tous les saints (by Jorge Amado): reviewed by Camus, 7
Bakunin, Mikhail, 126
Bandung Conference, 159
Barthes, Roland, 114
Bayet, Albert, 120
Beck, Beatrice, 150
Ben Bella, Ahmen, 228n1
Béraud, Henri, 86, 94, 226n14
Berdyaev, Nicholas, 8
Bergery, Gaston, 81, 225n11
Bernard, Jacqueline, 60
Bidault, Georges: elected president of C.N.R., 59; snubbed by de Gaulle, 73; mentioned, 65, 155
Block-Michel, Jean: conversations with Camus, 165, 166; mentioned, 162
Blum, Léon: French premier in 1936, 5; and nonintervention in Spanish Civil War, 9–10; disarmament proposals of, 50; tried at Riom, 226n23; mentioned, 16, 48
Blum-Violette Project: reforms in Algeria proposed in, 27; mentioned, 29, 38, 99
Bois, Elie-J., 50
Bolshevik Revolution, 8, 74, 105, 106
Bony and Laffont (French Gestapo chiefs), 83
Bordeaux (France), 54

Bourdet, Claude: member of Combat network, 55; association with Camus in 1944, 60, 61; on Camus and politics, 80, 123; succeeds Camus as editor of *Combat,* 107; mentioned, 56, 60, 65, 95

Bourgeoisie: Camus's criticism of, 78–80

Brasillach, Robert, 83, 86, 225n12

Cachin, Marcel, 120, 230n3

Caligula, xiv, 49

Camus, Albert: in Algiers, 3; expelled from Algeria, 3; early views on social and political questions, 4; and communism, 6, 8, 65–66, 75, 105, 119–20, 122–23, 124, 141, 158, 159; attitude toward U.S.S.R., 6, 8, 41, 104, 106, 124, 139, 159–60, 220n8; and revolution, 7–8, 61, 65, 70–76, 95–96, 105, 126–27, 132–33; and Spanish Civil War, 9, 10; and freedom, 14–16, 90–91, 147–48; and working class, 17, 122–23, 150–51; critical of French political leaders, 17–18, 64–65, 67, 77–78; and Greece, 25, 32, 41, 128–29, 133–34, 147; on elimination of poverty, 29–30, 33; on peace and disarmament, 48–49, 50, 222n1; reaction to outbreak of World War II, 48–50, 51–54, 62–64, 66; on history, 49, 106, 136; attempts to enlist, 52; illness of, 52, 60, 115; marriage, 54; in Resistance, 59–61, 65–68; and death penalty, 66–67, 84–85; and violence, 66–70, 95, 104, 105, 124–25, 132, 164; critical of bourgeoisie, 70–80; and Resistance in postwar period, 73, 75–76, 84–85, 86, 91–92, 107–8, 132; visits U.S. and Canada, 103–4; rejects historical determinism, 103–4, 119, 127–28;

and Marxism, 105, 106, 127–28, 138–39; on dangers of cold war, 106, 115–17; early works of, misunderstood, 109–12; and the Absurd, 110–11; and existentialism, 110–11, 161; and progressist intellectuals, 113–14, 115, 152–53, 159–60, 161–62; and Crusade for World Federation, 115–16; proletarian background of, 122; quarrel with Sartre, 137–39; resigns from UNESCO, 145; visit to Italy and Greece, 147; reaction to Hungarian revolt, 158–59, 162; defends West, 159; receives Nobel Prize, 163–64; death, 168. *See also* Pensée de Midi; titles of Camus's works

—and Algeria: attitude toward Moslems, 6, 29–30, 37–38; criticism of French colonial policies, 18–19, 35–36, 99; attitude toward European Algerians, 25, 44–45, 101–2, 164–65; defense of nationalist movements, 26, 36–39, 99; proposals for reforms, 28, 31, 32–33, 33–36, 101–2; sense of pride in being Algerian, 39–40; in his artistic universe, 40–41, 41–42, 45; reaction to Algerian War, 98–103, 155–57, 163–67, 234n32; appeal for truce, 156–57; proposals for settlement of Algerian War, 164–65. *See also* Algeria; *L'Etranger*

—as journalist: xii–xiii; for *Alger-Républicain,* 3; editor of *Soir-Républicain,* 3, 21, 46–47; for *Paris-Soir,* 3, 54; on role of press, 20–21, 47; co-founder of *Rivages,* 40; for *Combat clandestin,* 60–62; editor-in-chief of *Combat,* 61, 96, 103, 104, 106–8, 186–89; for *L'Express,* 147, 148

(F.L.N.): Algerian nationalist movement, 102, 166, 227n7; mentioned, 156, 164
Front National (Resistance network), 56
Front Populaire. *See* Popular Front
Front Républicain: Camus and, 148, 153–54; formation of, 151–52, 232n5; and 1955 general election, 154–55

Gaulle, Charles de: Camus's interview with, 166; mentioned, 57, 72, 73, 75, 86, 97, 100, 155, 165, 223n1
Gérin, René, 81, 225n11
Germano-Soviet Pact, 56
Germany: and causes of World War II, 48; political responsibility by people of, 62; proposals for disarmament of, 222n1; *See also* Nazis; Nazism
Gide, André: Camus on, 13; mentioned, 40
Gillibert, Jean: Camus's letters to, 130, 157
Gimont, Marcel, 188, 189
Giono, Jean, 7
Giraudoux, Jean: Minister of Information in 1939–40, 47
Gouin, Félix, 89
Greece: Kabylia compared to, 25, 32; influence on Camus, 32, 41, 128–29, 133–34; Camus's visit to, 147; mentioned, 116. *See also* Pensée de Midi
Grenier, Jean, xii, 11, 220n12
Grenier, Roger, 188
La Guerre de Troie n'aura pas lieu: (by Giraudoux), 47
Guibert, Armand, 12

Hadj, Messali, 6, 220n5
Hamlet (by Shakespeare): produced by Camus, 55

Hegel, Georg W. F., 127
Herriot, Edouard, 77
Hillary, Richard, 159, 223n15
Historical determinism: Camus's views on, 103–4, 119, 127–28
Historical dialecticism. *See* Historical determinism
History: Camus's views on, 49, 106, 136
Hitler, Adolph, 46, 48, 50, 103
Hitlerism. *See* Nazism
Hodent, Michel: Camus's defense of, 21–23; mentioned, 51, 59
L'Homme révolté: publication of, xii, 124, 136–37; ideas later expressed in, 7, 8; analysis of, 124–36; artist and artistic creation discussed in, 128–29; controversy over, 137–39, 140–42; mentioned, 6, 71, 75, 115, 152, 153
Hungarian revolt: reaction to, in France, 158; Camus's reaction to, 158–59, 162
Hungary. *See* Hungarian revolt

Ibarruri, Dolores: Camus's review of articles by, 10
Imperialism, 48
Isvolski, Hélène, 8
Italy: Camus's visit to, 147

Jeanson, Francis: and controversy over *L'Homme révolté*, 137
"Jonas" (*L'Exil et le royaume*): adapted from "La Vie d'artiste," 143, 144
Jouvenel, Renaud de, 78
Joxe, Louis, 228n1
Les Justes, 71

Kabylia: compared to Greece, 32. *See also* Algeria
Kessous, Aziz, 100
Krim, Belkacem, 227n1

Republique de Mali